COGNITIVE MODELS
OF PSYCHOLOGICAL TIME

COGNITIVE MODELS
OF PSYCHOLOGICAL TIME

Edited by

Richard A. Block
Montana State University

 LAWRENCE ERLBAUM ASSOCIATES, PUBLISHERS

1990   Hillsdale, New Jersey   Hove and London

Lawrence Erlbaum Associates, Inc., Publishers
365 Broadway
Hillsdale, New Jersey 07642

Library of Congress Cataloging-in-Publication Data
Cognitive models of psychological time / edited by Richard A. Block.
   p. cm.
   ISBN 0-8058-0359-9
   1. Time perception.   I. Block, Richard A., 1946-
BF468.C55 1990
153.7´53--dc20   89-37741
                                                          CIP

Printed in the United States of America
10 9 8 7 6 5 4 3 2 1

Contents

Contributors

Richard A. Block
Department of Psychology
Montana State University
Bozeman, MT 59717, U.S.A.

Scott S. Campbell
Institute for Circadian Physiology
677 Beacon Street
Boston, MA 02215, U.S.A.

Janet L. Jackson
Institute of Experimental
    Psychology
University of Groningen
Kerklaan 30
9751 NN Haren,
    The Netherlands

Mari Riess Jones
Department of Psychology
The Ohio State University
404-C West 17th Avenue
Columbus, OH 43210, U.S.A.

Frederick T. Melges†
Department of Psychiatry
Duke University Medical Center
Durham, NC 27710, U.S.A.

John A. Michon
Institute of Experimental
    Psychology
University of Groningen
Kerklaan 30
9751 NN Haren
    The Netherlands

---

† Deceased

Suchoon S. Mo
Department of Psychology
University of Southern Colorado
Pueblo, CO 81001, U.S.A.

Robert Patterson
Department of Psychology
Montana State University
Bozeman, MT 59717, U.S.A.

H. L. Roitblat
and **K. N. J. Young**
Department of Psychology
University of Hawaii at Manoa
Honoloulu, HI 96822, U.S.A.

Jeffery J. Summers
and **Bruce D. Burns**
Department of Psychology
University of Melbourne
Parkville, Victoria 3052
    Australia

Dan Zakay
Department of Psychology
Tel-Aviv University
Ramat-Aviv
69978 Tel-Aviv, Israel

Preface

The study of time is receiving increasing interest in the sciences and humanities. The International Society for the Study of Time, which was founded in 1966, has now held seven conferences. The subject of time is also becoming more accessible to the general public. Perhaps the best example of this is the fact that Stephen W. Hawking's book, *A Brief History of Time* (Bantam Books, 1988) has remained on the best-seller list throughout much of this past year.

When I first considered editing a book on the subject of psychological time, I thought that there was a serious need for one that critically reviewed the numerous cognitive models appearing in the extant literature. In organizing this volume, therefore, I told contributors that the book had the working title, *Cognitive Models of Psychological Time.* I assumed that each contributor would emphasize how his or her own work related to that subject. The chapters in this volume do, indeed, address psychological time from the point of view of cognitive models: The subject index contains 37 sub-entries under the heading "Model," which is not that many fewer than the 61 sub-entries under the heading "Time." Fortunately, however, the contributors ventured considerably beyond a strict interpretation of the subject. As a result, the chapters turned out to be much more general, more interesting, and more important than I would have thought possible.

A number of people deserve sincere thanks for helping produce this volume. I thank my family for patiently enduring my long hours in front of my computer; it is to them that I dedicate the result of my efforts. Judith Suben, my editor at Erlbaum, provided encouragement and editorial suggestions. John Eagleson, the production editor, was also extremely helpful. Martha Jane Craft, my secretary, assisted me in numerous ways. I also thank the anonymous people at Microsoft for their Word 5.0, those at Bitstream for their Fontware, and those at Hewlett-Packard for their Laserjet Series II printer; without their work, I would not have enjoyed editing and producing this volume nearly as much as I did. The contributors, however, deserve utmost thanks for their excellent work and for meeting (most of) my unrealistic deadlines. In particular, I wish I were able to express my sincere gratitude to Frederick Melges, the author of the final chapter in this volume. A few weeks after he completed his chapter, I was saddened to learn of Dr. Melges' death. Those of us working in the field of the psychology of time have lost an outstanding scholar and colleague.

Bozeman   *Richard A. Block*

Introduction

Richard A. Block
Montana State University

The nature of time-related behavior and experiences was one of the first topics that psychologists began to investigate experimentally at the inception of the discipline in the late 1800s. Although empirical work was already underway by about 1865 (Michon & Jackson, 1985), in many ways the continuing study of psychological time is traceable to three 100-year old publications (Guyau, 1890/1988; James, 1890; Nichols, 1891). The many empirical studies that psychologists have conducted since that time reveal that psychological time is extremely complex: There appear to be no simple answers, nor any innocent questions. No simple model can purport to explain the variety of temporal behaviors and phenomena that are experienced by individuals.

Research on the psychology of time has addressed such wide-ranging topics as biological rhythms, duration experiences, and cultural tempos. As a result, models of psychological time have assumed a number of orientations: biopsychological, behavioral, cognitive, developmental, psychoanalytic, and social-psychological. This volume emphasizes cognitive models and some of the research that has been conducted in order to clarify them. Chronobiological and behavioral models that address cognitive psychological issues are also included.

Most of the chapters in this volume focus on models and the evidence that rejects or supports them. A brief clarification of the meaning of the term *model* is in order. As used here, a model is a description that helps us understand a phenomenon or process that is not directly observable. This volume considers a mixture of models and theories. At present, the cognitive psychology of time needs useful, interesting, and testable ideas; such ideas may come from empirical observations or may be induced from formal models.

Chapter 1, by Richard A. Block, reviews various models of psychological time, most of which have had a major impact on the field. Some models pertain directly to the view of time as succession, some to the view of time as duration, and some to the view of time as temporal perspective. The view of time as succession is reviewed by considering models that focus on phenomena related to the psychological moment, the psychological present, and memory for temporal order. The view of time as duration is reviewed by considering models that focus on experienced and remembered duration, including chronobiological models, behavioral models, internal-clock models, attentional models, memory models, and a general contextualistic model. Most of these models are limited in scope and explanatory power, although some are complementary. Models of temporal perspective are the least well developed, but studies on how temporal perspective is altered in people displaying psychiatric illnesses (e.g., schizophrenia) represent a promising line of research.

Chapter 2, by John A. Michon, also surveys the field of time psychology from the perspective of a cognitive scientist. He argues that the traditional view of time psychologists—that of time as duration—is overly narrow. As an alternative, Michon asserts that we must consider a broader set of time-related phenomena, such as the perception of rhythmic patterns, the planning of future action, and the temporal structure of narrative events. Underlying these phenomena is the biological necessity that organisms "stay in tune with a dynamic, unfolding outside world" (p. 55). In order to do so, people use different kinds of representations, ranging from concrete dynamic scenes, to semi-abstract analogical schemes, to formal theories of time. Michon provides a number of fascinating examples of these representations.

Chapter 3, by Dan Zakay, discusses issues concerning the impact of methodological choice, which is a critical consideration because "subjective time is . . . not separable from its measurement" (p. 60). The choice of methodology influences the form of model that a particular researcher might propose. Because "the pattern of temporal experiences and their relationships with the events in the objective world depend on the context within which they are taking place" (p. 60), a contextualistic approach may be a valuable way to handle enigmas in the literature on psychological time. Zakay's careful and systematic consideration of the implications of time estimation methods is, to my knowledge, the best available such guide for beginning and more advanced time researchers.

Chapter 4, by Robert Patterson, is the first of several in this volume that focus on models with strong biopsychological underpinnings. Patterson describes research that has a bearing on psychological-moment models, models that have attempted to explain the fine structure of successiveness. Patterson focuses on the proposal that a central (i.e., cortical) pacemaker controls the sampling of perceptual information in a way that is immune from influence of stimulus parameters. He concludes that this assumption of psychological-moment models has not really been adequately tested, largely because investigations have employed stimuli now known to elicit persistence at sub-cortical levels of the visual system. He asserts that the available evidence on cortical mechanisms provides no support for the notion of a central, fixed-duration intermittency underlying perception.

Chapter 5, by Scott S. Campbell, reviews chronobiological work that pertains to human estimation of long durations (i.e., many minutes to hours). Although research on circadian rhythms may initially seem to relate little to cognitive studies of time estimation, Campbell's synthesis of research findings leads to fascinating conclusions about the system underlying human time-related behavior and judgment. Specifically, the human timekeeping system displays two properties that are not usually associated with clocks, whether the usual, external clocks or the "internal clocks" proposed by some theorists. Campbell calls these properties *sluggishness* and *sloppiness*. The system is sluggish in that free-running circadian rhythms typically have periods slightly longer than 24 hr, which apparently relates closely to the finding that humans isolated from all temporal cues experience a subjective hour that averages about 1.12 hr. The system is sloppy in that, without ordinary environmental cues and behavioral controls, it is quite labile: As a result, "long-term time estimation frequently becomes a guessing game" (p. 115). Findings in this area do not support the notion that human time-related behavior and judgment are mediated in an important way by an internal clock or clocks similar to those which underlie circadian rhythms and timing in non-human animals. Instead, evidence seems to limit the role that internal-clock mechanisms play in human tuning to temporal contingencies.

Chapter 6, by H. L. Roitblat and K. N. J. Young, takes a comparative approach to the study of time as duration and time as succession. In the first half of the chapter, they review research on interval timing in nonhuman animals (e.g., rats and pigeons). This research has led to an understanding of various properties of an inferred internal clock in animals: It is a countup timer, similar to a stopwatch, which times up (rather than down), scales time linearly (rather than logarithmically), and can be stopped. In the second half of the chapter, Roitblat and Young review research on sequential behavior; that is, how animals represent the order in which events occur relative to one another. The available evidence leads them to conclude that "animals form and use hierarchical coherent representations of serially structured events" (p. 149).

Chapter 7, by Janet L. Jackson, continues the focus on time as succession. She reviews cognitive work on such temporal memory judgments as order, spacing, and position, as well on as on autobiographical memory (mostly concerning recency). She addresses three major questions concerning temporal information that underlies these judgments. First, what kind of information serves as a temporal attribute (the *what* issue)? Jackson argues that "intrinsic order constitutes the functional stimulus for temporal judgments" (p. 169). Second, is this information encoded at the time other, nontemporal information is acquired, or is it only constructed during retrieval (the *when* issue)? Jackson's view is that the temporal order of items is contextually anchored at the time of acquisition by means of a study-phase rehearsal process. Third, is this information processed automatically, or is it necessarily the result of deliberate effort (the *how* issue)? On this issue, Jackson concludes that "making temporal judgments involves deliberate or controlled information processing" (p. 173).

Chapter 8, by Jeffery J. Summers and Bruce D. Burns, discusses several kinds of cognitive approaches to timing in human movement sequences. The information-processing approach contains constructs such as the motor program and the internal clock. The activation, or connectionist, approach postulates that timing nodes control the activation of movement components. The ecological, or action-system, approach argues that movement timing is a consequence of the dynamic functioning of coordinative structures. Summers and Burns conclude that "no single mechanism can account for timing behavior in the motor domain" (p. 182). Instead, any of a variety of mechanisms and sources of information may be used to control the spatiotemporal patterning of the components of a movement sequence. Some available evidence suggests that the particular mechanism that a person adopts appears to be a consequence of his or her selection of strategy upon interacting with the specific demands of the ongoing task.

Chapter 9, by Mari Riess Jones, considers phenomena associated with time in music and other rhythmic structures. Music is, after all, one of the most time-involving human creations, and it should come as no surprise that the psychology of music and the psychology of time are intimately intertwined. Jones considers two kinds of relative time that form a part of the structure of all event sequences: temporal changes relative to space or spacelike changes (the motional properties of events) and temporal changes relative to each other (the rhythmic properties of events). Jones characterizes these two properties as they pertain to music and music perception, and she carefully considers two general kinds of models of psychological time. Clock models can handle some of the phenomena of relative time found in music, but (reminiscent of Campbell's conclusions in chapter 5) they can apparently do so only if the interval relations that they code are labile, or "stretchable." Dynamic event structure models, which focus on a person's sensitivity to higher-order temporal relationships, present a flexible alternative to clock models, especially in their description of event-related expectancies.

Chapter 10, by Suchoon S. Mo, considers how particular kinds of abnormality characterizing schizophrenia relate to cognitive research investigating the processing of temporal information. He discusses the distinction between two kinds of duration information: prior time information, which is temporal information about a to-be-experienced duration, and posterior time information, which is temporal information from a currently-experienced duration. He argues that schizophrenics show a reversal of these two kinds of information: Whereas nonschizophrenics are largely unaffected by prior time information, schizophrenics are greatly affected by it. Furthermore, Mo discusses evidence showing that the "brain hemisphere laterality associated with time information in schizophrenics is a mirror image . . . of that in nonschizophrenics" (p. 247). He concludes that what we call *insanity* may be a result of abnormal ways of processing prior and posterior temporal information.

Chapter 11, by the late Frederick T. Melges, summarizes some clinical observations on the breakdown of temporal perspective in acutely ill psychiatric patients. He also considers the relationships between the way a person construes temporal perspective and the person's maintenance of a sense of identity. His central thesis is that "the sense of identity is related to the continuity of temporal perspective, especially future time perspective" (p. 256). In support of this thesis, Melges reviews evidence suggesting that temporal disintegration induces depersonalization, and that the discontinuity of temporal perspective relates to a diffused sense of identity. He points to the importance of time in human cognition when he further speculates that "the essence of self-consciousness may reside in the capacity to observe oneself through time" (p. 265). Cognitive psychologists may be making a serious mistake by focusing primarily on succession and duration. In doing so, they have largely relegated the problems concerning temporal perspective to those who study personality and its breakdown in clinical patients. Melges argues that temporal perspective is the most permanent aspect of psychological time, and perhaps the most important: "Within the framework of temporal perspective, momentary changes of sequence, rate, and rhythm are evaluated" (p. 257). Duration experiences, also, probably depend heavily on temporal perspective, although the ways in which this might occur are largely unresearched and, thus, unknown.

The research and theorizing on time-related behavior and experience that is reviewed in this volume has had little influence on topics that are considered to be in the mainstream of the experimental psychology of sensory, perceptual, and cognitive processes. If anything, the amount of influence may be decreasing. A striking example is that the original edition of Stevens's *Handbook of Experimental Psychology* contained a widely cited review chapter on "Time Perception" (Woodrow, 1951), whereas the recent two-volume second edition of this handbook (Atkinson, Herrnstein, Lindzey, & Luce, 1988) does not contain a chapter on psychological time. In the 37 years between these two editions, most psychologists have continued to rely on time as an independent variable, much as physicists use t in their equations. With few exceptions, studies in which time is a dependent variable (i.e., those in which psychological time is measured) have not made any substantial impact on theorizing or model building in cognitive psychology. Perhaps this is because it remains unclear how extensively psychological time might influence the wide range of behaviors and experiences characteristic of organisms. The present volume is needed in order to extend the range of connections with more mainstream literature in the area of cognitive science. The contributors to this volume collectively argue that psychological time can no longer continue to be ignored by psychologists who propose models of nontemporal behavior, because nontemporal behavior does not exist.

REFERENCES

Atkinson, R. C., Herrnstein, R. J., Lindzey, G., & Luce, R. D. (1988). *Stevens' handbook of experimental psychology* (2 vols.). New York: Wiley.

Guyau, J.-M. (1988). *La genèse de l'idée de temps* [The origin of the idea of time]. In J. A. Michon, V. Pouthas, & J. L. Jackson (Eds.), *Guyau and the idea of time* (pp. 37-92). Amsterdam: North-Holland. (Original work published 1890)

James, W. (1890). *The principles of psychology* (Vol. 1). New York: Holt.

Michon, J. A., & Jackson, J. L. (1985). Introduction: The psychology of time. In J. A. Michon & J. L. Jackson (Eds.), *Time, mind, and behavior* (pp. 2-17). Berlin: Springer-Verlag.

Nichols, H. (1891). The psychology of time. *American Journal of Psychology, 3*, 453-529.

Woodrow, H. (1951). Time perception. In S. S. Stevens (Ed.), *Handbook of experimental psychology* (pp. 1224-1236). New York: Wiley.

1 Models of Psychological Time

Richard A. Block
Montana State University

Psychological time consists of three major aspects: succession, duration, and temporal perspective. *Succession* refers to the sequential occurrence of events (i.e., changes), from which an organism may perceive successiveness and temporal order. *Duration* refers to several different characteristics of events. Every event persists for a certain duration, which an individual may encode and remember. Events are separated by time periods, or intervals, that may contain other events, and the length of intervals plays a role in various aspects of psychological time. A relatively unified series of events forms an episode that continues for a certain duration, which an individual may encode and remember. *Temporal perspective*, the third aspect of psychological time discussed here, refers to an individual's experiences and conceptions concerning past, present, and future time.

This chapter reviews models and evidence concerning each of these three aspects of psychological time. It also focuses on problems with, or weaknesses of, the various models. No existing model can handle the variety of experimental evidence on psychological time.

MODELS OF PSYCHOLOGICAL TIME AS SUCCESSION

In the literature on psychological time, researchers have been somewhat less concerned with time as succession than with time as duration

1

(Michon, chapter 2, this volume). Nevertheless, considerable research has investigated judgments of simultaneity, successiveness, and temporal order of rapidly occurring, very brief-duration events. This work has been grounded primarily in models of biopsychological and sensory-perceptual processes. Researchers studying memory have done considerable recent work on issues and models concerning how people encode and remember the temporal order of events occurring over longer periods of time.

Simultaneity and Successiveness

Some classic studies on psychological time investigated the temporal resolution of perceptual systems. Various phenomena occur if brief stimuli are presented in such a way that the stimulus-onset asynchrony (i.e., the interval between the onset times of two stimuli) is less than several milliseconds. The perceptual systems differ somewhat in this regard, especially audition and vision, the two that researchers have studied most. An added complication is that certain kinds of phenomena occur when stimuli strike the same sensory-receptor areas (e.g., the same position on the cochlea of an ear or on the retina of an eye), whereas somewhat different phenomena occur when stimuli strike different receptor areas.

The monaural or binaural presentation of two brief auditory stimuli separated by less than a few milliseconds produces an experience of simultaneity—subjects fail to discriminate the two stimuli from a single stimulus. However, the auditory system is still extremely sensitive to relatively small temporal differences. Under optimal conditions, Exner reported successiveness if the stimulus-onset asynchrony of two binaurally presented stimuli was as short as about 2 ms (see Hirsh & Sherrick, 1961). If two auditory stimuli are presented dichotically (i.e., one stimulus to each ear) with a stimulus-onset asynchrony less than about .5 ms, people experience them as a single stimulus. Under these conditions, the perceptual phenomenon is spatial, rather than temporal: A sound source located away from the median plane normally produces such slight differences in asynchrony, and these differences are a cue that enable a person to localize the sound source. If the stimulus-onset asynchrony of two dichotically presented stimuli is greater than several milliseconds, however, people experience successiveness, with one stimulus located to the left and one to the right of the median plane.

Exner also reported that if two binocularly presented stimuli occur with a stimulus-onset asynchrony less than about 44 ms, they seem to be a single, unchanging stimulus. If stimuli repeatedly strike the same retinal areas with slightly longer interstimulus intervals, people experience flicker−temporal discontinuity of the stimuli. Other phenomena occur under conditions in which stimuli strike different retinal areas. Westheimer and McKee (1977) found that if two 100-ms visual stimuli strike spatially adjacent positions on a retinal surface, people report apparent movement of a single stimulus, even if the stimulus-onset asynchrony is very short (e.g., 3-10 ms). (Perhaps concomitantly, under these conditions they can also judge temporal order fairly reliably. As I mention later, however, people cannot always judge temporal order reliably under conditions in which they can discriminate successiveness reliably.) As the stimulus-onset asynchrony of two stimuli increases (e.g., 120 ms for two 100-ms stimuli, or an interstimulus interval of 20 ms), apparent movement becomes optimum, but it nevertheless depends on stimulus parameters (Kahneman & Wolman, 1970). At still longer intervals, people experience successive stimuli, but no apparent movement.

Psychological Moment

A number of studies have investigated several slightly different central (i.e., cortical) intermittency models of what Stroud (1955) originally called the *moment*, or "the least timewise element of psychological experience" (p. 180). These models, which have mostly fallen from whatever favor they originally had, are usually collectively called *psychological-moment*, or *perceptual-moment*, models. They originated with observations that people experience apparent simultaneity if a very short interval separates two or more brief visual stimuli. Although these models propose a central pacemaker immune to specific sensory-perceptual influence, virtually all of the studies investigating psychological-moment models have used visual stimuli (see Patterson, chapter 4, this volume).

Stroud's (1955, 1967) original proposal, which is usually called a *discrete-moment* model, claims that all incoming information is processed in nonoverlapping (i.e, temporally discrete) samples or scans and that the temporal order of stimuli within a scan is not preserved. Allport (1968) proposed a major alternative, a so-called *travelling-moment* model, which asserts that information is processed as if it is perceived through a continuously moving, fixed-duration window, rather than as if it is perceived in discrete, nonoverlapping samples. Regardless of model (discrete moment or travelling moment), early speculation linked the moment with a hypothetical scanning reflected in the alpha rhythm, which is 8-12 cycles/s, or about 100 ms/cycle. Different investigators have obtained varying evidence on the duration of this hypothetical time span of integration. For example, researchers have estimated the moment at about 90 ms (Hylan, 1903), 50-200 ms (Stroud, 1955), 140-170 ms (White, 1963), and 70-100 ms (Allport, 1968).

Although psychological-moment models such as Stroud's propose a central, neural pacemaker that is uninfluenced by external events, stimulus parameters such as duration and intensity heavily influence estimates of the moment. Efron (1970) found that the minimum duration of a visual or auditory perception is about 130 ms, and he suggested that this finding is interpretable in terms of persistence of vision. Efron and Lee (1971) compared predictions of moment and persistence explanations. Their results, which are consistent with a persistence model, reject any psychological-moment model in which a central pacemaker or internal clock dictates a fixed sampling period that is uninfluenced by stimulus parameters. Prior research on the psychological moment may have involved dynamic properties of sensory systems rather than any central temporal pacemaker. Breitmeyer (1984) reviewed evidence showing that "the existence of a psychological moment can be as easily explained by persistence" at peripheral levels of the visual system, and so "the notion of the psychological moment is conceptually superfluous" (p. 94). In addition, failures to link internal-clock models with the alpha rhythm of about 10 cycles/s (e.g., Treisman, 1984) weaken the frequently proposed neurophysiological basis for a fixed-duration moment of about 100 ms.

Patterson (see chapter 4, this volume) discusses relationships between psychological-moment models and recent research, which suggests that several kinds of neural persistence accompany the visual analysis of information. He concludes that although research has not adequately tested psychological-moment models, no available evidence supports the notion of a central, fixed-duration intermittency with a period of about 100 ms.

Some other research seems to reveal the operation of briefer kinds of intermittences in time-related estimates and productions, and this has led to models that hypothesize a smallest unit of psychological time, or a so-called *time quantum*. Geissler (1987), for example, reviewed analyses of various kinds of time-related response measures that suggest a time quantum with a duration of approximately 4.5 ms. Kristofferson (1980) identified a step function underlying duration discrimination in well-practiced human subjects. Based on this step function, Kristofferson concluded that the time quantum does not have a fixed periodicity; instead, it may double and halve, assuming values of about 13, 25, 50, and 100 ms. The origins of these values of the hypothetical time quantum remain obscure. At present, no research unambiguously reveals the existence of a central, neural pacemaker that may underlie the concept of a psychological moment or time quantum; there probably is none.

Psychological Present

If an event or a sequence of events lasts for more than a few seconds, people experience what most theorists call the *psychological present* or *conscious present*.   James (1890), who called it the *specious present*, suggested the metaphor of "a saddle-back . . . on which we sit perched, and from which we look into two directions into time" (p. 609).

Controversy about the upper limit of the psychological present continues, especially concerning what this implies about the attention and memory systems that may underlie the phenomenon. Boring (1933/1963) said that the "conscious present can certainly include a rhythmic grouping that occupies a second or a second and a half, and that with somewhat less 'immediacy' . . . may extend to include a rhythm of a quarter or perhaps even half a minute" (p. 135). More recent evidence reveals that the upper limit of the psychological present is much shorter than this. Pöppel (1972) reported evidence suggesting a process with a period between 4 and 7 s, which he said is roughly equivalent to the time span of the conscious present. Michon (1978) concluded that the width of the psychological present is highly variable, but that the upper limit is about 7 or 8 s. Fraisse (1984) said that the psychological present averages about 2 to 3 s, with an upper limit of about 5 s. As examples of content that are part of the psychological present, Fraisse cited the perception of a telephone number, a simple sentence, or a unified rhythmic pattern. These are typical examples of content that is maintained in an activated state, or in a hypothetical short-term memory store. Block (1979) agreed that the psychological present is limited to about 5 s and suggested that this limit is related to the dynamic functioning of the short-term store.

No single temporal-judgment paradigm or method allows us precisely to measure the duration of the psychological present. To my knowledge, little or no evidence reveals any discontinuity in the experiencing of durations or intervals over the range from about 1 s through tens of seconds. The lack of any discontinuity is probably a reflection of the continuous transitions between dynamically different information-processing components, at least as far as the experiencing of a psychological present is concerned. Stated somewhat differently, the psychological present "is a highly flexible tuning process that is dynamically fitting the temporal width of the field of attention . . . to the sequential structure of the pattern of events" (Michon, 1978, p. 89).

The perception and production of rhythm, as in a piece of music or in a series of coordinated movements, depends on structural and dynamic properties of the information-processing systems underlying the psychological present (see Jones, chapter 9, this volume). If a musical or other rhythmic tempo is very slow, the limits of the psychological present may be exceeded, and a person may need to effortfully strive to synthesize what seems like a relatively nonunified piece. Thus, the experiencing of rhythm (or the lack of it) apparently involves an awareness of durations of events and of intervals between events maintained in information-processing systems involved in the construction of a psychological present (cf. Woodrow, 1951).

Memory for Temporal Order

Perhaps in interaction with human cognitive processes, information relating to the ordering of events from earlier to later gives rise to the common idea that the progression of time may be represented as a line or an arrow. The continuously integrated functioning of perceiving, remembering, and anticipating processes apparently produces a relatively automatic awareness of the successive ordering of events. This is a fundamental aspect of all temporal experiences beyond those that merely produce an experience of successiveness without the ability to discriminate temporal order. The primary psychological basis for the encoding of order relationships between events relates to the dynamic characteristics of information processing: In the process of encoding an event, a person remembers related events which preceded it, anticipates future events, or both (cf. Hintzman, Summers, & Block, 1975; Tzeng & Cotton, 1980).

Under conditions in which the same sensory-receptor areas are stimulated, trained observers can discriminate reliably (i.e., at 75% accuracy) the temporal order of two events (rather than merely discriminate two stimuli from one stimulus) only if the interval separating the events is greater than several milliseconds. Hirsh and Sherrick (1961) found a temporal-order threshold of about 20 ms for auditory, visual, and tactile stimuli. No one has yet identified a specific sensory-perceptual or cognitive process that underlies this 20-ms threshold, however; and any such threshold apparently depends on stimulus variables such as intensity, size, and position (cf. Westheimer & McKee, 1977).

If a person encodes a series of stimuli that occur with relatively long (e.g., 1 or 2 s) interstimulus intervals separating them, we can assume that order discrimination is essentially perfect at the time of the initial encoding. Several related questions then arise: How long does a person retain information about temporal order? What factors influence the accuracy of long-term temporal-order judgments? What are the implications of this level of accuracy on models of memory for temporal order and on models of memory in general?

Hintzman and Block (1971) investigated the ability of subjects to remember the approximate serial position of an event in a series of relatively homogeneous events, such as a word in series of words. Even though subjects were not forewarned about the subsequent position-judgment task, they were able to remember serial positions with a reasonable degree of accuracy. The slope of the function relating judged position and actual position serves as an index of the encoding and remembering of time-related information (see Schab & Crowder, 1988). Hintzman and Block found that this slope is greatest over the first 7-10 words in a series (a temporal span of about 35-50 s), and that the slope is more gradual, although still positive, across the remainder of the positions.

Subjects can also remember the relative spacing of pairs of related events, such as words, in a homogeneous series, as well as the distribution of repetitions of an event in each of two such series presented successively (Hintzman & Block, 1971, 1973; Hintzman et al., 1975). In addition, the accuracy of judgments of relative primacy or recency is greater for pairs of events which occurred in the initial positions in a series, a finding that mirrors the strong primacy effect seen in the slope of the position-judgment function (Marshall, Chen, & Jeter, 1989).

These findings support models in which time-related information about events and relationships among events is encoded as part of the memory of an event. Converging evidence suggests that this information, a so-called *time tag*, is contextual in nature (Hintzman & Block, 1971, 1973; Hintzman, Block, & Summers, 1973; Tzeng, Lee, & Wetzel, 1979). Contextual elements include implicit associations to an event or to other events in an episode, mood states, internal physiological cues, and conspicuous external events. The primacy effect in serial-position and relative-recency judgments, as well as the positive time-order effect in duration judgment (discussed later), suggest that changes in contextual elements occur more rapidly near the start of a new episode. Within an episode, a somewhat different process, called *study-phase retrieval*, serves to encode information concerning the relative recency of events. In this process, an event that is related in some way to a current event is retrieved, along with its contextual elements, and information concerning this retrieval is associated with the current event (Hintzman et al., 1975; Tzeng & Cotton, 1980).

Jackson (1985, 1986; see also chapter 7, this volume) has argued that, at least under certain circumstances, information-processing strategies influence the accuracy of judgments of position, recency, and similar temporal-memory judgments. For example, subjects' use of more elaborative mnemonic strategies increase the accuracy of their subsequent position judgments. In addition, subjects remember the temporal position of words in a list more accurately if the words are concrete (e.g., door) rather than abstract (e.g., truth). Further, cuing subjects to forget words impairs temporal-order judgments involving those words (Jackson & Michon, 1984). Jackson (1986) concluded that "relative order judgments may indeed reflect some automatic encoding of intrinsic order, but . . . such coding is not sufficient to enable subjects to perform more complex temporal judgment tasks adequately" (pp. 81-82).

The finding that subjects can make accurate serial-position, order, and other temporal-memory judgments even though they are not forewarned that the experimenter will ask them to do so suggests that at least some temporal or contextual information is encoded automatically. In addition, some researchers (e.g., Auday, Sullivan, & Cross, 1988) have found no influence of forewarning subjects about the forthcoming temporal-judgment task on the accuracy of subsequent serial-position and relative-recency judgments. Exactly what kinds of temporal information are encoded relatively automatically and what kinds are encoded only deliberately remains an unresolved issue. In addition, the precise role that contextual information plays in each kind of temporal judgment task must be clarified.

Memory researchers who have investigated recency and temporal-order judgments have traditionally employed a relatively simple methodology: Event a occurs, then an unfilled interstimulus interval, then Event b, and so on. However, actual relationships between events are more complex than the simple before/after relationship that is the focus of this memory research. Allen and Kautz (1985) argued that 13 primitive relationships form the basis for all knowledge about the temporal relationship between any two (or more) durations. In addition to the before/after relationship, the relationships between two durations (of events or of episodes) include: equals, meets/met by, overlaps/overlapped by, starts/started by, during/contains, and finishes/finished by. The human information-processing system probably does not automatically encode all of these relationships, so a person frequently must infer relationships among events much later than at the time that the events occurred. Future research might profitably focus on this issue.

MODELS OF PSYCHOLOGICAL TIME
AS DURATION

If an event lasts for less than a few milliseconds, it seems instanta-neous—without duration. If an event or episode persists for longer than a few milliseconds, people experience, remember, and may therefore be able to judge duration. A person is typically more aware of the duration of a time period if various factors influence him or her in such a way that the duration seems lengthened rather than shortened. Judgments of time periods in the range from about one-half second to a few minutes tend to be fairly veridical in that judged duration is related to actual duration in an approximately linear way, with a slope of about 1.0 (Allan, 1979; Michon, 1975, 1985). In the range from minutes to hours and days, judged time also shows this veridical function if the usual variety of events mark the passage of time. If such markers are absent, the experienced duration of a time period is somewhat shortened compared to its actual duration, as well as more variable. Experiments studying the estimation of long time periods (i.e., those on the order of hours) reveal a slight shortening of experienced duration: Subjects tend to verbally underestimate 1-hr periods and tend to produce a subjective hour that averages about 1.12 hr (discussed later, as well as in Campbell, chapter 5, this volume). Because estimates of relatively long durations may relate to the tendency of circadian rhythms to free-run with periods slightly longer than 24 hr (Aschoff, 1984, 1985), biological factors may be involved.

Experienced Duration and Remembered Duration

James (1890) asserted that duration in passing lengthens when "we grow attentive to the passage of time itself" (p. 626), whereas duration in retrospect lengthens as a function of "the multitudinousness of the memories which the time affords" (p. 624). Fraisse (1963) proposed that "direct time judgments [are] founded immediately on the changes we experience and later on the changes we remember" (p. 234). By emphasizing that psychological time involves changes, Fraisse avoided a common pitfall: As discussed later, explanations that refer to attention to time or to temporal information processing must be qualified, because time itself is not a stimulus (see Gibson, 1975). However, changes serve as referents, or cues, to use in experiencing, remembering, and judging time.

During much of this century, descriptions and interpretations of experimental findings often failed to acknowledge the distinction between duration in passing and duration in retrospect. Diverse findings that appeared to conflict merely involved different methods of obtaining temporal judgments. Even if interpretations were reasonable, descriptions of findings often did not reflect the true kind of duration judgment studied. For example, an otherwise excellent article investigating judgment of duration in retrospect is marred by the title, "Time Went By So Slowly," which suggests that the article concerns judgment of duration in passing (Loftus, Schooler, Boone, & Kline, 1987).

Most researchers recognize the importance of distinguishing between these two fundamentally different kinds of duration experiences, and some researchers have experimentally investigated the differences between the two. Experimenters study the distinction by varying instructions to subjects, using either a prospective paradigm or a retrospective paradigm (see Zakay, chapter 3, this volume). In a prospective paradigm, the experimenter tells a subject beforehand that the experimenter subsequently will ask the subject to judge the duration of a time period. Because each subject can be asked to make many such judgments for different time periods, researchers have used the prospective paradigm frequently. Hicks, Miller, Gaes, and Bierman (1977) called the temporal experience studied in the prospective paradigm "the experience of time-in-passing" (p. 443). I prefer to call it *experienced duration*. In a retrospective paradigm, the experimenter gives a subject vague instructions about the task, and only after the experimental time period does the experimenter ask the subject to judge its duration. I call the temporal experience studied in this paradigm *remembered duration*.

This distinction is intimately related to the different methods of duration judgment. When an experimenter uses a method like verbal estimation or comparison, he or she may use either a prospective or a retrospective paradigm. However, when an experimenter uses the method of production, the paradigm must be a prospective one, because the experimenter must inform the subject about the task before the subject can produce the required duration. The method of reproduction is a hybrid form of paradigm, because the experimenter may or may not inform the subject before the presentation of the to-be-reproduced duration, but the subject must make the actual reproduction prospectively.

The operational distinction between prospective and retrospective paradigms involves instructions to subjects, and so it is best to view these paradigms as influencing subjects' temporal outlook. Recent research shows that the prospective outlook and the retrospective outlook differ because of the way in which they interact with other experimental factors to influence underlying cognitive processes. For example, Brown (1985; Brown & Stubbs, 1988) found that prospective verbal estimates and reproductions are longer (and also more accurate) than retrospective judgments. Brown (1985) found little or no other difference between the two experimental paradigms, and Brown and Stubbs (1988) suggested that "a common timing process may underlie judgments under prospective and retrospective conditions" (p. 307).   Nevertheless, other researchers have reported reliable differences between the two paradigms in the influence of various factors on duration judgments. Hicks, Miller, and Kinsbourne (1976) found that prospective duration judgments of a task are shortened if subjects process more information. In the prospective paradigm, it appears that subjects' allocation of attention to more difficult tasks or more complex stimuli restricts their allocation of attention to time-related information, such as contextual changes (cf. Brown, 1985).

In a retrospective paradigm, attention to time-related information has a more limited influence on duration judgments.   Instead, people remember the duration of a time period by relying both on event information and on contextual information associated with the episode. If a person can retrieve a greater number of events, he or she remembers the duration of a time period as being longer (Ornstein, 1969; Vroon, 1970). However, people do not simply base retrospective duration judgments on the degree of recallability of events from the time period (Block, 1974; Loftus et al., 1987); other factors are involved.   Even if people do sometimes use this kind of strategy, they undoubtedly do not attempt to retrieve all available memories of events from the time period. Instead, they probably rely on an availability heuristic—roughly, they remember a duration as being longer to the extent that they can easily retrieve a few of the events that occurred during the time period.

A slightly different proposal is that retrospective "duration judgments are based on memory for the amount of processing done" (Miller, Hicks, & Willette, 1978, p. 178). However, it is unclear how subjects are able to estimate the amount of processing done and how this kind of estimate differs from an estimate of the ease of retrieval of events.   Other processes, such as a person's implicit assessment of the amount of contextual change during the duration, also play an important role (see later). However, the processes involved when subjects assess contextual change remain just as obscure as those involved when subjects assess availability of events or amount of processing.

Chronobiological Models

The normal environment affords information related to many kinds of cyclic change. Cycles involving wakefulness and sleep, light and dark, work and rest, and cold and warmth form a salient part of our lives. Even if few changes occur in a person's external environment, changing thoughts and other internal events, proprioceptive cues, and biological consequences of internal rhythms may be salient enough to afford the person an important and useful frame of reference in time.

Some chronobiologists have recently studied relationships between duration judgments and biological rhythms (see Campbell, chapter 5, this volume). More typically, though, chronobiological research investigates relationships between endogenous biological rhythms and organisms' cyclical behaviors, such as those revealed in circadian cycles of activity level, feeding, and sleeping. Their research, which uses such diverse species as honeybees, hamsters, and humans, is based on a model in which a central pacemaker (or several pacemakers) underlies and controls cyclical behaviors (see Figure 1.1).

Researchers are beginning to identify and understand the underlying brain processes, but they remain elusive (Johnson & Hastings, 1986). In some species, research has identified a specific circadian pacemaker. For example, the suprachiasmatic nuclei of some rodents apparently contain neural mechanisms which regulate behavioral cycles. As an organism's nervous system develops, cyclical external cues called *zeitgebers* ("timegivers"), such as the daily onset of light, synchronize these pacemakers. If there are no abrupt changes, once *zeitgebers* have served this function they may play a relatively minor, corrective role. Cyclical behaviors continue on an approximately 24-hr (i.e., circadian) cycle even if an organism is isolated from all exogenous changes (see Aschoff, 1984). Under conditions that are not well understood, some people who are isolated from *zeitgebers* may show an internal desynchronization of some rhythms from others, suggesting that the "circadian system consists of a multiplicity of oscillators . . . kept in synchrony by the zeitgebers" (Aschoff, 1984, p. 446).

Chronobiologists typically study cyclical behaviors by seeking the physiological basis of such oscillators or pacemakers. The prototypical chronobiological model shown in Figure 1.1 seems necessary to explain the regulation of cyclical behavior. However, most extant chronobiological models are limited: They do not consider whether various strategies of the organism influence circadian rhythms. For example, a person may choose when to sleep and when not to sleep following time-zone shifts that produce so-called *jet-lag* experiences; this choice may influence overt

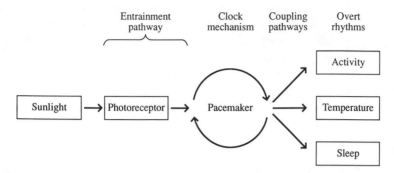

Figure 1.1. A chronobiological model of cyclical (i.e., circadian) behaviors. (After Johnson & Hastings, 1986. Adapted by permission.)

behavioral rhythms. It may be fruitful to investigate potential ways in which such strategies modify the functioning of pacemakers that underlie biological rhythms, even if the account considers only a single category of time-related behavior, cyclical activity.

We also need to know much more about whether the pacemakers that apparently underlie circadian rhythms are involved in time-related behaviors and experiences other than overt rhythms. Fortunately, some data are now available on the relationships between experienced duration and circadian rhythms in humans. Aschoff (1985; see also Aschoff, 1984) studied people living for a period ranging from 7 days to more than 30 days in an environment that afforded no exogenous time cues. During this period, Aschoff asked his subjects to make two kinds of duration judgment. Long-duration judgments required them repeatedly to produce a 1-hr duration: They were told to signal every subjective hour (except, of course, during sleep epochs). Short-duration judgments required subjects to produce a verbally stated duration ranging from 10 to 120 s.

For present purposes, Aschoff's most important finding is that the short-duration productions were not related to the long-duration productions. Long-duration productions of a 1-hr period averaged slightly longer than 1 hr, and each person's mean production correlated positively with his or her duration of wakefulness as well as with the length of the circadian (i.e., sleep-wake) cycle. In contrast, short-duration productions were not correlated with either of these variables. Although Aschoff found considerable individual differences in short-duration productions, on the average these productions were fairly accurate (e.g., the mean production of a 10-s duration was 11.7 s and that of a 120-s duration was 116.8 s). Thus, processes involved in making short-duration judgments apparently differ from those involved in making long-duration judgments. However, the short and the long productions may have differed only because of differences in the methods used to obtain them: Long-duration productions were subject-initiated, whereas short-duration productions were experimenter-initiated. As Aschoff noted, his findings must be replicated in an experiment that uses the same method to investigate both short- and long-duration experiences.

Campbell (1986) studied the "estimation of empty time" in people restricted to an isolation unit that afforded only minimal temporal cues. In contrast to Aschoff, Campbell prohibited his subjects from engaging in activities like reading, exercising, listening to music, and so on. At various relatively long intervals (ranging from 5.2 to 23.5 hr) during a 60-hr isolation period, he asked participants to estimate the time of day. The participants verbally underestimated these intervals, and Campbell concluded that their mean subjective hour actually lasted about 1.12 hr. Lavie and Webb (1975) had found that subjects who are not strictly isolated (that is, they could engage in various kinds of activity) verbally underestimated long intervals to about this same extent. So we cannot attribute Campbell's finding that subjects verbally underestimated long intervals to the lack of activity or stimulation afforded by a monotonous environment. In addition, Campbell found that this shortening of experienced duration was about the same proportion as the mean proportion by which a person's free-running subjective day was lengthened. Campbell (chapter 5, this volume) discusses this characteristic of the human circadian system, which he calls its *sluggishness*. He also discusses the considerable variability in subjects' duration experiences, a characteristic which reveals what he calls the *sloppiness* of the circadian system.

Although biological rhythms influence psychological time, time-related experiences and behaviors involve more than the relatively simple biological processes that chronobiological models describe. Earlier in this century, however, some theorists adopting biological or biochemical models made some far-reaching claims. Consider now a historically separate, yet theoretically related, kind of model.

Internal-Clock Models

Hoagland (1933, 1966) attributed various kinds of time-related behaviors and judgments to a single mechanism: chemical processes in the brain. He called this mechanism a *master chemical clock*. The proposed mechanism is somewhat analogous to the modern conception of biological rhythms in that it relies on the notion that activity in "certain parts of the brain" (Hoagland, 1933, p. 283) underlies psychological time. However, Hoagland's chemical clock differs in other ways. First, it is more hypothetical: Hoagland was unable to identify a specific brain area, such as the suprachiasmatic nuclei, that is involved. So far, neurological evidence has failed to find Hoagland's master chemical clock, other than the processes involved in the circadian system. The circadian system, however, pertains to longer time periods than the seconds-to-minutes periods to which Hoagland's model most directly applies. Second, Hoagland's model contains no notion of *zeitgebers*, or entraining stimuli. Third, the explanatory burden of this model lies mostly outside the domain of cyclic behaviors. Instead, Hoagland's model attempts to explain aperiodic duration experiences, such as the experience of time-in-passing over brief periods.

Without speculating about a possible biochemical or neural basis, Treisman (1963) extended Hoagland's notion by proposing a model of what he called the *internal clock* (see Figure 1.2). In this model, a pacemaker produces a regular series of pulses, although the pulse rate increases as an organism's specific arousal level increases. A counter records the number of pulses that arrive at a given point, and the result is entered into a store or into a comparator mechanism. A verbal selective mechanism (a long-term memory store containing verbal labels, such as *20 sec*, *1 min*, etc.) assists in retrieving useful information from the store.

Treisman (1984) recently attempted to determine whether the frequency of this hypothetical pacemaker is related to the well-known alpha rhythm. The alpha rhythm is frequently mentioned as a possible source of (or reflection of) the kind of pacemaker involved in a hypothetical internal clock. Treisman recorded EEGs of subjects while they produced 4-s durations in a darkened cubicle. His data failed to support the notion that arousal, which is presumably reflected in alpha frequency, is correlated with the frequency of the hypothetical pacemaker. These data also do not support the notion that a common pacemaker may influence both the alpha-rhythm generator and the frequency of the hypothetical pacemaker in an internal-clock system. In short, this evidence offers no empirical support for any relatively simple internal-clock model, and there is no known neurophysiological basis for the components of Hoagland's (1933) and Treisman's (1963) models. Furthermore, it is questionable whether this descriptive model is needed to explain temporal behaviors and experiences.

Some contemporary behavioral psychologists, especially those who collect the kinds of data needed to make inferences about cognitive processes in animals, have also explored internal-clock models. They

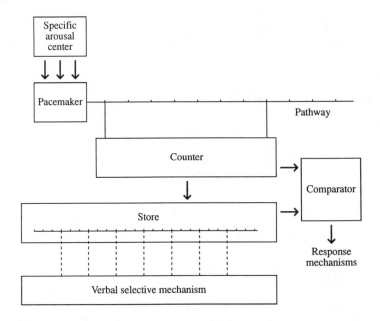

Figure 1.2. A model of a hypothetical internal clock. (From Treisman, 1963. Reprinted by permission.)

typically investigate behavioral responses of animals such as pigeons and rats during relatively short time periods (e.g., seconds to minutes). The general finding is that animals are sensitive to different interval schedules of reinforcement. Many behavioral psychologists propose that interval-schedule responding relies on an event-independent timer, or internal clock.

Figure 1.3 illustrates a general behavioral model of this hypothetical internal clock (see, for example, Church, 1984; Roitblat, 1987, and chapter 6, this volume); note that it is strikingly similar to Treisman's (1963) model (see Figure 1.2). It assumes that the internal-clock mechanism consists of a pacemaker, a switch, and an accumulator. The pacemaker, operating somewhat like a metronome, generates more or less regularly spaced pulses, as in Treisman's model. This assumption of the model fits nicely with the finding that in various species subjective duration and actual duration are apparently linearly related. At the onset of a relevant external timing signal, the switch engages and the accumulator begins to count pulses. The switch is included in the model

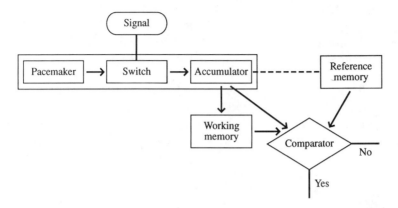

Figure 1.3. A model of time-related behavior in animals. (From Church, 1984. Reprinted by permission.)

to handle the finding that an interrupted timing signal may stop the accumulation of pulses from the pacemaker, as revealed by temporally displaced responding. This implies that the internal clock functions like a stopwatch. (This feature represents a difference between this model and Treisman's model, which has no counter-stopping mechanism.) A reference memory retains information about the approximate number of pulses that elapsed before past reinforcement. A working memory holds the current total pulse count. The response rate on an interval schedule increases in probability as a comparison (by the comparator mechanism) of working memory and reference memory reveals a similar count of pulses.

Because this timing scheme can time various kinds of signals, it is somewhat flexible. However, the model is limited in the sense that it does not take into account other potentially important factors, which are more prominent in humans than in other animals. For example, activities (such as strategies) of an organism during a time period influence its time-related behaviors, but this model is silent on that issue. Evidence suggests that children, for example, use an "external clock" to time an interval; that is, they engage in various repetitive movements that take an appropriate amount of time while they wait for reinforcement (Pouthas, 1985).

A serious question about all internal-clock models concerns whether they can be generalized to handle evidence on human timing and temporal judgment. These models seem unable to explain why cognitive kinds of factors (e.g., strategies) influence temporal behavior and experience. No existing internal-clock model includes a mechanism whereby these factors influence the basic functioning of the hypothetical pacemaker; indeed, the pacemaker in these models is relatively autonomous (immune to external influence). In addition, these models focus mainly on experienced duration (that is, prospective interval timing). Thus, they differ considerably from cognitive-process models that can easily handle remembered duration and that emphasize how controlled strategies interact with other factors in complex ways to influence temporal experiences. Internal-clock models seem best suited to handle relatively simple relationships, such as that between body temperature, arousal, and response rate. Thus, internal-clock models propose what may be an oversimplified view of the complex set of processes that underlie psychological time.

Related to this is the problem of why human duration judgments are sometimes so inaccurate, especially for an organism that is said to possess an internal clock. For example, Loftus et al. (1987) found that the mean remembered duration of a 30-s videotape was about 150 s. Cognitive models, which propose that a variety of different factors influence remembered duration, can explain the inherent inaccuracy of human duration judgments more convincingly than can internal-clock models. An alternative view is that people make such inaccurate duration judgments only when they must "translate" a duration experience into a conventional verbal unit (e.g., "It was about 142 s"). If, instead, they may produce temporal judgments by responding nonverbally, as other animals do, their interval timing may be much more accurate (see, for example, Slanger, in press).

In short, internal-clock models proposed by behavioral psychologists investigating interval timing in nonhuman animals seem limited. Most cognitive psychologists agree that these models are incomplete, and they think that other models of time-related behavior and experience are more valid. Animal models are interesting, but unless they consider the role that cognitive factors play, we probably cannot generalize them very easily to human psychological time. In this regard, Richelle and his colleagues (e.g., Richelle & Lejeune, 1980; Richelle, Lejeune, Perikel, & Fery, 1985) have made considerable progress: They have done comparative research involving several species, including humans, and they have included a role for cognitive factors. Perhaps as a result, Richelle et al. (1985) were able to pose a provocative question: "Why not admit that there are as many clocks as there are behaviors exhibiting timing properties?" (p. 90).

Cognitive psychology is not without its own internal-clock models, however: Some researchers studying human movement timing have also proposed internal-clock models. Lashley (1951) proposed that practiced movement sequences are structured as individual elements organized into chunks that are executed as part of a what he called a *motor program* for the action sequence. Because Lashley proposed that a motor program is executed without the need for feedback, the program needed some sort of internal-control process for timing the elements of the program. Researchers have searched for a common mechanism, such as an internal clock, which is able to stabilize motor programs in the face of changes in states of the performer, changes in contextual stimuli, changes in equipment or instruments used for the performance, and so on. They have had some successes. However, the important question of how movement sequences are timed is still largely unresolved, as is the question of whether recourse to an internal-clock mechanism is needed (see Summers & Burns, chapter 8, this volume).

Attentional Models

Several theorists have proposed attentional models of psychological time in which terms like *attention to time* and *temporal information processing* play a major explanatory role (e.g., Hicks et al., 1976; Thomas & Weaver, 1975; Underwood & Swain, 1973). In this section, I review some of the evidence relating to these attentional models, and I suggest several sources of inadequacy in the elaboration of them.

Thomas and his colleagues (Thomas & Brown, 1975; Thomas & Weaver, 1975) developed and tested a mathematical model concerning how attentional allocation influences perceived duration. This model has the benefit of being an explicitly formulated and, thus, easily criticized attentional model of psychological time, which is why I am focusing on it here. The model may be expressed as the functional equation: $\tau(I) = a\ f(t,I) + (1 - a)\ g^*(I)$. The basic notion of the model is that the perceived duration (τ) of an interval containing certain information (I) is monotonically related to the weighted average of the amount of information encoded by two processors, a temporal information processor, or timer [$f(t,I)$] and a nontemporal information processor [$g^*(I)$]. Attention is divided between the two processors, which function in parallel. Perceived duration is weighted (with probability parameter a) to optimize the reliability of the information that each processor encodes, because as more attention is allocated to one processor, the other becomes more unreliable. That is, as a approaches 1, the subject encodes more temporal information, and as a approaches 0, the subject encodes more nontemporal information.   To the extent that little stimulus information occurs during the to-be-judged duration, more attention is allocated to temporal information, and f(t,I) is more heavily weighted; to the extent that considerable information occurs, more attention is allocated to nontemporal information, and g*(I) is more heavily weighted.

Thomas restricted the range of applicability of this model to duration judgments of stimuli presented for less than 100 ms, and it is not surprising that his data generally fit the model.   Moreover, Michon (1985) stated that this model provides a good generic model of temporal information processing, even that involving much longer time periods. I have some reservations about this, because the extension of this model to longer time periods is post hoc, and some data seem to reject this extension of the model (e.g., Michon, 1965; Vroon, 1970).   Consider Vroon's experiments, which investigated how an information-processing task influences the remembered duration of a 60-s time period.

In one experiment, Vroon presented subjects with two time periods, each of which contained a series of high- and low-pitched tones, and their task was simply to attend to the tones.   One time period was filled with more stimuli than the other: Subjects heard 60 rather than 30 tones. Vroon found that subjects remembered the duration of the time period containing more tones as being longer.   Along with other models that I discuss later, Thomas' model can explain this finding.   It assumes that if a person encounters a greater amount of information, he or she allocates greater attention to the processing of this nontemporal information [g*(I)], and remembered duration lengthens as a result.

In another experiment, Vroon required subjects to respond actively to the presented information; they had to classify each tone as being either low-pitched or high-pitched and respond appropriately.   These results reveal the opposite effect: Remembered duration was shorter if subjects processed a greater amount of information.   In this case, the remembered duration of the time period could not have been based on nontemporal information [g*(I)], or the finding would have been the same as before.   It must, therefore, have been based on temporal information [f(t,I)].   Taken by itself, this explanation seems reasonable, because a person should be able to encode more temporal information under conditions of reduced information-processing demands.   However, it is incorrect to assume that subjects encoded more reliable temporal information in Vroon's second experiment than in his first, because in the second experiment subjects performed a more attention-demanding information-processing task.   Thus, the explanations that Thomas' model provides are post hoc and unconvincing.

Another difficulty is that this kind of model does not take into account changes in arousal level or variations in level of alertness attributable to circadian rhythms and other biological factors. It assumes that there is a constant pool of attentional resources. A more general model more along the lines of Kahneman's (1973) resource model of attention appears to be needed. Kahneman proposed that arousal influences the total attentional resources available to be allocated at any moment to meet information-processing demands. Thus, temporal information processing is influenced not only by characteristics of the stimulus information that a person is processing, but also by momentary arousal level and, hence, total available resources. We need this kind of amendment to Thomas' model to account for findings that increased alertness, such as when a person is under the influence of stimulants like methamphetamine, lengthens duration experience (Frankenhaeuser, 1959).

Thomas' model is also too passive: Stimulus information alone determines the allocation of attention, and strategies are not involved. Some recent research focuses on information-processing strategies (Jackson, chapter 7, this volume; Michon, 1989; Michon & Jackson, 1984). A person selects and uses particular strategies, such as kinds of attentional deployment and mnemonic involvement, depending on the ways in which he or she interprets and approaches an information-processing task. In spite of these problems, Thomas' model has played an important role in guiding research and theories on psychological time.

Consider another attentional model. Underwood (1975) proposed that duration experience is positively related to the degree of attentional selectivity that an information-processing task requires. Some evidence supports this notion. For example, Underwood and Swain (1973) found that subjects remembered as being longer in duration a prose passage which presumably required greater attentional selectivity for its analysis than one that presumably required less attentional selectivity. Other studies, however, have not found the expected influence of attentional manipulations on remembered duration (Brown, 1985; Gray, 1982). The possible ways in which a person's attentional selectivity influences the remembered duration of a time period are unclear. Attentional selectivity probably interacts in complex ways with task demands and information-processing strategies. To explain some other findings, Underwood (1975) also mentioned the amount of attention a person pays to time itself. Some experiments on experienced duration support the claim that this factor is important (see Block, George, & Reed, 1980). However, this explanation lacks specificity (see later).

A theoretical problem with attentional models of psychological time, including both Thomas' (Thomas & Brown, 1975; Thomas & Weaver,

1975) model and Underwood's (1975; Underwood & Swain, 1973) model, lies in the similar concepts of attention to time and temporal information processing. Several theorists have attempted to explain the finding that experienced duration is longer than remembered duration (e.g., Brown, 1985) by saying that in a prospective paradigm a person attends to the passage of time itself and that this kind of attentional deployment lengthens duration experience. This explanation is vacuous without some additional specification of the information to which a person attends when he or she deploys attention in this way. The term *time perception* is widely used to refer to processes involving psychological time (e.g., Allan, 1979; Woodrow, 1951). Gibson (1975) stressed that the perception of time is an insoluble problem: He said that "there is no such thing as the perception of time, but only the perception of events and locomotions" (p. 295). Thus, terms like *attention to time* and *temporal information processing* are unacceptably vague without an accompanying specification of time-related attributes to which a person is attending (see Zakay, chapter 3, this volume). Along these lines, Michon and Jackson (1984) proposed that the principal attributes that qualify as temporal information are the simultaneity and order of events. In addition to these external stimulus attributes, temporal information probably also includes changes in internal attributes, including proprioceptive information, moods or emotions, kinds of cognitive processes, and so on. What, then, does it mean to attend to time itself? The answer may be that it involves an awareness of changes (or the lack of such changes) in events or cognitions occurring during a time period. This awareness seems to be characteristic of a person adopting a prospective outlook on an ongoing episode.

Memory-Storage Models

Some early philosophers who speculated about time-related experiences realized that time is intimately connected to memory processes. Aristotle (c. 330 B.C.) said that "only those animals which perceive time remember, and the organ whereby they perceive time is also that whereby they remember" (McKeon, 1941, pp. 607-608). More recently, cognitive psychologists have proposed a number of different memory models in attempts to explain duration experiences.

Ornstein (1969) was an early critic of internal-clock models. He obtained considerable evidence suggesting that these models cannot parsimoniously explain why information-processing activities, such as the ways in which a person encodes information, strongly influence remembered duration. Ornstein argued that remembered duration is a cognitive construction based on what he called the *storage size* in memory taken up by encoded and, later, retrievable stimulus information. If a person encodes more stimuli during a time period, or if the person encodes the stimuli in a more complex way, the experience of duration lengthens. Ornstein also provided evidence that information supplied after a time period influences remembered duration, presumably by influencing the accessibility of stored information.

It appears that the storage-size model is seriously flawed. Ornstein reported that people remember the duration of a time period as being longer if they had viewed a more complex figure than if they had viewed a less complex figure. Subsequent experiments challenge this fundamental prediction of the storage-size model and clarify the way in which complexity influences remembered duration (Block, 1978). Subjects do not necessarily judge a sequence of stimuli as being longer in duration if the individual stimuli are more complex than if they are less complex. However, they do remember a more complex sequence of stimuli (i.e., one in which a natural sequence of stimuli is randomized) as being longer in duration than a less complex sequence. These data suggest an alternative explanation of Ornstein's findings on effects of stimulus complexity: Instead of storage size per se, the variability of a person's encodings (i.e., the cognitive context) may be the critical factor, and subjects encode a greater number of different interpretations of a more complex stimulus than of a less complex stimulus. In other words, changes in cognitive context are critical, not the inherent complexity of individual stimuli.

In another experiment, Ornstein found that information provided to subjects after an information-processing task influences the remembered duration of the task. In contrast, Predebon (1984) reported that subjects comprehend and recall a prose passage better if they receive prior thematic information, but prior thematic information does not influence the remembered duration of the passage. Predebon interpreted these findings in terms of a contextual-change model (see later): Remembered duration is based on the overall amount of change in cognitive context during a time period, not on the size of the storage space occupied by memories of stimulus events.

Ornstein proposed the storage-size model during a period in which cognitive psychology was using the metaphor of the mind as programs running in a digital computer. Even though the storage-size model had several advantages over internal-clock models, it is based on an implausible memory metaphor. Compared to memory processes in digital computers, human memory functions in a more interconnected way, reflecting a continual reorganization of previously encoded information. As Estes (1980) succinctly put it: "Human memory does not, in a literal sense, store anything; it simply changes as a function of experience" (p. 68). Ornstein's storage-size model cannot easily handle findings revealing the importance of changes in contextual factors. I now discuss these experiments, along with resulting memory-change models.

Memory-Change Models

More than a century ago, the physicist Mach (1883/1942) said that "time is an abstraction, at which we arrive by means of the changes of things" (p. 273). James (1890) agreed, saying that "awareness of change is . . . the condition on which our perception of time's flow depends" (p. 620). Guyau (1890/1988) outlined a contemporary-sounding view in which, among other things, cognitive factors influence time judgments. Guyau's factors included the number of events, the number of differences among them, the amount of attention paid to them, and various associations to the events. As the middle of this century approached, internal-clock models became influential, and cognitive models receded into the background. One exception was the work of Frankenhaeuser (1959), who conducted a series of important experiments in which she asked subjects to estimate durations. Frankenhaeuser concluded that the amount of mental content during a duration, which several factors influence, is a critical determinant of duration experience. Fraisse (1963) concluded that "psychological duration is composed of psychological changes" (p. 216). Gibson (1975) said that "external stimuli . . . provide a flow of change, and it is this we perceive rather than a flow of time as such" (p. 299).

Block and Reed (1978) reported evidence suggesting that important changes during a time period do, indeed, influence the remembered duration of it. These changes include those in variables such as background stimuli, interoceptive stimuli (e.g., posture, temperature, nausea), and the psychological context—that is, "what the subject is thinking about," or "the internal monologue" (Bower, 1972, p. 93). Specifically, Block and Reed found that subjects remembered a duration as being longer to the extent that changes in process context had occurred. Process context changes occur when a person employs different kinds of cognitive processes as he or she engages in various tasks or strategies of encoding during a time period. This kind of information is apparently encoded as an integral part of the memory representations of stimulus events. Block and Reed proposed what they called a *contextual-change* model of remembered duration. According to this model, remembered duration involves a cognitive reconstruction based on retrieving contextual information that is stored as an integral part of the memory encodings of events, rather than a reconstruction based on retrieving stimulus information per se. The greater are the encoded and retrievable contextual changes, the longer is the remembered duration of a time period.

Process context changes are not the only kind of change that influence remembered duration. Block (1982) investigated environmental context as another potentially salient source of contextual changes. Subjects' previous experience in a particular environment (a room containing an experimenter, various objects, and so on) shortened the remembered duration of a subsequent time period spent in that environment. One interpretation of this finding is that more contextual changes occur during a time period spent in unfamiliar surroundings. This explanation is supported by the additional finding that if the encoding of environmental context is different in some way during a second time period, the relative duration of that time period lengthens. Further, different kinds of contextual factors do not simply produce additive effects on remembered duration (Block, 1982, Experiment 3). Instead, subjects apparently assess remembered duration by integrating the combined influence of different kinds of factors; and in doing so, some factors are more salient than others.

Several additional tests of the contextual-change model support only one of two versions of it. One version offers a rather mechanistic explanation: It says that the critical factor is the number of different contextual associations connected with the memory traces of stimulus events. (This interpretation resembles the complexity-of-coding notion of the storage-size model.) This contextual-association version of the model cannot explain why subjects remember an imagery task that maximizes the number of varied contextual associations as being shorter, rather than longer, than an imagery task that minimizes the number of varied contextual associations (Block, 1986). This finding contradicts the notion that the encoding of varied contextual associations is critical. Another version of the model says that an overall change in context from a preceding duration to the to-be-judged duration, which is encoded during the to-be-judged duration, is the critical factor underlying remembered duration. This version, which is less specific than the contextual-association version, could not be rejected. Remembered duration was influenced by an interaction between performance of a preceding imagery task and performance of a specific kind of imagery task during the to-be-judged duration. Thus, any contextual-change model must accommodate interactions of contextual factors.

A person's processing activities (e.g., encoding strategies) interact with the kind of information-processing task in which the person is engaged. This interaction in turn influences the remembered duration of the task (Block, 1986). Consider Michon's (1965) and Vroon's (1970) findings on the influence of information-processing on duration judgments, which are embarrassing both to attentional models (e.g., Thomas & Weaver, 1975) and to storage-size models (e.g., Ornstein, 1969). As noted earlier, Vroon found that the way in which the amount of presented information influences remembered duration depends on whether subjects actively process the information. The contextual-change model offers an explanation for this interaction: For each item which a person must actively process, correspondingly less attention is available for a subject to encode contextual changes occurring during the duration. If a person must make a greater number of overt decisions about presented information, he or she encodes and remembers fewer contextual changes.

The contextual-change model predicts a positive time-order effect in retrospective judgments of duration, especially if fairly long time periods and a comparative duration-judgment task are used. A positive time-order effect is the finding that (with all other factors equal or counter-balanced) subjects remember the first of two equal time periods as being longer than the second (for reviews, see Block, 1982, 1985a). More generally, a positive time-order effect is also revealed in longer retrospective judgment of durations presented earlier in a series of several durations (see Brown & Stubbs, 1988). The contextual-change model says that a subject encodes more changes in contextual elements during a relatively novel experience, such as during the first of several durations, and that this lengthens remembered duration. Two additional findings support the notion that contextual changes influence the positive time-order effect. The effect is eliminated if the environmental context prevailing during the second of two durations is different from that prevailing during the first (Block, 1982). The effect is also eliminated if changes in emotional context that would ordinarily occur during the first duration occur instead during a preceding time period (Block, 1986). Note that the positive time-order effect is somewhat counter-intuitive. For example, Ornstein's (1969) storage-size model predicts just the opposite, a negative time-order effect attributable to "items dropping out of storage" (p. 107). Although Ornstein did not mention it, some of his data seem to reveal a positive time-order effect rather than a negative one (see Block, 1986).

A difficulty with the contextual-change model is that its explanations tend to be circular, because it does not propose any independent way of measuring the amount of change in cognitive context. (There is, similarly, no independent way of measuring storage size in the storage-size model.)   However, recent studies of components of event-related potentials (brain-wave changes accompanying the processing of events) suggest a possible psychophysiological measure.   Some researchers have hypothesized that the P300 (also called P3) component reflects a process called *context updating* (Donchin & Coles, 1988), although this hypothesis is a controversial one (see Verleger, 1988 and the commentaries on Donchin and Coles' article).

Another problem with the contextual-change model is that it is difficult to ascertain which specific cognitive processes are involved when a person remembers the amount of contextual change during a time period. This problem is like that encountered in attempting to ascertain the specific processes involved when a person assesses the amount of attention allocated to some information, the amount of information processed by the person, or the amount of storage space required by some information.

MODELS OF PSYCHOLOGICAL TIME
AS TEMPORAL PERSPECTIVE

Temporal perspective involves ways in which people view and relate to issues concerning past, present, and future.   These phenomena are uniquely psychological in that modern physics has no need for the conception of time's passage from past to present to future (Fraser, 1987).   The fundamental time-related equations of physics concern only the relative ordering of events (i.e., earlier/later).   As noted earlier, people tend to view time as a dimension or continuum evolving from the past through the present and into the future.   Alternatively, the common perspective is that of a succession of events approaching from the future, being experienced in the present, and receding into the past.

From a cognitive viewpoint, the psychological present usually consists of a mixture of remembrances of past events, responses to present events, and anticipations of future events.   However, little or no cognitive work addresses how temporal perspective may be derived from the psychological present (but see Michon, 1978).

Issues concerning temporal perspective and its vicissitudes arise from several different sources.   Questionnaire research reveals that beliefs about the relative importance of the past, the present, and the future vary considerably between individuals (e.g., Block, Saggau, & Nickol, 1983-84).   Temporal perspective apparently varies more between individuals from different countries than between individuals from the same country (Block, Buggie, & Saggau, in preparation).   Cross-cultural investigations are an important, if rather under-utilized way, to study temporal perspective.

Perhaps the most important work on temporal perspective is that which investigates the ways in which psychiatric disorders disrupt or otherwise modify an individual's temporal perspective. Melges (chapter 11, this volume) reviews this fascinating literature and theorizes about the implications for normal temporal perspective.

Literature on altered states of consciousness, such as those induced by techniques of hypnotism or concentrative meditation, reveals additional information about the range of potential temporal perspectives (for a review, see Block, 1979). As people experience altered states of consciousness, they report unusual kinds of experiences. In some states, the construction and maintenance of temporal perspective seems suspended, and people concurrently report a quality of temporal experiencing that is best characterized by the term *timelessness*. Although experiences of timelessness are usually somewhat ineffable, one recurring kind of description is that they involve an altered mode of temporal perspective in which "divisions of time, including divisions into past, present, and future, are [experienced as] . . . illusion. Events do not 'happen' or 'occur,' they 'are'" (LeShan, 1976, p. 92). One explanation of this kind of phenomenon is that processes involving working or activated memory, which ordinarily encode the current context in which ongoing events are occurring, do not function in the way that they usually do. In other words, a person may experience timelessness if the momentary environmental or psychological conditions prevent him or her from constructing a cognitive context in which to interpret an episode. Under these conditions, a person does not maintain the usual assumptions about time and reality, and attention diverts from external events to internal processes. A person experiences and remembers the duration of such a time period only with great difficulty. This kind of experience represents an interesting limiting case for cognitive models of psychological time, especially those involving the formation and maintenance of temporal perspective.

A GENERAL CONTEXTUALISTIC FRAMEWORK

A general contextualistic framework provides a useful summary of various important factors that influence psychological time, many of which I discussed in this chapter and in other recent reviews (Block, 1985a, 1985b, 1989a, 1989b). This framework is called *contextualistic* because it emphasizes factors surrounding an event or episode which influence an organism's encoding of, conceiving of, and responding to the event or episode. The framework includes four kinds of factors that influence psychological time.

The four factors, or clusters of variables, are: characteristics of the time experiencer, contents of a time period, activities during a time period, and time-related behaviors and judgments. Important characteristics of the time experiencer include such variables as species, sex, personality, interests, temporal perspective, and previous experiences. The contents of a time period include various attributes of events, such as their number, complexity, modality, duration, and so on. Although an organism may attend primarily either to external events or to thoughts, experience is always a mixture of activated representations of both external and internal events. An organism's activities during a time period range from relatively passive nonattending to external events through more actively controlled processes, such as strategies in which a person engages in the process of acquiring information. The kinds of activities in which an organism engages are mainly influenced by previously learned strategies, by instructions that an experimenter provides, and by the events that occur during a duration. Finally, changes in time-related behaviors occur as an experimenter or an environment demands various temporal judgment or estimation—simultaneity, rhythm, order, spacing, duration, and so on.

None of these factors operates in isolation from the others: If one factor changes, it interacts with the other factors in different ways. Because many experiments on psychological time study only one or two factors in relative isolation, the findings of these studies tell us relatively little. The resulting models can handle only those factors that theorists have chosen to investigate, and only under relatively special conditions.

This general contextualistic framework helps to clarify experimental findings and process models, especially by highlighting what they are omitting (see Block, 1989a). I emphasize that this framework is a descriptive, or heuristic, one; it is neither a process model nor a formal (e.g., mathematical) model. A limitation is that this framework does not reveal which factors or which interactions are the more important ones. Another problem is that this framework does not precisely indicate the ways in which the factors interact. Many of the interactions remain relatively obscure and not well understood. A more complete understanding of the complexities of psychological time will be possible only after researchers have experimentally investigated the complex interactions among the factors and generated more specific, process models. The main contribution of this framework is to emphasize the factors that may be needed in any relatively complete model of psychological time.

SUMMARY AND CONCLUSIONS

This chapter evaluated models concerning several aspects of psychological time—as succession, as duration, and as temporal perspective.

Experiences of successiveness, or the primary psychological encoding of order relationships between events, involves dynamic information-processing characteristics: In the process of perceiving and encoding an event, a person remembers related events which preceded it, anticipates future events, or both. The notion of a fixed-duration psychological moment arose largely from experiments that are now thought to involve visual persistence; the available evidence does not support the notion of a central pacemaker or internal clock. Similarly, the experiencing of a psychological present is probably related to the temporal dynamics of short-term, or activated, memory. Some time-related information about events and relationships between events is apparently encoded automatically, whereas other information is only encoded deliberately.

The experience of duration in passing may differ from that in retrospect. Experienced duration depends on variables such as the amount of attention to temporal information, whereas remembered duration involves contextual changes encoded in memory. Models of psychological time as duration vary considerably. Chronobiological models typically attempt to explain diverse cyclical behaviors by seeking the physiological basis of a pacemaker or pacemakers in the brain of the organism. Some psychologists have also explored the notion of a pacemaker—a collection of brain processes that generates a series of pulses or other cyclical marker events which may underlie temporal experiences. However, these internal-clock models seem unable to explain the diverse ways in which cognitive kinds of factors influence temporal behavior and experience. As an alternative, many cognitive psychologists believe that the experience of duration is related to the storage size in memory of information that occurred during a time period. Another interesting class of model is that which emphasizes the deployment of attention, including the concept of attention to temporal information. However, changes in cognitive context during a time period influence remembered duration, and a contextual-change model provides a better account of recent evidence than do storage-size and attentional models.

Phenomena of temporal perspective involve experiences and conceptions concerning the past, the present, and the future. Temporal perspective differs between individuals, and it often changes radically when a person experiences altered states of consciousness, including those related to psychiatric illnesses. At present, no comprehensive model is able to account for the formation and maintenance of temporal perspective.

A general contextualistic framework summarizes interactions of four kinds of factors that influence psychological time: characteristics of the time experiencer, contents of the time period, the person's activities during the time period, and the person's time-related behaviors and judgments. Although this framework clarifies experimental findings and process models, it does not indicate the precise ways in which the factors interact.

ACKNOWLEDGMENTS

I thank John Michon and Robert Patterson for helpful comments on this chapter. Preparation of the chapter was supported, in part, by a grant from the College of Letters and Sciences, Montana State University.

REFERENCES

Allan, L. G. (1979). The perception of time. *Perception & Psychophysics, 26*, 340-354.

Allen, J. F., & Kautz, H. A. (1985). A model of naive temporal reasoning. In J. R. Hobbs & R. C. Moore (Eds.), *Formal theories of the commonsense world* (pp. 251-268). Norwood, NJ: Ablex.

Allport, D. A. (1968). Phenomenal simultaneity and the perceptual moment hypothesis. *British Journal of Psychology, 59*, 395-406.

Aschoff, J. (1984). Circadian timing. In J. Gibbon & L. Allan (Eds.), *Timing and time perception* (pp. 442-468). New York: New York Academy of Sciences.

Aschoff, J. (1985). On the perception of time during prolonged temporal isolation. *Human Neurobiology, 4*, 41-52.

Auday, B. C., Sullivan, C., & Cross, H. A. (1988). The effects of constrained rehearsal on judgments of temporal order. *Bulletin of the Psychonomic Society, 26*, 548-551.

Block, R. A. (1974). Memory and the experience of duration in retrospect. *Memory & Cognition, 2*, 153-160.

Block, R. A. (1978). Remembered duration: Effects of event and sequence complexity. *Memory & Cognition, 6*, 320-326.

Block, R. A. (1979). Time and consciousness. In G. Underwood & R. Stevens (Eds.), *Aspects of consciousness: Vol. 1. Psychological issues* (pp. 179-217). London: Academic Press.

Block, R. A. (1982). Temporal judgments and contextual change. *Journal of Experimental Psychology: Learning, Memory, and Cognition, 8*, 530-544.

Block, R. A. (1985a). Contextual coding in memory: Studies of remembered duration. In J. A. Michon & J. L. Jackson (Eds.), *Time, mind, and behavior* (pp. 169-178). Berlin: Springer-Verlag.

Block, R. A. (1985b). World models for the psychology of time. *Teorie & Modelli*, *2*(Suppl. 1), 89-111.

Block, R. A. (1986). Remembered duration: Imagery processes and contextual encoding. *Acta Psychologica*, *62*, 103-122.

Block, R. A. (1989a). A contextualistic view of time and mind. In J. T. Fraser (Ed.), *Time and mind: Interdisciplinary issues* (pp. 61-79). Madison, CT: International Universities Press.

Block, R. A. (1989b). Experiencing and remembering time: Affordances, context, and cognition. In I. Levin & D. Zakay (Eds.), *Time and human cognition: A life-span perspective* (pp. 333-363). Amsterdam: North-Holland.

Block, R. A., Buggie, S. E., & Saggau, J. L. (in preparation). *Beliefs about time in Japan, Malawi, and the United States*.

Block, R. A., George, E. J., & Reed, M. A. (1980). A watched pot sometimes boils: A study of duration experience. *Acta Psychologica*, *46*, 81-94.

Block, R. A., & Reed, M. A. (1978). Remembered duration: Evidence for a contextual-change hypothesis. *Journal of Experimental Psychology: Human Learning and Memory*, *4*, 656-665.

Block, R. A., Saggau, J. L., & Nickol, L. H. (1983-84). Temporal Inventory on Meaning and Experience: A structure of time. *Imagination, Cognition and Personality*, *3*, 203-225.

Boring, E. G. (1963). *The physical dimensions of consciousness*. New York: Dover. (Original work published 1933)

Bower, G. H. (1972). Stimulus-sampling theory of encoding variability. In A. W. Melton & E. Martin (Eds.), *Coding processes in human memory* (pp. 85-123). Washington, DC: Winston.

Breitmeyer, B. G. (1984). *Visual masking: An integrative approach*. New York: Oxford University Press.

Brown, S. W. (1985). Time perception and attention: The effects of prospective versus retrospective paradigms and task demands on perceived duration. *Perception & Psychophysics*, *38*, 115-124.

Brown, S. W., & Stubbs, D. A. (1988). The psychophysics of retrospective and prospective duration timing. *Perception*, *17*, 297-310.

Campbell, S. S. (1986). Estimation of empty time. *Human Neurobiology*, *5*, 205-207.

Church, R. M. (1984). Properties of the internal clock. In J. Gibbon & L. Allan (Eds.), *Timing and time perception* (pp. 566-582). New York: New York Academy of Sciences.

Donchin, E., & Coles, M. G. H. (1988). Is the P300 component a manifestation of context updating? *Behavioral and Brain Sciences*, *11*, 357-373.

Efron, R. (1970). Effect of stimulus duration on perceptual onset and offset latencies. *Perception & Psychophysics*, *8*, 231-234.

Efron, R., & Lee, D. N. (1971). The visual persistence of a moving stroboscopically illuminated object. *American Journal of Psychology*, *84*, 365-375.

Estes, W. K. (1980). Is human memory obsolete? *American Scientist*, *68*, 62-69.

Fraisse, P. (1963). *The psychology of time* (J. Leith, Trans.). New York: Harper & Row.

Fraisse, P. (1984). Perception and estimation of time. *Annual Review of Psychology*, *35*, 1-36.

Frankenhaeuser, M. (1959). *Estimation of time: An experimental study*. Stockholm: Almqvist & Wiksell.

Fraser, J. T. (1987). *Time: The familiar stranger*. Amherst, MA: University of Massachusetts Press.

Geissler, H.-G. (1987). The temporal architecture of central information processing: Evidence for a tentative time-quantum model. *Psychological Research, 49,* 99-106.

Gibson, J. J. (1975). Events are perceivable but time is not. In J. T. Fraser & N. Lawrence (Eds.), *The study of time II* (pp. 295-301). New York: Springer-Verlag.

Gray, C. (1982). Duration differences: Attentional demand or time error? *Perception, 11,* 97-102.

Guyau, J.-M. (1988). *La genèse de l'idée de temps* [The origin of the idea of time]. In J. A. Michon, V. Pouthas, & J. L. Jackson (Eds.), *Guyau and the idea of time* (pp. 37-90; translation pp. 93-148). Amsterdam: North-Holland. (Original work published 1890)

Hicks, R. E., Miller, G. W., Gaes, G., & Bierman, K. (1977). Concurrent processing demands and the experience of time-in-passing. *American Journal of Psychology, 90,* 431-446.

Hicks, R. E., Miller, G. W., & Kinsbourne, M. (1976). Prospective and retrospective judgments of time as a function of amount of information processed. *American Journal of Psychology, 89,* 719-730.

Hintzman, D. L., & Block, R. A. (1971). Repetition and memory: Evidence for a multiple-trace hypothesis. *Journal of Experimental Psychology, 88,* 297-306.

Hintzman, D. L., & Block, R. A. (1973). Memory for the spacing of repetitions. *Journal of Experimental Psychology, 99,* 70-74.

Hintzman, D. L., Block, R. A., & Summers, J. J. (1973). Contextual associations and memory for serial position. *Journal of Experimental Psychology, 97,* 220-229.

Hintzman, D. L., Summers, J. J., & Block, R. A. (1975). Spacing judgments as an index of study-phase retrieval. *Journal of Experimental Psychology: Human Learning and Memory, 1,* 31-40.

Hirsh, I. J., & Sherrick, C. E. (1961). Perceived order in different sense modalities. *Journal of Experimental Psychology, 62,* 423-432.

Hoagland, H. (1933). The physiologic control of judgments of duration: Evidence for a chemical clock. *Journal of General Psychology, 9,* 267-287.

Hoagland, H. (1966). Some biochemical considerations of time. In J. T. Fraser (Ed.), *The voices of time* (pp. 312-329). Amherst, MA: University of Massachusetts Press.

Hylan, J. P. (1903). The distribution of attention. *Psychological Review, 10,* 373-403, 498-533.

Jackson, J. L. (1985). Is the processing of temporal information automatic or controlled? In J. A. Michon & J. L. Jackson (Eds.), *Time, mind, and behavior* (pp. 179-190). Berlin: Springer-Verlag.

Jackson, J. L. (1986). *The processing of temporal information.* Doctoral dissertation, University of Groningen, The Netherlands.

Jackson, J. L., & Michon, J. A. (1984). Effect of item concreteness on temporal coding. *Acta Psychologica, 57,* 83-95.

James, W. (1890). *The principles of psychology* (Vol. 1). New York: Henry Holt.

Johnson, C. H., & Hastings, J. W. (1986). The elusive mechanism of the circadian clock. *American Scientist, 74,* 29-36.

Kahneman, D. (1973). *Attention and effort.* Englewood Cliffs, NJ: Prentice-Hall.

Kahneman, R., & Wolman, R. E. (1970). Stroboscopic motion: Effects of duration and interval. *Perception & Psychophysics, 8,* 161-164.

Kristofferson, A. B. (1980). A quantal step function in duration discrimination. *Perception & Psychophysics, 27,* 300-306.

Lashley, K. S. (1951). The problem of serial order in behavior. In L. A. Jeffress (Ed.), *Cerebral mechanisms in behavior: The Hixon symposium* (pp. 112-146). New York: Wiley.

Lavie, P., & Webb, W. B. (1975). Time estimates in a long-term time-free environment. *American Journal of Psychology, 88,* 177-186.

LeShan, L. (1976). *Alternate realities.* New York: Evans.

Loftus, E. F., Schooler, J. W., Boone, S. M., & Kline, D. (1987). Time went by so slowly: Overestimation of event duration by males and females. *Applied Cognitive Psychology, 1,* 3-13.

Mach, E. (1942). *The science of mechanics* (5th ed., T. J. McCormack, Trans.). LaSalle, IL: Open Court. (Original work published 1883)

Marshall, P. H., Chen, C.-Y., & Jeter, B. S. (1989). Retrieval influences on tests for the automaticity of the encoding of temporal order information. *American Journal of Psychology, 102,* 39-52.

McKeon, R. (Ed.). (1941). *The basic works of Aristotle.* New York: Random House.

Michon, J. A. (1965). Studies on subjective duration: II. Subjective time measurement during tasks with different information content. *Acta Psychologica, 24,* 205-219.

Michon, J. A. (1975). Time experience and memory processes. In J. T. Fraser & N. Lawrence (Eds.), *The study of time II* (pp. 302-313). New York: Springer-Verlag.

Michon, J. A. (1978). The making of the present: A tutorial review. In J. Requin (Ed.), *Attention and performance* (Vol. VII, pp. 89-111). Hillsdale, NJ: Lawrence Erlbaum Associates.

Michon, J. A. (1985). The compleat time experiencer. In J. A. Michon & J. L. Jackson (Eds.), *Time, mind, and behavior* (pp. 20-52). Berlin: Springer-Verlag.

Michon, J. A. (1989). Timing your mind and minding your time: In J. T. Fraser (Ed.), *Time and mind: Interdisciplinary issues* (pp. 17-39). Madison, CT: International Universities Press.

Michon, J. A., & Jackson, J. L. (1984). Attentional effort and cognitive strategies in the processing of temporal information. In J. Gibbon & L. Allan (Eds.), *Timing and time perception* (pp. 298-321). New York: New York Academy of Sciences.

Miller, G. W., Hicks, R. E., & Willette, M. (1978). Effects of concurrent verbal rehearsal and temporal set upon judgments of temporal duration. *Acta Psychologica, 42,* 173-179.

Ornstein, R. E. (1969). *On the experience of time.* Harmondsworth, England: Penguin.

Pöppel, E. (1972). Oscillations as possible basis for time perception. In J. T. Fraser, F. C. Haber, & G. H. Müller (Eds.), *The study of time* (pp. 219-241). Berlin: Springer-Verlag.

Pouthas, V. (1985). Timing behavior in young children: A developmental approach to conditioned spaced responding. In J. A. Michon & J. L. Jackson (Eds.), *Time, mind, and behavior* (pp. 100-109). Berlin: Springer-Verlag.

Predebon, J. (1984). Organization of stimulus events and remembered apparent duration. *Australian Journal of Psychology, 36,* 161-169.

Richelle, M., & Lejeune, H. (1980). *Time in animal behavior.* Oxford: Pergamon Press.

Richelle, M., Lejeune, H., Perikel, J.-J., & Fery, P. (1985). From biotemporality to nootemporality: Toward an integrative and comparative view of time in behavior. In J. A. Michon & J. L. Jackson (Eds.), *Time, mind, and behavior* (pp. 75-99). Berlin: Springer-Verlag.

Roitblat, H. L. (1987). *Introduction to comparative cognition.* New York: Freeman.

Schab, F. R., & Crowder, R. G. (1988). The role of succession in temporal cognition: Is the time-order error a recency effect of memory? *Perception & Psychophysics, 44,* 233-242.

Slanger, T. G. (in press). Evidence for a short-period internal clock in humans. *Journal of Scientific Exploration.*

Stroud, J. M. (1955). The fine structure of psychological time. In H. Quastler (Ed.), *Information theory in psychology: Problems and methods* (pp. 174-205). Glencoe, IL: The Free Press.

Stroud, J. M. (1967). The fine structure of psychological time. *Annals of the New York Academy of Sciences, 138,* 623-631.

Thomas, E. A. C., & Brown, I. (1975). Time perception and the filled duration illusion. *Perception & Psychophysics, 16,* 449-458.

Thomas, E. A. C., & Weaver, W. B. (1975). Cognitive processing and time perception. *Perception & Psychophysics, 17,* 363-367.

Treisman, M. (1963). Temporal discrimination and the indifference interval: Implications for a model of the "internal clock." *Psychological Monographs, 77* (Whole no. 576).

Treisman, M. (1984). Temporal rhythms and cerebral rhythms. In J. Gibbon & L. Allan (Eds.), *Timing and time perception* (pp. 542-565). New York: New York Academy of Sciences.

Tzeng, O. J. L., & Cotton, B. (1980). A study-phase retrieval model of temporal coding. *Journal of Experimental Psychology: Human Learning and Memory, 6,* 705-716.

Tzeng, O. J. L., Lee, A. T., & Wetzel, C. D. (1979). Temporal coding in verbal information processing. *Journal of Experimental Psychology: Human Learning and Memory, 5,* 52-64.

Underwood, G. (1975). Attention and the perception of duration during encoding and retrieval. *Perception, 4,* 291-296.

Underwood, G., & Swain, R. A. (1973). Selectivity of attention and the perception of duration. *Perception, 2,* 101-105.

Verleger, R. (1988). Event-related potentials and cognition: A critique of the context updating hypothesis and an alternative interpretation of P3. *Behavioral and Brain Sciences, 11,* 343-356.

Vroon, P. A. (1970). Effects of presented and processed information on duration experience. *Acta Psychologica, 34,* 115-121.

Westheimer, G., & McKee, S. P. (1977). Perception of temporal order in adjacent visual stimuli. *Vision Research, 17,* 887-892.

White, C. T. (1963). Temporal numerosity and the psychological unit of duration. *Psychological Monographs, 77* (Whole no. 575).

Woodrow, H. (1951). Time perception. In S. S. Stevens (Ed.), *Handbook of experimental psychology* (pp. 1224-1236). New York: Wiley.

2 Implicit and Explicit Representations of Time

John A. Michon
University of Groningen

During most of the first century of its existence as a more or less distinct subject within the domain of experimental psychology, the study of time has manifestly been a *psychophysics of duration.* To a large extent, experimenters have dealt with the curious fact that time will now seem to fly and then again appear to drag intolerably. In literature as well as in personal, everyday experience this is perhaps the most remarkable feature of our experience of a changing world. Absolute thresholds (the minimum amount of time that we perceive as an enduring moment) and relative thresholds have been determined as a function of all sorts of physical, physiological, and cognitive variables. In these experiments intervals are compared, produced, reproduced, or estimated (e.g., Gibbon & Allan, 1984; Macar, 1985; see also Zakay, chapter 3, and other chapters in this volume).

Methodologically and conceptually, the psychophysics of time has been consistent with the behavioristic tradition in experimental psychology. Models have usually been of the "clock-and-regulator" type. This implies that, whatever variable is studied for its effect on the subjective rate of flow, it is considered to affect the rate of an internal clock which, as a result, will slow down or speed up, thus creating the subjective feeling of time dragging or accelerating (Treisman, 1963). Irrespective of the details of the numerous models in this tradition, they all rely strongly on a clock metaphor and as such they may in fact be reduced to simple variations on the theme of *time measurement* or *chronometry* (e.g., Fraser, 1982).

With the arrival of cognitive psychology, this reductionist approach to the experience of time has changed. In recent years the temporal aspects of cognition and the cognitive aspects of temporality have begun to converge, on their way to become an integrated, fairly substantial topic within the domain of general experimental psychology. Time psychologists have become concerned with the syntactic (rhythmic) and semantic (conceptual) properties of time, the planning of future action, the temporal structure of speech and language, event perception and the narrative structure of event sequences, episodic and autobiographical memory, the subjective value of time, and several other topics. In particular, the relation between time experience and memory organization has come under close scrutiny.

From the cognitive point of view the experience of time is not primarily the perception or retention of duration. On the contrary, duration is in fact a rather abstract outcome, a derived and highly formal product of the mind. Even in its nonverbal disguises, experimentally dressed as the comparison between intervals or the reproduction of a preceding interval, a highly public and language-dominated convention is clearly at work.

If I claim that duration is a product of the mind, the question is what it is derived from, or at least what the function is of this apparently extremely well-developed and well-maintained abstraction. My answer, as it emerges from this chapter, is that the experience of time is the conscious product of processes that enable us to cope with the sequential contingencies of reality. And duration is only one abstract aspect of this product. Memory is the ensemble of the processes that temporally organize our experiences. This view of memory as process or strategy deviates from some conventional views that treat memory as a reservoir of facts and rules. The reasons become clear in the course of my argument, but the view presented here is consistent with that of at least a number of other authors. Schank (1986), for instance, pointed out that "the test of an effective understanding system . . . is not the realism of the output it produces, . . . but rather the validity of the method by which that output is produced" (p. 11).

In summary then, time is not just duration, it is not even duration in the first place. Time is more, and the question remains what it has been for more than 15 centuries: *"Quid enim est tempus?"* – "What then is time?"

THE DUAL NATURE OF TIME EXPERIENCE

With the arrival of cognitive psychology it has become acceptable again to talk about intentionality. Brentano's century-old claim, that the fundamental property of mental processes is that they are always about or directed at something, is once more taken seriously. Certain topics that were once prominent in phenomenological psychology as it was propagated especially by Brentano, Husserl, and Merleau-Ponty are once more attracting attention (see e.g., Brockelman, 1985; I. Miller, 1984; Sherover, 1975). The experience of time is such a topic. Time has, right from the beginning, occupied a very central position in phenomenological psychology. Both Brentano and Husserl considered it one of the fundamental "constituent" factors of experience.[1]

Phenomenological analysis has, in particular, highlighted the dual nature of time in human behavior. This duality finds expression in *action* and *reflection*, respectively.

In the phenomenological view the first temporal mode is an implicit, direct tuning of human action to the dynamics of the surrounding world. Action, our concrete, intentional behaving in a given situation, takes place in an immediate action field (called the Now or, with a German term, the *Präsenzfeld*) in which retentions of earlier experiences and anticipations about the future are implied. The temporal structure or *temporality* of behavior, that is, their dynamics, their timing, their tuning to the objects and events that they are about (the so-called *intentional objects*), is not normally accessible to introspection. The temporality of our behavior is, in other words, cognitively impenetrable. An action *expresses* time but is not defined by any temporal representation, that is, by relations in terms of duration, order, date, and so forth, in a person's consciousness. This form of temporality builds on what Schacter (1987) called *implicit memory*. It is the form of memory that expresses itself in and through our knowledge or performance but that cannot be represented in propositional (verbal) terms (see e.g., Richardson-Klavehn & Bjork, 1988).

In contrast, the second temporal mode distinguished in phenomenological analysis deals with time viewed as past, future, order, or duration. It is the conceptual structure by means of which humans express their

---

[1] I wish to emphasize that the phenomenology of time in its present interpretation is not in terms of the idealistic, philosophical form it takes in Husserl's later work, and most certainly does not take the form of the psychologically meaningless, metaphysical obfuscations of Heidegger.

awareness of temporal relations between events and their reflections on their action. Reflection makes the action that is the object of reflection into an intentional object, and the *implicit* Now in which that action is taking place thereby becomes an *explicit* temporal object, an event that lasts so long and that can be placed at such a place in an explicit temporal dimension past-present-future, that is, in a historical context: "To be self-conscious means to be aware of oneself as a temporal relation . . . as a set of narratively shaped active temporal relations in the progressive tense" (Brockelman, 1985, p. 76).   Past experiences are localized at a point in the remembered past, expectancies are projected as events that are still to happen in a future that gradually comes closer and closer. Conscious reflection being cognitively penetrable, it enables the organism to plan its actions and to adaptively tune to the prevailing circumstances in the world.

TIME IN COGNITIVE PSYCHOLOGY

The question considered next is what psychological views of time look like if they are considered to be a regular subject within the domain of cognitive psychology. In order to answer this question I choose a definition for *time* that I have been using for some years and with a great deal of satisfaction: "Time is the conscious experiential product of the processes that allow the (human) organism to adaptively organize itself so that its behavior remains tuned to the sequential (i.e., order) relations in its environment" (Michon, 1985, p. 20). The merit of this definition is that time is defined, not as a thing with attributes or a property of the existential mode of things, but as a process or ensemble of processes that is capable of generating the entire conceptual structure that we conventionally call *time*.

This definition is consistent with the dual character of the cognitive architecture that I discussed earlier in this chapter. In the first place, it claims that there are processes that allow us to tune to the course of events in the external world or that, with another phrase, allow us to maintain a dynamic, interactive relation with our environment of a kind that the innocent bystander would qualify as "smooth" or "effortless." An important implication is, moreover, that time as such plays no role in these tuning processes. Whether or not the duration of a movement is long or short is not dependent on a direct manipulation of the duration parameter, but of other dynamic parameters, such as force, or momentum.   The definition also implies that time is the consciously experienced product of this tuning process. That is, we must look for a process or ensemble of processes that can explain (or reproduce) the entire spectrum of conscious temporal experiences.

THE HUM IN THE BASEMENT

The philosopher Lawrence (1986) has compared the implicit temporality of automatic, unattended behavior with "the hum in the basement," with the noises your central heating or your washer are making but that you will not notice until one day they stop inadvertently. Such behavior can express highly complex temporal relations, but one will not find time as an explicit control parameter in the control structure (see Summers & Burns, chapter 8, this volume). The quality (smoothness, precision) of an automatic action relies on other factors. This fact is, physically speaking, fairly trivial but psychologically speaking it is not: After all it is conceivable that duration as such might have a causal influence, even in the case of automatic behavior, if only pure duration would be explicitly represented in a neural code. There is, however, little evidence for such an encoding, except for the various biological rhythms that, however, have comparatively long periods (month, day, 90 minutes).

Thomassen and Teulings (1985; Teulings, 1988) have shown that relevant control parameters of handwriting are the force exerted and the kinematic properties of the hand-arm system, but not duration as such. Systematic variations in the conditions under which the writing was produced clearly revealed influences from the former parameters on letter forms, whereas there was no such systematic effect on the duration parameter as such (see also Jones & Boltz, 1989; Shaffer, 1985). Time is a product, not a building brick, of behavior.

A second line of research is concerned with the question of whether time is an automatic byproduct of other information-processing activities. This research (e.g., Jackson, 1986; Michon & Jackson, 1984; see also Jackson, chapter 7 in this volume) has shown that such temporal information is not encoded unless it is explicitly attended to. The conclusion is that time (in the sense of duration, epoch, etc.) is not only not represented explicitly in automatic behavior, but in addition that we are not capable of forcing someone to construct such a representation, even if we explicitly try to induce it by inputting exact temporal information: Explicit training of the duration of muscle twitchings is not likely to improve one's chance of winning an Olympic gold medal.

Visual perception proceeds in a highly parallel and automatized fashion. One may therefore expect that in this domain there will be no explicit representation of time. Gibson (1969, 1975) has pointed this out very explicitly. He has repeatedly emphasized that time is not a perceptual dimension, but a construction a posteriori, based on the dynamic structure of the perceptual field. Again, this supports my thesis that time in conscious experience is a derived entity. Because psychology is still very much dominated by Kant's transcendental view of time and space, this claim may still seem revolutionary. It is, however, at least a century old. As early as 1885 the French philosopher Guyau made the point in great detail and very eloquently (Michon, Pouthas, & Jackson, 1988).

Although there is a considerable body of research into the perception of "natural" movement (e.g., recognizing the gait of people moving about "anonymously" and the encoding of abstract movement patterns), there is no research on record to find out if time (duration) as such plays a role in the identification and retention of such patterns of action. The ease with which people can understand and retain even very disorderly cinematographic information adds to the plausibility that duration as such is either not coded at all, or else is coded only very indirectly and incompletely.

THE CONCEPTUALIZATION OF TIME

The experience of time—that is, the perception, meaning, and use of time as duration, past, now, future, and so on—is inextricably associated with conscious information processing, with the reflective mode of thinking, or with whatever other name this relation may have received in the literature. Temporal cognition belongs to the declarative domain of knowledge. The representation of temporal relations, therefore, is a form of high-level cognition and should be accessible to the same sort of empirical methods that apply to problem solving, decision making, comprehension, or explanation. In this light, a relevant question is why explicit representations of time are, in fact, at all necessary. A first good reason is an impasse in the process of action tuning. A person may for instance be in a situation for which he or she has no appropriate automatic behavioral procedures available. The second reason is one of communication. In order to understand each other, people must be able to give orderly and ordered accounts of their behavior. Such is the structure of narrative.[2]

In this context, time is conceived as a conceptual structure—a mental model in the sense of Johnson-Laird (1983)—a structure that is designed

---

[2] It might be added, however, that people seem capable of learning to deal with highly complicated temporal relations in narrative with surprising ease.

specifically to represent and solve problems that emerge whenever the tuning process fails for some reason or other.   An example of this function of mental models is the temporal organization required to repair a vacuum cleaner.   Unless one already happens to be an experienced vacuum cleaner mechanic, one is helped a great deal by treating the disassembling task as a temporal problem and by relying on an order scenario.   The many parts are to be located on the workbench in the order in which they were removed, and successful reassembling mostly depends on following the proper reverse of this order, because the other important question of where and how the part is to be reinstalled can frequently be answered by considering the shape of the various units.   A nut simply "asks" to be mounted on a bolt.

Time as a conceptual structure can take three forms—literal or verisimilar, metaphorical, and formal—that are functionally more or less equivalent.   In each case we are dealing with a temporal schema enabling us to specify sequences of events for later reconstruction, or for anticipating future events.   The difference seems to reside mostly in the level of abstraction that is required to match a representation with the temporal structure of the concrete episode that it represents.

THE VERISIMILAR REPRESENTATION
OF TIME: BEING REMINDED

Many situations in which humans must, in one way or another, represent temporal relations explicitly are extremely trivial—much more trivial, in any case, than the maintenance of a vacuum cleaner.   Generally speaking, information processing in these circumstances might be automatic, but frequently the actor is asked for an explanation or a suggestion. Take, for instance, the question, "How far is it to the post office?".   The answer may well be stated as "About 20 minutes if you keep walking like this" or "Maybe 10 minutes if you are in a good condition."   The informer must have a representation of spatial distances and must also be able to superimpose on this representation a time scale that can be calibrated on the basis of relevant external information, in this case the observed or inferred walking pace of the inquirer.[3]

Humans normally have access to a large repertoire of temporal standards for concrete, everyday, "natural" events, associated with scenarios (scripts, frames), not only in order to efficiently execute routine

---

[3] There may be considerable cultural differences at play in this case.   In large parts of Europe my description stands, but elsewhere (viz. the U.S.A.) it may not.

activities, but also in order to explain and communicate.   Classic temporal phenomena like the acceleration and deceleration of the subjective flow of time can actually be explained more appropriately in terms of deviations from the expectations raised by a scenario one is reminded of (e.g., Jones, 1976, 1985; Jones & Boltz, 1989; Michon, 1967, 1985; Shepard, 1984), than in terms of internal counters, clocks, or memory registers that allow estimates of passed or passing duration in terms of the number or complexity of events that take place during an interval.   Jones and Boltz (1989), for instance, demonstrated this by comparing judgments of the durations of "natural" melodies with those of structurally malformed melodies. The latter induce grossly inadequate expectations in the subject about their endpoint. As a result, the subject may experience and judge the malformed melody as being either shorter or longer than a corresponding "natural" melody.

We do not yet know in sufficient detail how temporal relations are represented in these concrete scenarios. Shepard (1984) has, in a long series of experiments, studied the manipulation of mental images of two- and three-dimensional objects. The time it takes to execute such a mental manipulation—the rotation of a three-dimensional block shape, for instance—is found to be proportional to the extent and complexity of the movement in mental space. But this finding in itself does not tell us very much about the explicit representation of the temporal relations involved in such manipulations. Shepard remained silent on the physical properties, or rather the represented physical properties, of his mental objects. Do his mental shapes have mass or density? There should be differences between the properties of an image of a cube made of mental styrofoam and one made of cast mental iron—or is it mental cast iron? The important questions are to what extent mental models of real processes are in fact dynamic models, and to what extent the properties of these models are coherent and consistent with, say, Newtonian mechanics. This question has come under scrutiny only in recent years.

The burgeoning field of qualitative or naive physics deals with precisely these questions (e.g., DiSessa, 1983; Freyd, 1987; Hobbs & Moore, 1985). Findings from this research seem to point out that representations of a fair number of elementary physical processes—such as magnetic attraction, free fall, friction, or collision—may indeed be fairly consistent across subjects and that, moreover, they tend to be more consistent with an Aristotelian worldview than with the views of Newton, let alone Einstein. Although Newton has taught us, for instance, that a stone, when thrown, will no longer be subject to the force of the throw, we still seem to believe with Aristotle that the force of the throw—its impetus—will "go with the stone" and only gradually fade, causing the stone to slow down.

Despite this increased attention, cognitive psychologists have not yet answered the question of whether or not the representation of temporal relations in the mental world is consistent with the physical laws that appear to hold in this world. Apart from Piaget (1946), Mashhour (1964), and Montangero (1977, 1985), the verisimilar representation of time in basic scenarios of real-time events has not yet been studied in any detail. The latter authors have all dealt with the question of whether or not the basic kinematic relation *distance* = *velocity* × *time* holds subjectively. Piaget did show that this is the case only in the advanced stages of human development. Montangero, working in the tradition of Piaget, did confirm this, but he went much farther. He presented considerable evidence for a triadic conceptualization of time: time in relation to distance and velocity; time in relation to frequency and number; and time in relation to states and transitions between states. At the earlier stages of development humans deal with time in each of these representational domains independently (and even incoherently). Only later do the separate triads merge into a single consistent model with one concept of time. This supports the century-old view, phrased in a most interesting cognitivist way by the French philosopher Guyau (1890/1988), that establishment of a consistent representation of time is a matter of strenuous cognitive effort.[4]

Mashhour (1964) made an attempt to show that Stevens' power law holds not only for distance, velocity, and duration separately, but that there is even a power relation that holds between these three variables. In other words, qualitative kinematics is apparently consistent with a relation of the form:

$$(distance)^\alpha = (velocity)^\beta \cdot (time)^\tau$$

Within certain constraints Mashhour did indeed find fairly stable values for α, β, and τ within subjects, suggesting that numerical estimates of the duration of simple events are consistent with the qualitative physics that an individual subject happens to entertain.

The verisimilar representation of time is not restricted to the microlevel of events. Schank (1982, 1986), among others, has proposed, with great force of arguments, that human behavior in everyday life is steered by scenarios, explicit representations of remembered situations that are sufficiently close to the prevailing circumstances to serve as a guide for further action. This approach to dynamic memory reiterates

---

[4] See Michon, Pouthas, and Jackson (1988) for a translation of Guyau's original text and an extensive discussion of Guyau's views on the origin of the idea of time.

and develops Guyau's view that memory is simply the way of effectively and efficiently using the strategies by which we organize our knowledge representations (Guyau, 1890/1988). Guyau's theory of dynamic memory is beautifully reflected in Schank's theory; but, unlike Schank, Guyau focused directly on the fundamental significance of the representation of time as a cognitive strategy.

An Illustration: Political Timing

Schank's position implies that "the best brains connect everything with everything else and so are constantly reminded" (Schank, personal communication, 1987). To be flooded with reminiscences is, however, a mixed blessing. Luria (1968), in his penetrating analysis of the mind of a mnemonist relates various examples of his subject "S." being overwhelmed by memories and images upon reading even a simple poem. More specifically, as many authors have pointed out, the correspondence between the episode one is reminded of and the present situation may indeed be coincidental and thus provide the wrong guideline for action that no "tweaking" can redress. Reason and Embrey (1985) emphasized this in the context of the likelihood of major catastrophes. Neustadt and May (1986) did pretty much the same in their analysis of major political disasters, one of which was the Vietnam adventure of the United States. To prevent such disasters, or at least to reduce their likelihood, Neustadt and May suggested that every plausible scenario for action be subjected to a very careful time-path analysis. What they mean by this can be illustrated by the following example.

When, in 1964, President Lyndon B. Johnson was facing the decision of whether to make a military commitment in Vietnam, almost everybody involved was reminded of the unsuccessful French campaign in the early 1950s. On the basis of this analogy Johnson decided to actively support the basically weak and instable government of South Vietnam. In the process of deliberation preceding this unfortunate decision no attempt was made to see whether or not the temporal relations between the key events in both episodes (the French example and the expected development of the actual situation) did indeed match to a sufficient degree. The Americans thought they could draw a parallel with the final years of the French campaign. Accordingly, they felt they would be able to avoid the mistakes the French had made at that time. In hindsight, however, it turned out that the actual situation in Vietnam developed along the line that had characterized the early years of the French campaign in Indo-China. The false parallel suggested that it would be possible to eliminate the Viet-Cong with a limited commitment. The correct parallel would have pointed to the fact that the United States, with an extremely weak and corrupt ally, would be defeated in a guerrilla war against a determined enemy that could rely on a massive support from an equally determined North Vietnam.[5]

THE FIGURATIVE REPRESENTATION
OF TIME: METAPHORS

Attempts at activating a verisimilar scenario from one that would be able to derive an appropriate representation of temporal relations may fail. Frequently it is impossible to be reminded of such a scenario because no comparable events have been experienced in the past.   Sometimes reminding is unsuccessful because the objects and relations that need to be represented lack a concrete, perceptual basis. In these cases memory search must be extended so as to include analogies (metaphors) that allow at least a number of relevant properties and relations to be represented coherently by means of a conceptual structure that is borrowed from another semantic domain. The term *metaphor* actually refers only to the verbal expression of such an analogy, but is frequently used instead of the term *analogy*.

Carbonell (1982) described in detail the process by which an analogy or metaphor is selected and adapted as a substitute for a verisimilar scenario. If someone is confronted with events for which he or she has no appropriate verisimilar scenario, the constraints on memory search will be relaxed. The requirements for a sufficient match between the analogy and the actual situation depend on the purpose for which the analogy (metaphor) is activated. This means that an acceptable analogy must at least be capable of representing the goal structure and the strategies for action. If we wish, for example, to adopt the analogy "time is our enemy," then it must, in the first place, mean something to make war against and to defeat time (e.g., Rifkin, 1987) and, in the second place it must be possible to give meaning and content to such strategies as attacking, ambushing, or killing time. Other implied characteristics, however, such as functional relations (e.g., between regiments and platoons), physical attributes (e.g., the metallurgical composition of a bullet) need not be taken into consideration. When an effective analogy is established, the next step in the process of fitting it to the prevailing

---

[5] There is in such cases always a Cassandra, someone destined to see more clearly but to be overruled. In the present case this role was played by the Under Secretary of State, George Ball. For the details, see Neustadt and May (1986).

situation is to determine its extended reading—that is, its useful range of application in the target domain.

There exists a tremendous number of temporal metaphors. *Bartlett's Familiar Quotations* (Bartlett, 1980), for instance, gives more than 600 remarkable statements about time (not counting the many related quotations about hours, years, clocks, etc.). From this set I have been able to distill some 40 essentially different metaphors: time as destroyer or as healer, time as receding or approaching, time as flying or dragging, time as substance or container, and so on. Time, it appears from this list, is absolutely relative: For every conceptualization there is also its opposite.

The 40-odd characteristic metaphors for time can be classified quite easily in terms of a very limited set of core metaphors. Lakoff and Johnson (1980), in their discussion of the metaphors we live by, distinguished between simple metaphors that establish an orientation, an ontological categorization, or a personification of a single concept or event, and the more complex structural (or generative) metaphors that entail a whole network of properties, relations, and implications.

Of the last category, spatial metaphors are nearly always dominant. This again was pointed out already by Guyau (1890/1988), who explained the fact in an evolutionary framework. He argued that the development of the idea of time derives from the child's reaching out in space to what it has not yet, from the distance between "the goblet and the lips" (p. 34). Because of this spatial origin, later conceptual representations of time are likely to refer more or less naturally back to the spatial domain. Guyau's argument has been reinforced in recent times by several authors, for instance by Clark (1973) who, in an analysis of time in the language of the child, found evidence for "a thoroughly systematic spatial metaphor, suggesting a complete cognitive system" (p. 62). Gruber (1976) made an attempt to formalize this observation in his so-called *thematic relation hypothesis.* He maintained that there is a forced preference for spatial analogies in many (if not all) semantic domains, with precise (and perhaps innate) substitution rules that prescribe which attributes and relations of the target domain are mapped onto the spatial domain (see Jackendoff, 1983, for a detailed discussion). In this context I should not fail to mention the emphasis that is currently being placed on the role of visual imagery (physical envisionment, or *Anschaulichkeit* in German) in scientific discovery and the understanding of complex formal relations. Studies by Holland, Holyoak, Nisbett, and Thagard (1986); A. I. Miller (1986); Langley, Simon, Bradshaw, and Zytkow (1987); and Larkin and Simon (1987) all seem to support the contention that one picture (sometimes) tells us more than ten thousand words.

An Illustration: The Bureaucracy of Time

Mixed metaphors (or mixed analogies) are sometimes extra powerful. Whereas space and, by implication, spatial analogies are inherently inert or passive, an active secondary metaphor may easily "stimulate" a static spatial metaphor. The colonization of time, for instance, turns out to be an enterprising, if not aggressive, extension of the spatial metaphor. It has found serious application in the domain of space-time geography and transportation (Burns, 1979), and is also frequently used or implied in sociological analyses of modern cultural phenomena (Nowotny, 1989). Refrigerators, automatic dishwashers, and day-care centers are recognized as the advanced weaponry of the colonists (Burns, 1979, p. 107).

A successful metaphor will affect the cognitive style and the activity patterns of a society. The metaphor "Time is money," for instance, can be taken to be the most "western" of all metaphors of time. It suggests that it is possible to treat time as a valuable, scarce commodity. "Time is money" not only generates a tremendous array of applicable expressions for temporal relations, but it induces patterns of behavior that are unknown or that are looked upon with contempt or puzzlement in the so-called "mañana cultures." An extravagant time management is one of the potentially harmful consequences of applying this structural metaphor.

Time management may indeed deteriorate into a pathological ritual. Around his 20th birthday, a rather important Dutch novelist and literary critic Lodewijk van Deyssel (1864-1952) decided, as he wrote at the time, "to impose on myself an iron temporal discipline and to document in minute detail all the mechanical aspects of my intellectual functioning; one and the other with the aim of collecting the building bricks for a science concerning the properties and functioning of my brain."[6] This mental bureaucracy which, incidentally, on occasion affected Van Deyssel's creativity, allowed him, on the other hand, to retain the extreme equanimity that he felt he needed. "Like the workings of my body . . . the temporal performance in the course of the days of my life may be investigated, in order to achieve as much as possible, an uninterrupted and desired state of mind . . . I now feel in this paper life-administration not more and not less than a (relative) omnipotence." The rituals that enabled Van Deyssel to live a totally regulated life were supported by printed routine orders, memoranda tacked to the bedposts, and alarm clocks. And yet Van Deyssel's rules and regulations did not

---

[6] The details and the quotations from Van Deyssel's unpublished diaries were taken from an article by H. G. M. Prick in the periodical *Hollands Diep* (28 February 1976; vol. 1, no. 5).

always work. Thus, in spite of eight impressive precautions implemented on the previous night, he succeeded in oversleeping on June 29th, 1891. Among other things, he overslept, he said, "because my spouse has neither awakened me, nor told me to rise."

Now, a century later, time management has become a flourishing branch of industry. Time management is *big business*. Time not only must be divided, it must also be conquered, invested, shared, saved, and accounted for. Some people own a whole library of do-it-yourself books on the subject. All these book contain extensive discussions, exercises, and advice about how to manage the days and parts of days and parts of parts of days, and in particular—and that is where the pathology creeps in again—about the records one should keep for later evaluation. If you want to invest your time in this kind of activity you can procure a pound-heavy time-management agenda with dozens of different types of sheets and tables. Here we see the ultimate *reductio ad absurdum* of the temporal organization of behavior: the malignant growth of a metaphor, and the bureaucratic substitute for a personal history, a genuine diary.

THE FORMAL REPRESENTATION
OF TIME: RECEIVED VIEWS

The philosopher Goodman (1984) summarized the problem of establishing an appropriate representation of the world around us as follows: "We make visions, and true visions make worlds" (p. 34). In other words, of all our attempts to construct representations of reality only a few are strong enough to support a view of the world. The same is true of some representations of time that have proved so successful that we have become convinced that they simply must be telling us something essential about the temporal structure of nature. This conviction has made it possible to develop conceptual structures that are so coherent and consistent that we may call them *theories of time*.

The most conspicuous example would seem to be the clock metaphor, derived from early ideas about the harmony of spheres and the polyphonic chanting in the church. Szamosi (1986) pointed out that in particular this latter activity represents an artistic and chronometric achievement of the first order—the mastery of time in the range of actual behavior—but that as an achievement it is based on no less than 5 centuries of intense experimentation and practice.

The clock metaphor, ultimately formalized in the 17th century in Newton's mechanics, is particularly visible in theories that deal with periodic phenomena such as pendulums or waves, and in related mathematical methods such as Fourier analysis. Early in the 20th century the classical clock metaphor has disappeared somewhat behind a truly spatial theory of time. That was when Einstein, Poincaré, and Weyl introduced time as an integral part of the relativistic spacetime in which time, distance, and motion are integrated by means of a fundamental invariant, the (finite) speed of light.

Both the clock metaphor and this spatial conception of time deny the ultimate reality of time. Classical physics has for centuries attempted to rid itself of time, and relativistic spacetime physics is no different in this aim (Park, 1985). But these attempts have been less than totally successful. They have been based on the assumption that time is in principle symmetric, that is, reversible. There are natural phenomena, however, that seem to fundamentally contradict this assumption. All metaphors that represent time as the destroyer, the healer of all wounds, the teacher, or the river Lethe, give expression to the archetypal insight that what is done is done. The crystallization of this insight was achieved with the formulation of thermodynamics in the middle of the 19th century. Since then, several other "arrows of time" have been defined (e.g., Horwich, 1987; Morris, 1985). Despite attempts to explain these asymmetries away, some arrows have proved to be very resistant, and some have even attained the status of axiomatic theory (e.g., Prigogine, 1980; Rosen, 1985).

An Illustration: The Geological Time Scale

Although formal representations of time do not always require five centuries to develop as in the case of musical chronometry, their construction nevertheless requires a substantial period of time. Geology, for instance, undoubtedly one of the sciences of time, has struggled at least a century and a half with its image of "deep time," that is the relation between the structure and localization of strata and their age.

Recently, Gould (1987) has given a lively account of this struggle. In a book that explains the roles of "time's arrow and time's cycle" in the establishment of a received view of geological time he offered an analysis of the respective roles that have been played by two fundamental and quite popular metaphors of time—the pointed arrow and the circle—in the development of scientific geology during the 18th and 19th centuries. The founding fathers of geology were in fact facing two major conceptual problems. First they had to free themselves from the totally inappropriate time scale of the biblical Book of Genesis. By the middle of the 18th century, evidence had accumulated that required a conceptual extension of the age of the world from several thousands to several millions, and perhaps even hundreds or thousands of millions of years. Second, they had to come to grips with an apparent conflict between the evident changes in the morphology of the earth and its inhabitants—both a sign of time's arrow—on the one hand, and the physically inspired wish to formulate general, uniform, and constant laws and processes of nature on the other hand.

It is easy to appreciate the importance of the latter point. If the physical laws that govern sedimentation and mountain formation, or the origin and extinction of live species do not remain constant over time, then every attempt at describing the history of the planet Earth and of life on Earth is basically futile and every bit as arbitrary as the time scale of Genesis. The solution that the early geologists initially saw for this dilemma was to assume that the observed changes were essentially cyclical. Thus, a change in one direction would eventually be "compensated" by a change in the opposite direction. Periods of mountain formation and erosion would eternally alternate "with no vestige of a beginning, no prospect of an end" as one of them wrote in 1788 (James Hutton, cited in Gould, 1987, p. 79).

This discussion about arrows and cycles in geology has not survived the 20th century's taste for dialectic synthesis, but traces can still be found in the distinction that biologists and paleontologists make between analogy and homology. *Analogy* is evidence for the fact that nature will occasionally repeat itself—as it did, for instance, with the torpedo-shaped bodies of aquatic animals—for the simple reason, that good designs are scarce in this universe. *Homology*, on the other hand, "represents similarity through inheritance and [thereby] determines a historical time" (Gould, 1987, p. 197-198).

THE FORMALIZATION OF ACTION
PLANNING: A UNIFICATION

Attempts, in the 1960s, to develop temporal logics that allow us to determine the truth value of propositions about complex relations between points in time, the so-called *instant logic*, have met with considerable success. Then in the course of the 1970s the so-called *interval logic* was added to the repertoire, allowing similar exercises with propositions about the relations between (finite) time intervals (e.g., Van Benthem, 1983). From then on developments have been impressive.

There is an eminently practical reason for this acceleration that derives from the fact that temporal logic constitutes a formalization of the ways people seem to deal with their verisimilar and figurative representations of time.

Temporal logics—there are several of them—may be considered as computational theories for describing complex temporal relations and for action planning (see e.g., Georgeff & Lansky, 1987). Until recently, artificial intelligence had few ways of dealing with temporal relations between events. For many applications the absence of algorithms for string manipulation is no serious matter. In the game of chess for instance there are strings of moves and positions, but the world changes only during and as a result of a particular move. Beyond that the world is frozen. Compare this, however, with an automobile approaching an intersection. While this happens the driver looks at the road in front of him and observes a car is approaching from the left. In order to cross in front of this second car the driver decides to accelerate, but just then a child dashes out. In this case string manipulation to compute the consequences of different serial actions and their outcomes is required (Aasman, 1988; Michon, 1988). Recently, several methods have been developed for the dynamic planning of action, most of which use the results of one or the other temporal logic.

Consider a robot charged with the task of storing, transporting, and delivering goods inside a warehouse. If this robot decides it must take Box A, which is located under Box B on Shelf C in Room D, and bring it to Room E to put it in Corner G before Event H takes place in Room D, then this simple chain of actions is fundamentally affected by anything that happens in the mean time, while the robot is at its job. Anything that happens to any object in this world that is not a direct consequence of an action of the robot will affect the truth and falsity of a great many propositions about this world. The maintenance of truth in the representation the robot has of its world is a computationally explosive problem and the robot will soon find itself left "buried in thought." This would happen because, at least initially, models of action planning were based on straightforward and exhaustive algorithms for updating the truth values of propositions—all propositions—about the world. But stagnation in the execution of actions is likely to occur even if certain logical or physical restrictions apply, such as the insight that an object cannot be in two different places at the same time or that a door must be open if one wishes to proceed from one room to the next.[7] The question is how the

---

[7] The truth maintenance problem is similar to the many-body problem in mechanics. The effect of A on B and that of A on C will affect the interaction between B and C. Consequently the combined effects of B and C on A will be affected, so that the effect of A of on B and on C will change as well, and so the computation "explodes."

robot can constrain its problem space sufficiently to avoid the dreaded computational explosion and at the same time remain capable of dynamically adapting to environmental change. This seems to me one of the most fundamental problems that any plausible theory of intelligence that incorporates temporal phenomena will have to solve. Although this problem has been known in various disguises for many centuries, dating back at least to Zeno of Elea (e.g., Grünbaum, 1968), it has recently attracted much attention in its formulation as the *frame problem* (McCarthy & Hayes, 1969; Pylyshyn, 1988).

More recent models for temporal planning try to avoid the frame and truth maintenance problems altogether. They do not proceed from separate frames or actions with their conditions and results, but from string of elements, *chronicles*, that represent an action sequence or episodic progression from its inception to the present instant (e.g., Lansky, 1987). Planning implies the choice of one of (perhaps infinitely) many possible worlds that are consistent with the course of events up to the present point in time, and that in addition meet the action constraints imposed by the present circumstances. This approach avoids the problem of dealing with the world as a succession of inert states that requires an explosive amount of truth maintenance if action is to be taken. It is not clear, however, whether models that are based on the concept of string or chronicle can indeed cope successfully with the computational divergence.

These are some of the trends toward formalized theories of action. Their impact will be enhanced by the added modeling possibilities offered by parallel architectures—in the form of distributed networks (Rumelhart, Smolensky, McClelland, & Hinton, 1986), perhaps, or in the form of parallel rule-matching systems such as Soar (Laird, Newell, & Rosenbloom, 1987). In many respects these trends seem to match the psychological insights into the mental representation of time that I have reviewed in the preceding sections of this chapter, from concrete intentional action, to verisimilar scenarios, to representations of generative metaphors, and finally to formal conceptions of what time is. They provide the foundations for a more explicit and detailed theory about the processing of temporal information and the way humans stay tuned to the dynamic world around them.

SUMMARY AND CONCLUSIONS

In its first century, the experimental study of human time experience has been almost entirely a *psychophysics of duration*. Only recently, with the emergence of cognitive psychology, a much broader array of temporal phenomena has become the subject of empirical study, including the perception of rhythmic patterns, the planning of future action, and the narrative structure of complex events. In this chapter I have argued for the position that time as duration is in fact an advanced abstraction, a form of representation which derives from a functionally much more basic biological requirement: the need to stay in tune with a dynamic, unfolding outside world. Mental representations of time enable us to achieve behavioral and cognitive coherence of successions of real events, or episodes. If these events pertain to our personal history, this "narrative closure" leads to the identity of what we call our *self*. Cognitive representations of time span a continuum from highly veri-similar, concrete dynamic scenes, to semi-abstract analogical schemes, and from there to formalized, axiomatic theories of time. The remark-able instability of time's rate of flow is the most pronounced aspect of subjective time and the principal dependent variable of the psychophysics of time. It is derived from the use humans make of these various types of representation while they are "tuning in" on the sequen-tial contingencies of their environment.

REFERENCES

Aasman, J. (1988) Implementations of car-driver behaviour and psychological risk models. In J. A. Rothengatter & R. A. de Bruin (Eds.), *Road user behaviour: Theory and research* (pp. 106-118). Assen, The Netherlands: Van Gorcum.

Bartlett, J. (1980). *Bartlett's familiar quotations* (15th ed.). Boston, MA: Little, Brown.

Brockelman, P. (1985). *Time and self: Phenomenological explorations.* New York: Crossroad.

Burns, L. D. (1979). *Transportation: Temporal and spatial components of accessibility.* Lexing-ton, MA: Heath.

Carbonell, J. G. (1982). Metaphor: An inescapable phenomenon in natural language compre-hension. In W. G. Lehnert & M. U. Ringle (Eds.), *Strategies for natural language processing* (pp. 415-434). Hillsdale, NJ: Lawrence Erlbaum Associates.

Clark, H. H. (1973). Space, time, semantics, and the child. In T. E. Moore (Ed.), *Cognitive development and the acquisition of language* (pp. 27-63). New York: Academic Press.

DiSessa, A. (1983). Phenomenology and the evolution of intuition. In D. Gentner & A. L. Stevens (Eds.), *Mental models* (pp. 15-33). Hillsdale, NJ: Lawrence Erlbaum Associates.

Fraser, J. T. (1982). *The genesis and evolution of time: A critique of interpretation in physics.* Amherst, MA: University of Massachusetts Press.

Freyd, J. J. (1987). Dynamic mental representations. *Psychological Review, 94,* 427-438.

Georgeff, M. P., & Lansky, A. L. (Eds.). (1987). *Reasoning about actions and plans.* Los Altos, CA: Morgan Kaufmann.

Gibbon, J., & Allan, L. (Eds.). (1984). *Timing and time perception.* New York: New York Academy of Sciences.

Gibson, J. J. (1969). *The ecological approach to visual perception*. Boston, MA: Houghton Mifflin.

Gibson, J. J. (1975). Events are perceivable but time is not. In J. T. Fraser & N. Lawrence (Eds.), *The study of time II* (pp. 295-301). New York: Springer-Verlag.

Goodman, N. (1984). *Of mind and other matters*. Cambridge, MA: Harvard University Press.

Gould, S. J. (1987). *Time's arrow, time's cycle: Myth and metaphor in the discovery of geological time*. Cambridge, MA: Harvard University Press.

Gruber, J. S. (1976). *Lexical structures in syntax and semantics*. Amsterdam: North-Holland.

Grünbaum, A. (1968). *Modern science and Zeno's paradoxes*. London: Allen & Unwin.

Guyau, J.-M. (1988). *La genèse de l'idée de temps* [The origin of the idea of time]. In J. A. Michon, V. Pouthas, & J. L. Jackson (Eds.), *Guyau and the idea of time* (pp. 37-90; translation pp. 93-148). Amsterdam: North-Holland. (Original work published 1890)

Hobbs, J. R., & Moore, R. C. (1985). *Formal theories of the common sense world*. Norwood, NJ: Ablex.

Holland, J. H., Holyoak, K. J., Nisbett, R. E., & Thagard, P. R. (1986). *Induction: Processes of inference, learning, and discovery*. Cambridge, MA: MIT Press.

Horwich, P. (1987). *Asymmetries in time: Problems in the philosophy of science*. Cambridge, MA: MIT Press.

Jackendoff, R. (1983). *Semantics and cognition*. Cambridge, MA: MIT Press.

Jackson, J. L. (1986). *The processing of temporal information*. Doctoral dissertation, University of Groningen, The Netherlands.

Johnson-Laird, P. N. (1983). *Mental models*. Cambridge: University of Cambridge Press.

Jones, M. R. (1976). Time, our lost dimension: Toward a new theory of perception, attention, and memory. *Psychological Review, 83*, 323-355.

Jones, M. R. (1985). Structural organization of events in time. In J. A. Michon & J. L. Jackson (Eds.), *Time, mind, and behavior* (pp. 192-214). Berlin: Springer-Verlag.

Jones, M. R., & Boltz, M. (1989). Dynamic attending and responses to time. *Psychological Review, 96*, 459-491.

Laird, J. E., Newell, A., & Rosenbloom, P. S. (1987). Soar: An architecture for general intelligence. *Artificial Intelligence, 33*, 1-64.

Lakoff, G., & Johnson, M. (1980). *Metaphors we live by*. Chicago, IL: University of Chicago Press.

Langley, P., Simon, H. A., Bradshaw, G. R., & Zytkow, J. M. (1987). *Scientific discovery: Computational explorations of the creative process*. Cambridge, MA: MIT Press.

Lansky, A. L. (1987). A representation of parallel activity based on events, structure, and causality. In M. P. Georgeff & A. L. Lansky (Eds.), *Reasoning about actions and plans* (pp. 123-159). Los Altos, CA: Morgan Kaufmann.

Larkin, J. H., & Simon, H. A. (1987). Why a diagram is (sometimes) worth ten thousand words. *Cognitive Science, 11*, 65-100.

Lawrence, N. (1986). The origins of time. In J. T. Fraser, N. Lawrence, & F. C. Haber (Eds.), *Time, science, and society in China and the West: The study of time V* (pp. 23-38). Amherst, MA: University of Massachusetts Press.

Luria, A. R. (1968). *The mind of a mnemonist*. New York: Basic Books.

Macar, F. (1985). Time psychophysics and related models. In J. A. Michon & J. L. Jackson (Eds.), *Time, mind, and behavior* (pp. 112-130). Berlin: Springer-Verlag.

Mashhour, M. (1964). *Psychophysical relations in the perception of velocity*. Stockholm: Almqvist & Wiksell.

McCarthy, J. M., & Hayes, P. J. (1969). Some philosophical problems from the standpoint of artificial intelligence. In D. Michie & B. Meltzer (Eds.), *Machine intelligence* (Vol. 4, pp. 463-502). Edinburgh: Edinburgh University Press.

Michon, J. A. (1967). *Timing in temporal tracking*. Assen, The Netherlands: Van Gorcum.

Michon, J. A. (1985). The compleat time experiencer. In J. A. Michon & J. L. Jackson (Eds.), *Time, mind, and behavior* (pp. 20-52). Berlin: Springer-Verlag.

Michon, J. A. (1988). Should drivers think? In J. A. Rothengatter & R. A. de Bruin (Eds.), *Road user behaviour: Theory and research* (pp. 508-517). Assen, The Netherlands: Van Gorcum.

Michon, J. A., & Jackson, J. L. (1984). Attentional effort and cognitive strategies in the processing of temporal information. In J. Gibbon & L. Allan (Eds.), *Timing and time perception* (pp. 298-321). New York: New York Academy of Sciences.

Michon, J. A., Pouthas, V., & Jackson, J. L. (Eds.). (1988). *Guyau and the idea of time*. Amsterdam: North-Holland.

Miller, A. I. (1986). *Imagery in scientific thought*. Cambridge, MA: MIT Press.

Miller, I. (1984). *Husserl, perception, and temporal awareness*. Cambridge, MA: Bradford Books/MIT Press.

Montangero, J. (1977). *La notion de durée chez l'enfant de 5 à 9 ans* [The notion of time in 5- to 9-year old children]. Paris: Presses Universitaires de France.

Montangero, J. (1985). The development of temporal inferences and meanings in 5- to 8-year old children. In J. A. Michon & J. L. Jackson (Eds.), *Time, mind, and behavior* (pp. 279-287). Berlin: Springer-Verlag.

Morris, R. (1985). *Time's arrows: Scientific attitudes toward time*. New York: Simon & Schuster.

Neustadt, R. E., & May, E. R. (1986). *Thinking in time: The uses of time decision makers*. New York: Free Press.

Nowotny, H. (1989). Mind, technologies, and collective time-consciousness: From the future to an extended present. In J. T. Fraser (Ed.), *Time and mind: Interdisciplinary issues* (pp. 197-216). Madison, CT: International Universities Press.

Park, D. (1985). Brain time and mind time. In J. A. Michon & J. L. Jackson (Eds.), *Time, mind, and behavior* (pp. 53-64). Berlin: Springer-Verlag.

Piaget, J. (1946). *Le développement de la notion de temps chez l'enfant* [The child's conception of time]. Paris: Presses Universitaires de France.

Prigogine, I. (1980). *From being to becoming: Time and complexity in the physical sciences*. San Francisco: Freeman.

Pylyshyn, Z. (1988). *The frame problem*. Hillsdale, NJ: Lawrence Erlbaum Associates.

Reason, J. T., & Embrey, D. E. (1985). *Human factors principles relevant to the modelling of human errors in abnormal conditions of nuclear and major hazardous installations*. (Report prepared for the European Atomic Energy Community under contract EC1 1164-B7221-84-UK). Dalton, Lancashire, England.

Richardson-Klavehn, A., & Bjork, R. A. (1988). Measures of memory. *Annual Review of Psychology, 39*, 475-543.

Rifkin, J. (1987). *Time wars: The primary conflict in human history*. New York: Henry Holt.

Rosen, R. (1985). *Anticipatory systems: Philosophical, mathematical and methodological foundations*. Oxford: Pergamon Press.

Rumelhart, D. E., Smolensky, P., McClelland, J. L., & Hinton, G. E. (1986). Schemata and sequential thought processes in PDP models. In J. L. McClelland & D. E. Rumelhart (Eds.), *Parallel distributed processing: Vol. 2. Psychological and biological models* (pp. 7-57). Cambridge, MA: Bradford Books/MIT Press.

Schacter, D. L. (1987). Implicit memory: History and current status. *Journal of Experimental Psychology: Learning, Memory, and Cognition, 13*, 501-518.

Schank, R. C. (1982). *Dynamic memory: A theory of learning in computers and people*. Cambridge: Cambridge University Press.

Schank, R. C. (1986). *Explanation patterns: Understanding mechanically and creatively*. Hillsdale, NJ: Lawrence Erlbaum Associates.

Shaffer, L. H. (1985). Timing in action. In J. A. Michon & J. L. Jackson (Eds.), *Time, mind, and behavior* (pp. 226-241). Berlin: Springer-Verlag.

Shepard, R. N. (1984). Ecological constraints on internal representation: Resonant kinematics of perceiving, imagining, thinking, and dreaming. *Psychological Review, 91*, 417-447.

Sherover, C. M. (Ed.). (1975). *The human experience of time: The development of its philosophic meaning*. New York: New York University Press.

Szamosi, G. (1986). *The twin dimensions: Inventing time and space*. New York: McGraw Hill.

Teulings, H.-L. (1988). *The analysis of handwriting*. Doctoral dissertation, University of Nijmegen, The Netherlands.

Thomassen, A. J. W. M., & Teulings, H.-L. (1985). Time, size and shape in handwriting: Exploring spatio-temporal relationships at different levels. In J. A. Michon & J. L. Jackson (Eds.), *Time, mind, and behavior* (pp. 253-263). Berlin: Springer-Verlag.

Treisman, M. (1963). Temporal discrimination and the indifference interval: Implications for a model of the "internal clock." *Psychological Monographs, 77* (Whole no. 576).

Van Benthem, J. F. A. K. (1983). *The logic of time*. Dordrecht, The Netherlands: D. Reidel.

3 The Evasive Art of Subjective Time Measurement: Some Methodological Dilemmas

Dan Zakay
Tel Aviv University

Subjective time is one of the essential dimensions required by humans for orientation in their surrounding world. Navon (1978) suggested that "our conception of the world (or of stimuli in the world) is a hierarchy of dimensions, in which time occupies the first level and spatial dimensions occupy the second ones" (p. 227). Similarly, Michon (1985) claimed that behavior is under the control of time.

Despite this importance of time, however, no sense or sense organ by which time can be perceived directly is known, nor is it clear what information humans utilize to make time estimates. It seems that subjective time is a product of cognitive functioning and that "time experience can be understood as a manifestation of temporal information processes" (Michon, 1985, p. 31). Researchers since the emergence of experimental psychology have been trying to crack the secrets of information processing responsible for the sense of time. In order to achieve that goal, reliable and valid time-measurement tools are a must. Time, however, is a slippery entity, sensitive to the conditions under which it is measured. Bindra and Waksberg (1956) described this situation by saying that "despite the relatively simple design of time estimation studies, they are quite confusing to read, and an attempt to make generalizations from the results of different studies, gets one involved in many apparent or real contradictions" (p. 155). Because of this methodological status, investigators made an effort to define and categorize the factors that have an influence on subjective time's measurement (e.g., Allan, 1979; Block,

1985, 1988; Clausen, 1950; Fraisse, 1984; Hicks, Miller, & Kinsbourne, 1976; Wallace & Rabin, 1960; Zakay & Fallach, 1984).

Hicks et al. (1976) listed the following factors: (a) method of time estimation (e.g., absolute time judgment by production, verbal estimation, or reproduction, or comparative time judgment); (b) duration of the interval to be estimated; (c) the nature of processing required of the subject during the interval to be estimated (e.g., empty or filled interval); and (d) the nature of the measurement paradigm (e.g., a prospective paradigm in which the subject knows in advance that he or she will be required to estimate the elapsed time, or a retrospective paradigm in which the subject is told the nature of his or her task only after the target interval is over). A comprehensive model that ties together most of the factors relevant for time measurement is Block's (1989) contextualistic model of temporal experience. Block identified four types of factors that interact to influence temporal experiences: (a) The kind of temporal behavior involved. This factor refers to the type of time judgment utilized and the temporal dimension to be considered (e.g., simultaneity, successiveness, rhythm, order, spacing, or duration). (b) The characteristics of the time period that a person experiences. This factor refers to the external or internal events that occur during that period, and includes parameters like the number of events, their content, complexity, modality, and so on. (c) The characteristics of the experiencer. This factor refers to enduring or provisional personality traits, sex, past experience, and so forth. (d) Activity during the time period. This factor refers to what the experiencer is doing during the time period (e.g., the load of his or her information-processing behavior, his or her resource allocation policy, his or her expectations, the type of instructions provided by an experimenter, either prospective or retrospective, and so on. Block (1989) claimed that "a complete understanding of any kind of temporal experience is possible only if we consider complex interactions among all of these factors" (p. 334).

Because of the complexity of temporal experiences, the empirical data that were gathered from the beginning of research on subjective time were obscure and not explicable in terms of one simple theoretical framework. The outcome of this situation was the emergence of many models and theories, most of which were supported empirically. The solution to this enigma lies in the contextualistic approach, like that proposed by Zakay and Fallach (1984) and Block (1989), namely that the pattern of temporal experiences and their relationships with the events in the objective world depend on the context within which they are taking place. Subjective time is an entity that, like the path of the atom's elementary particles, is not separable from its measurement.

The pattern of the relationships between subjective duration and the information-processing load during an estimated interval can serve as an illustration. According to Ornstein's (1969) storage-size model, time estimation is a function of storage size, which, in turn, is a function of the complexity of information-processing required.

Accordingly, the greater the complexity of processing required, the greater the resulting storage size and thus the longer the corresponding time estimate. Support for Ornstein's model was obtained in several studies (e.g., Avant, Lyman, & Antes, 1975; Michon, 1965).

Block (1978), however, provided only qualified support for Ornstein's model: Remembered duration lengthened, just as he would predict, with a more complex sequence of events, but it was not influenced by the complexity of a single stimulus.

An opposing view is presented by attentional models (e.g., Hicks, Miller, Gaes, & Bierman 1977; Thomas & Brown, 1974; Zakay, Nitzan, & Glicksohn, 1983). They claim that duration estimation increased with the observer's attention to time, because the processing of temporal information demands mental effort. As a result, attention is divided between the processing of temporal and nontemporal information. The terms *temporal information processing, temporal information,* and the notion of attention within the frame of time estimation need further clarification. These terms look vague at first glance. Block (1979) suggested that "perhaps references to attention to time itself that are found in the literature on experienced duration can be understood in terms of attention to changes in contextual aspects of consciousness" (p. 196). The meaning of the former terms in the present chapter, is somewhat different. They are used as metaphors without pretension to describe a specific process. Several authors (e.g., Avant et al., 1975; Thomas & Brown, 1974; Thomas & Weaver, 1975) have proposed processing-time explanations of duration estimation. The idea is that somewhere in working memory, a cognitive timer or processor registers the number of times within a given interval that awareness to the passage of time takes place (e.g., Hicks et al., 1977). Metaphorically, each time a person is asking him or herself, "what time is it?"; or "how much time am I doing this?"; or "how much time should I wait until, . . . ?"; or "when will I finish this?"; and so forth, a registration is made in the cognitive timer. Attention to time is considered here as the energy that activates the counter. Hence, "temporal information" is not external but rather an internal input to the time processor. "Temporal information processing" is the process of registration in the time processor, and attention to time is manifested by being aware of time and by intentionally seeking information about objective time. The prediction, stemming from attentional models, is of a negative relation between task complexity and magnitude of time estimates. This prediction was supported in several studies (e.g., Burnside, 1971; Devane, 1974; Vroon, 1970; Zakay, 1989a). This fuzzy situation becomes clearer only if one considers the time-measurement paradigm. Hicks et al. (1976) found support for the prediction of a negative relation only within a prospective paradigm.

Zakay (1989b) found that, indeed, most of the studies in which the storage-size model was supported utilized a retrospective paradigm, whereas most of the studies in which attentional models were supported utilized a prospective paradigm. The different cognitive mechanisms underlying duration estimation under each of these paradigms interact with the information-processing load demanded by a task to be performed during a target interval to produce different duration experiences related to the same objective clock time.

This last illustration shed light on the importance of considering the methodological context while interpreting experimental results in the subjective time domain.

The purpose of this chapter is to analyze some of the major methodological factors and to point out the potential hazards that are thereby implicated in subjective time research, mainly in the domain of short interval estimation.

OBJECTIVE DURATION

The aspect of time estimation most widely studied is that in which observers are asked to estimate the duration of some event (see Michon, chapter 2, this volume).

Fraisse (1984) made a distinction between estimation and perception of duration. He said that "duration's estimation takes place when memory is used either to associate a moment in the past with a moment in the present or to link two past events, whereas perception of duration involves the psychological present" (p. 9). The psychological present is also termed the *indifference interval* or *indifference point* (Ornstein, 1969; Treisman, 1963). Block (1979) defined the *indifference point* as a "time period that is, on the average, neither overestimated nor underestimated" (p. 185). The indifference interval is usually considered to be about 500-700 ms, although estimates range from about 300 ms and up to 5 s or longer. As for other intervals, a common finding is that observers tend to overestimate brief intervals and to underestimate larger ones (Ward, 1975). Aschoff (1984, 1985) concluded that long and short time estimates are based on different mechanisms.

Fraisse (1984) suggested three categories of objective durations characterized by stimulating different temporal-related processes: (a) less that 100 ms, at which the perception is of instantaneity; (b) 100 ms to 5 s, in which perception of duration is part of the perceived present; and (c) above 5 s, in which duration estimation must involve memory mechanisms.

Although the validity of the boundaries of Fraisse's categories is not clear (for a more elaborated discussion of that point see Allan, 1979), the methodological implications are quite obvious: One has to use the appropriate objective duration in order to explore hypothesized temporal processes. Unfortunately, for practical reasons, the durations used in estimation research rarely exceed 1 min (Fraisse, 1984). This might limit our understanding of time-related processes that characterize the estimation of longer objective durations, as in Aschoff's (1984) study.

ESTIMATION METHOD

Bindra and Waksberg (1956), as well as Wallace and Rabin (1960) defined four major methods by means of which time intervals are judged in time estimation research.

1. Verbal estimation: the target interval duration is estimated verbally in terms of temporal units.
2. Time production: a predefined interval of a given length is produced.
3. Reproduction of time: the target interval is reproduced by means of some operation.
4. Comparison: two intervals are presented and the estimator is to judge which is longer.

This categorization is usually accepted in the literature (e.g., Block, 1989). Allan (1979) presented a more elaborated list of methods, classified under two major categories. The first category includes the methods of verbal estimation, magnitude estimation, category rating, production, ratio-setting, and synchronization. The ratio-setting method is actually equivalent to the reproduction method, but Allan differentiated between reproduction in which the proportion between the target and the reproduced intervals is 1.00, fractionation in which this proportion is less than 1.00, and multiplication in which this proportion is greater than 1.00. This differentiation is justified only from a theoretical point of view for analyzing the different cognitive processes that are involved in each case. This differentiation, however, is a posteriori and is not justified from a practical point of view of an experimenter who is designing his or her experiment.

Synchronization is a variant of the reproduction method that has two versions: "In one version, E [the experimenter] presents a fixed duration standard and S [the subject] responds in synchrony with its termination. In another version, E presents a series of brief events once per unit time and S reproduces a sequence of responses at the same rate" (Allan, 1979, p. 341). It can be claimed, however, that the number of actual estimation methods is higher than that just listed (see Table 3.1). Reproduction methods vary on the basis of the specific technique used (i.e., the subject presses a key for the estimated period that activates a hidden timer, or, the subject says "start" and then "stop" while the experimenter activates some measurement device following the subject's instructions, that is, turning on and off a light). The same is true for production of time.

Regarding comparison, this can be done by verbal categories or analogically where the experimenter presents the subject with two lines, one representing the length of the standard duration, and the other, which is longer, is used by the subject for demarcation of the length of the target interval. Although the variations between these methods might seem to be minor, the methodological implications are significant.

Researchers are actually using the entire repertoire of methods, but in most cases they give no explanation for the selection of a specific method. This is an undesirable situation because even slight nuances of the tools of measurement might affect the results obtained: It is conceivable that each method actually activates different time-related processes that lead to different responses. For instance, reproduction is considered to be more accurate and reliable than production and verbal estimation. Clausen (1950) noted that the method of verbal estimation resulted in less accuracy than the other methods. Block (1989) remarked that production and verbal estimation show more intersubject variability than reproduction and comparison. These, as well as other findings, support the assumption that perception of stimulus duration depends on the measurement method used (Doob, 1971; Hawkes, Ray, & Hayes, 1974). Indeed, Clausen (1950) pointed out that the methods of verbal estimation and production deal with the relation of subjective time to clock time, whereas the method of reproduction does not. His conclusion was that different functions were apparently involved. Block (1989) suggested that production and verbal-estimation methods use a "translation" of duration into conventional time units, whereas reproduction and comparison do not require this translation.

Carlson and Feinberg (1970) concluded that the validity and generalizability of time-judgment methods are uncertain. Allan (1979) argued that no single method can claim consistent superiority and that there is no significant correlation among methods.

The methodological implications stemming from the utilization of different estimation methods can be grouped into several categories, which are presented in the following sections, as well as summarized in Table 3.1.

Table 3.1
Methodological Implications of Time-Estimation Methods

Method	Judgmental type	Memory system involved	Engagement with temporal processes	Potential direction of a time-order error	Potential cognitive and perceptual biases
Verbal estimation	Absolute	STM or LTM[a]	Passive	Negative	1) Whole number response bias 2) Availability 3) Representativeness
Analogical comparison by lines' length	Relative	STM or LTM[a]	Passive	Positive	1) Anchoring, 2) Distortion of line's length perception
Active production	Absolute	STM	Active	Negative	Attentional distractions
Production by monitoring	Absolute	STM	Monitoring	Negative	Attentional distractions
Active reproduction	Relative and absolute	Mainly STM	Active	?[b]	Attentional distractions
Reproduction by monitoring	Relative and absolute	Mainly STM	Monitoring	?[b]	Attentional distractions

[a] Depends on length of duration.
[b] Signifies unpredictable direction.

Judgmental Processes

The methods can be categorized as either incorporating absolute judgment (i.e., verbal estimation and production) or relative judgment (i.e., comparison). Reproduction combines both types. When the subject is performing a reproduction he or she is making a comparison with some stored representation of the target interval's duration, but the reproduction phase itself is actually identical to time production. The standard of comparison used in a reproduction, however, is not as clear as in the comparison method.

It is of importance to pay attention to the type of judgmental processes involved because different cognitive processes characterize absolute and relative judgment (e.g., Wickens, 1984).

Memory Processes

Memory processes play different roles in the various estimation methods. Regarding the estimation of short intervals, verbal estimation, and production and probably reproduction as well, should involve short-term memory only, because the estimation is done during or immediately after the termination of the target interval. Hence, it can be assumed that some representation of its duration still exists in short-term memory when the estimation is carried out. This, however, is not the case regarding the comparison method, unless the total time period, including the standard and the target intervals, is very short.

The reason for that is that a standard interval is presented first followed by a target interval (or vice versa) and only then the estimation is made. Such a procedure should probably involve long-term memory, at least regarding some representation of the first of two presented intervals. These dissimilarities in memory role are another aspect of the essential differences among the estimation's methods.

Activity Versus Passivity of the Subject

Hawkes et al. (1974) noted that duration judgment may be more accurate when the perceiver is actively engaged in a task rather than merely passively observing. This is likely to be true regarding time estimation. Vroon (1970) found that when subjects behaved actively, experienced duration decreased with the number of processed bits. In the comparison method and probably the verbal-estimation method, the estimation is done without the perceiver being actively engaged with time-related processes during the estimation. In the production and reproduction methods, the perceiver is actively engaged with such processes during the time period. A somewhat different level of activity is involved in production or reproduction when the subject should stop some device operated by the experimenter. Here the subject is involved with monitoring the passage of time, rather than in actively producing it. The cognitive aspects underlying monitoring a process differ from those underlying active operation of that same process. This difference is responsible for increased latency and reduced detection accuracy (Wickens, 1984).

Time-Order Error

The time-order error in temporal judgments refers to the finding that the order of presentations influences the judgment. (An extensive discussion of this topic can be found in Allan, 1979.) Time-order error can be either positive or negative. In a positive time-order error, the first of two equal time intervals is judged to be longer in duration than the second interval, whereas in a negative time-order error the opposite is the case. Fraisse (1984) indicated that time-order errors are considered as either positive or negative, depending on the authors, the absolute duration, and the method. Block (1989) reported that in his studies of relatively long durations, using a retrospective paradigm, positive time-order errors are typically robust. Block (1979) suggested that a positive time-order error is caused because contextual elements, correlated with affective reactions such as boredom, change more rapidly at the start of a new experience. Time-order error is of specific significance in the comparison method. This methodological problem is usually dealt with by counterbalancing the presentation order of the standard and target intervals. This cure, however, is not necessarily complete because the two intervals are usually not equal in objective durations and hence it is not clear whether the magnitude of the time-order error is indeed balanced.

Cognitive and Perceptual Biases

Each one of the methods, because of its different nature, is prone to some specific cognitive or perceptual biases. The verbal estimation method is probably prone to a response bias of reporting the estimated durations in round numbers. For example, Hornik (1981) found that verbal estimation of time was done in multiples of 5 min. In order to prevent this bias, Hornik (1984) ordered subjects to estimate the time to the nearest minute.

Verbal estimation is probably prone to the cognitive biases of repre-sentativeness and availability (Tversky & Kahneman, 1974) as subjects can give the estimation on the basis of similarity of the task they performed during the target interval to a category of tasks whose durations are known to the subject or by using some retrieved examples.

The comparison method is probably prone to some perceptual biases. There is a danger of an anchor effect in temporal estimation, where a short anchor might pull judgments down and long anchors, up. This is probably related to the time-order error problem. Another, yet untested, perceptual bias might be caused by the length of lines used for the comparison. Because there is no standard line length common in the research literature, the ratio between length of lines representing the target and standard intervals might cause perceptual biases in estimating the length of the section marked by subjects. This assumption is based on Hartley's (1977) findings about the estimation of line length. In his experiment, a short standard was used to estimate the length of various lines. The results supported the hypothesis that subjects estimated line length by laying off a mental image of the standard along the target line.

ESTIMATION PARADIGM

The paradigm utilized for temporal judgment, as was already noted, is a major factor that influences temporal processes. Block (1989) claimed that it is critical to distinguish between prospective and retrospective judgment of duration. Prospective duration is referred to by Block (1974) as *experienced duration* in contrast with retrospective duration that is called *remembered duration*. This distinction reflects the divergence of temporal processes behind each paradigm. This difference was manifested by many empirical findings. Hicks et al. (1976) found that verbal estimates of time were an inverse linear function of response uncertainty under the prospective paradigm, but no significant function was obtained under the retrospective paradigm.

Similarly, Hicks et al. (1977) found that under the prospective paradigm, verbal estimates of time decreased monotonically with the increased processing demands of the task performed. This last finding is in contradiction with typical experimental results obtained under a retro-spective paradigm (e.g., Ornstein, 1969). It is plausible to assume that under a retrospective paradigm, time judgment must rely heavily on data stored in long-term memory, because the subject is not aware during the target interval itself that he or she should pay attention to the passage of time, and hence he or she should look post factum for traces of relevant information.   This is not the case, however, under a prospective paradigm in which the subject is aware in advance of the role of time in his or her task and as a result he or she can activate and utilize temporal-judgment processes.

The methodological implications of using the two paradigms are discussed in the following sections, and are also summarized in Table 3.2.

Memory Role

The connection between memory processes and experiences of duration was suggested by Michon (1975), who pointed out that different process-apparently underlie experiences of durations less than 500 ms and those

Table 3.2
Methodological Implications of Time Estimation Paradigms

Factor with implications	Estimation Paradigm	
	Retrospective	Prospective
Memory role	Primarily LTM	Primarily STM[a]
Engagement with time-related processes	Passive during the target interval	High during the target interval
Potential direction of a time-order error	Positive	Negative
Potential cognitive and perceptual biases	1. Anchoring 2. Availability 3. Representativeness	Attentional distractions
Presentation order	Can be presented only once, on first trial	Not a problem
Discrepancy between declared and perceived paradigms	Might be perceived as prospective	Not a problem
Immediacy of estimation	Estimation cannot be immediate	Estimation can be either immediate or remote

[a] Also LTM if the duration is long.

greater than 500 ms. He ascribed the difference to "the transition from immediate memory to short-term memory" (p. 304). As was mentioned earlier, it is conceivable to assume that retrospective estimations mainly involve long-term memory processes unless intervals are very short. Prospective estimations, rely mostly on short-term memory processes. The rational for this is that unless target intervals are very short, retrospective estimates mainly depend on stored information, whereas prospective estimates mainly depend on temporal information accumulated in the time processor, which is assumed to be a part of working memory, regardless of the length of the target interval.

There is, however, another strong argument, not mentioned so far in the literature, in favor of the dependency of time judgments under the retrospective paradigm on long-term memory. It should be remembered that the instructions for temporal judgment are, by definition, given to the subject after the termination of the target interval. This takes a significant time by itself, occupies the short-term storage and further removes the estimation phase from the target interval and significantly reduces the probability of finding traces of relevant information in short-term memory.

Activity Versus Passivity of Subjects

Tested under a retrospective paradigm, subjects are passive regarding time-related processes, during the target interval itself, whereas in a prospective paradigm, subjects can be actively engaged with time-related processes during that interval. One result of this dissimilarity might be that during the estimation phase retrospective judgment must utilize nontemporal information.

In both paradigms, the level of active engagement with temporal processes during the estimation phase depends on the specific estimation method used.

Time-Order Error

In some experiments researchers directly compare prospective and retrospective time estimation. It should be noted, however, that a retrospective judgment can be obtained from a particular subject only once, and this must be done on his or her first trial. It is clear that after his or her first retrospective time judgment, the subject already understands that he or she is participating in a time estimation experiment and hence all of the following trials will be prospective regardless of the experimenter's instructions.

Because of this order problem, any direct within-subjects comparison between retrospective and prospective estimation is a potential victim of a time-order error, which is usually positive in retrospective judgments, at least of relatively long durations (Block, 1989). The retrospective estimation, which by definition must be done first, has high probability of being longer than the following prospective judgments.

The order problem has two other implications on the utilization of a retrospective paradigm. One is that a within-subjects design is not feasible, the second is a difficulty in establishing the reliability of retrospective estimations.

Cognitive Biases

The dependency on long-term memory makes retrospective estimations vulnerable to cognitive biases such as representativeness, availability, and anchoring. Prospective estimations, on the other hand, should be vulnerable to external or internal attentional distractions that can increase or decrease the level of attentional resources directly devoted for temporal processes.

PERCEIVED VERSUS DECLARED ESTIMATION PARADIGMS

It is argued here that what really counts in time research is not what is the declared paradigm according to experimenters' instructions, but what is the subjective paradigm as perceived by subjects. This is a severe methodological trap into which it is easy to fall. It should be understood that the subject is engaged with speculating about the experimenter's hypotheses in the experiment and he or she is sensitive to perceive demand characteristics of the situation (Orne, 1962). As a result, subjects can interpret the demands as asking for a prospective time judgment despite experimenters' instructions. What counts is the existence of any contextual element that can create on behalf of subjects an expectation or an hypothesis related to the passage of time. Some common examples are listed in the following sections.

Presentation Order

It was already explained that only a first trial can be presented to any particular subject as retrospective. Any subsequent trials, are necessarily perceived by subjects as prospective. Lordahl and Berkowitz (1975) neglected this effect and successively exposed subjects to two retrospective sessions. They failed to obtain support for their predictions, and a possible explanation for this failure might be the subjects' perceived prospective situation of the second trial.

Removal of Watches

In many cases, when experimenters want to prevent subjects from simply telling the actual elapsed clock time, subjects are induced to take off their watches. For an example, McKay (1977) asked subjects "to remove their watches and jewelry because these metal objects some times interfere with our electronic recording equipment" (p. 186). Such instructions might lead subjects to suspect that the experiment is connected with time measurement. This assumption should, of course, be tested empirically.

Inducing Time Stress

The inducement of time stress might attract subjects' attention to the passage of time. This is a product of strategies that might be utilized by them in order to cope with the time stress (Tulga, 1978). The following is an example.

Hawkins and Meyer (1965) gave their subjects mechanical tasks, within a prospective paradigm. One task was easy to complete in the allotted experimental time, whereas the other was impossible to complete in the time allotted. The original intention of the experimenters was to manipulate information-processing load. It is highly probable, however, that time stress was induced. In this case, because the paradigm was prospective in the first place, no discrepancies between the perceived and declared paradigms should be expected. Still, there is potential confounding here between the prospective processes and strategies employed by subjects in order to handle the time stress.

Environmental Tempo

The existence of environmental tempo, like a metronome beat or subjects performing a tapping task (e.g., Michon, 1966) might attract subjects' attention to the passage of time. Both Frankenhaeuser (1959) and Ornstein (1969) found that time estimates obtained by the methods of comparison or verbal estimation were longer with the increasing beat of a metronome. Denner, Wapner, McFarland, and Werner (1963) reported that reproduced time estimates were longer with fast, rhythmic bodily activity. Zakay et al. (1983) found a positive relationship between the frequency of flickering of a white bulb and reproduced time estimation. Longest time estimates were obtained under fast external tempo (either visual or auditory) and shortest time estimates were obtained under slow external tempo.

A plausible explanation for all these results is that by attracting subjects' attention to the passage of time, the external tempo influenced the resource allocation policy so that more resources were allocated for temporal processes.

Occupation With the Passage of Time

In many cases, the very nature of a task given to subjects calls for occupation with the passage of time. This is typical in situations where subjects are instructed to wait for a pre-specified event to happen, and soon. In such cases, subjects actively engage in asking themselves "when will it happen" and estimate the elapsed time during the target interval, regardless of the experimenters instructions. An example of this is the well-known "watched pot" paradigm (e.g., Block, George, & Reed, 1980; Lordahl & Berkowitz, 1975). In a typical experiment subjects are asked to watch a pot of water until the water starts to boil. It is set so that the experimenter can control the length of the time period until boiling. In an experiment reported by Cahoon and Edmonds (1980), subjects were asked to wait in a waiting room until the experiment would begin. In the waiting room there was a glass coffee pot and a hot plate. Subjects were seated and divested of all metal objects "in order to ensure that a watch would not be available" (p. 115). Subjects in one group were told that there would be a delay in starting the experiment and were asked to call the experimenter when the water starts boiling. The control subjects were told about the delay in starting the experiment, but no reference to the pot was made. The experimenter then left the room for 240 s, and then returned and asked the subjects to write an estimate of the elapsed time. The results indicated that the experimental group gave significantly longer estimates as compared with the control group.

Although the declared paradigm is clearly a retrospective one, it is claimed here that the experimental procedure caused both groups to make prospective time judgments because all subjects were engaged with the delay. The experimental group, however, was manipulated to pay more attention to the passage of time, which resulted in longer duration estimates. It should be noted that the load posed by the task of watching a pot is mainly a load on temporal information processing. Of course, other explanations are possible, like those given by Cahoon and

Edmonds in support of Ornstein's (1969) storage-size model. However, because of this discrepancy between declared and potentially perceived paradigms no clear-cut theoretical conclusion is possible.

RESPONSE DELAY

If subjects are manipulated to make the duration judgment after some delay following the estimated interval, the result is a linear decline in accuracy with increasing delay. Hawkes, Warshan, and Ray (1973) found that for 10-30 s delays, the longer the delay, the greater the difference between objective and subjective durations.

Response delay, however, should be analyzed not only in terms of estimation accuracy but from the point of view of temporal processes as well. Zakay and Fallach (1984) called those paradigms in which duration estimation is done immediately upon the termination of the target interval, an immediate estimation, whereas a paradigm in which duration of an interval is estimated only after a given period of time was called remote estimation. It is important to note that both remote and immediate estimations are possible within the frame of a prospective paradigm, whereas only remote estimation is possible regarding a retrospective paradigm, because in a retrospective experiment the instructions always separate the estimation phase from the target interval. Zakay and Fallach (1984) claimed that direct accessibility of temporal information in working memory related to a specific interval decreases as a function of the time elapsing from the termination of that interval. As a result, prospective remote estimations depend on information stored in long-term memory and hence should be similar to retrospective estimations. On the basis of this rationale they hypothesized that the storage-size model should be supported under both retrospective and remote prospective estimations, whereas an attentional model (e.g., Hicks et al., 1977) should be supported only under an immediate prospective estimation. These predictions were indeed verified by Zakay and Fallach (1984). In this experiment, immediate and remote prospective duration estimation of tasks demanding low and high load of information processing were obtained via reproduction. In the immediate prospective estimation condition intervals during which a complex task was performed were estimated as shorter than equal intervals during which a simple task was performed.

In the remote prospective estimation condition, however, the difference between estimated durations of the simple and complex tasks was not significant, although the tendency was for longer estimates for the durations of the more complex task.

INTERACTION BETWEEN ESTIMATION PARADIGM, METHOD, AND RESPONSE DELAY

Block (1989) emphasized the role of complex interactions among contextual factors in determining temporal experience.   One such important interaction is that between estimation paradigm, method, and response delay.   I already mentioned that the combination of an immediate estimate with a retrospective paradigm is impossible. Another impossible combination is that of estimation by comparison with immediate prospective estimation.   The comparison method eliminates the immediacy of the estimate at least in respect to the first interval presented.   Another impossible combination is that of a retrospective paradigm with a production of time because by definition this entails a prospective estimate.   This situation does not permit a complete and systematic analysis of the separate influences of the paradigms, methods, and response delay on temporal experiences.   In some cases the combination of a specific paradigm and method might activate a unique temporal process.   For example, it is possible (although rare in the litera-ture) to make an estimate by comparison under a prospective paradigm. The resulting processes, however, should be different from that of comparative retrospective estimation.   The last can be described as an analogical comparison and the first as a comparison among two stored numbers.   It seems, therefore, that any combination of a paradigm, method, and a response delay should be considered as a unique time-estimation design.   These designs can be further analyzed in terms of their internal compatibility.

It is proposed here to differentiate between compatible designs, in which all elements rely on the same internal processes and incompatible designs in which this is not the case.   Compatible designs are assumed to evoke consistent memory processes (either short- or long-term memory), to attract subjects' attention toward or away from the passage of time without an internal conflict, and to be internally consistent with regard to all other methodological implications mentioned in Tables 3.1 and 3.2.

Incompatible designs, on the contrary, are assumed to evoke both short- and long-term memory processes, to attract subjects' attention simultaneously toward and away from the passage of time, and so forth.

The importance of this distinction is in that compatible designs enable controlled empirical testing of the influence of specific processes on time estimation, whereas in incompatible designs, various processes are confounded.

An example of a compatible design is that of an immediate prospective estimation done by reproduction, as all of the elements enable the utilization of temporal information stored in short-term memory.

Another compatible design is that of a retrospective estimation by comparison. Here, all the elements depend on information stored in long-term memory during the presentation of the intervals. Immediate prospective estimation by comparison, and delayed prospective estimation are examples of incompatible designs.

CONTENT AND STRUCTURE
OF THE ESTIMATED INTERVAL

Various aspects of the content and structure of an estimated interval might influence its estimated length, even without the investigator being aware of it.

Task Complexity

The influence of the complexity level of a task performed during an estimated period on the estimation is well known. I mentioned earlier that the relationship between complexity level and the length of an estimate is apparently linear but positive for retrospective estimates, and negative for prospective estimates.[1] It is difficult, however, to assess accurately the relative complexity of two tasks, as complexity can be interpreted in various ways, such as information-processing load, workload, attentional demands, time stress, and so on. It should be remembered that induced time stress increases the overall load as well (Tulga, 1978).

Usually, some objective criteria, like the amount of transmitted information (e.g., Hicks et al., 1977) or previous experimental findings about task performance are used for defining the complexity of a task.

There might be a problem because there may be individual differences in the perceived complexity of a given task. In order to overcome this problem it is possible to base the analysis on subjective ratings of task complexity (e.g., Zakay & Fallach, 1984).

---

[1] Hogan (1975) reported an inverted-U function relating complexity and retrospective estimates. The vast amount of research in this area, however, reports a positive linear function (e.g., Lyman & Avant, 1975; Michon, 1965; Ornstein, 1969).

Filled Versus Empty Time

A well-known phenomenon in literature on subjective time is the filled-duration illusion. It is generally reported in the literature (i.e., Coren, Porac, & Ward, 1984) that "filled" durations are estimated as longer in comparison with equal "empty" durations. This report, however, is not accurate because it does not consider the interaction with estimation paradigm. Zakay et al. (1983) asked subjects to estimate either empty intervals or filled intervals during which they performed verbal tasks at one of three levels of difficulty. Estimation was done by reproduction within the frame of a prospective paradigm.

They found that duration estimates were a decreasing function of tasks difficulty, but that durations for empty intervals were estimated to be longer than those for filled intervals. This is puzzling, because empty durations should be easiest in difficulty, not the most difficult. The whole notion of empty time however, is problematic because experimenters have no control over what a subject is doing internally during the empty intervals: He or she might be involved with complex or simple information processing or might be employing some time-estimation strategies like counting that are hidden from the experimenter. Poynter (1989) noted that the perception of empty time must be assumed to be influenced by processes that are not readily apparent, like discrete thoughts and other organismic events. Wallace and Rabin (1960) suggested that perhaps the distinction between filled and unfilled time is in the mind of the experimenter rather than in the experience of the subject.

Internal Estimation Strategies Employed by Subjects

The possibility that a subject employs estimation strategies was already pointed out, but this possibility exists not only regarding empty time but regarding filled intervals, as well. The methodological problem here lies in the possibility that learned strategies such as counting, in which even young children engage (e.g., Levin, 1989), might prevent the emergence of temporal experiences that are predicted on the basis of time-estimation models. Jackson (1985) obtained considerable evidence that individual differences in controlled strategies influence temporal information processing. Controlling the employment of such strategies is difficult. Lordahl and Berkowitz (1975) asked their subjects not to time the interval to be estimated, but this request not to count might cause a paradoxical effect and encouraged precisely that behavior (Cahoon & Edmonds, 1980).

Nevertheless, the possibility that subjects employ estimation strategies should be considered when designing and interpreting time-estimation experiments.

The Segmentation of the Estimated Interval

Fraisse (1963), Block and Reed (1978), Block (1982), and Poynter (1989) have all provided evidence for a change model of duration judgement.

The change approach assumes that judgment of duration is based on the ability to remember the sequence of events experienced during an interval. The amount of change experienced is a crucial factor according to this approach and judgment of duration depends on the number of perceived changes. "Change is the psychological index of time passage" (Poynter, 1989 p. 307). Poynter (1983) manipulated the amount of perceived changes by the number of high-priority events presented among a list of stimuli, where the high-priority events are those stimuli to which the subject should attend. It is assumed that these high-priority events serve as marker events. Indeed, Poynter (1983) and Poynter and Homa (1983) found that retrospective estimates increased as the number of high-priority events during the estimated interval increased. The methodological implication is that an estimated interval might be segmented by stimuli acting as high-priority events without the awareness of the experimenter. These high-priority events might of course influence the temporal judgment, especially under a retrospective paradigm. The differences in time-related processes characterizing brief versus long intervals might be partly explained by the higher probability that a longer duration is segmented in this manner.

The following section describes two undesired high-priority events that are common in experimentation.

Experimental Instructions as High-Priority Events. The instructions given by the experimenter are a significant stimulus for the subject that might serve as a high-priority event without the subject being aware of its influence. The following example of instructions that were given during a retrospective experiment serve as an illustration. Curton and Lordahl (1974) gave their subjects the instruction *ready*, the subject then turned over a task sheet. The instruction to *start* was then given, after which the required task was performed until the instruction to *stop* was given. At that time the subject gave his or her duration estimation. There are four events connected with the instructions (italicized here) that could be perceived as high-priority events and could segment the period, thus influencing the duration estimates.

Demarcation Signals. The signals indicating the onset and termination of the target interval may be the experimenter's instructions, two clicks, two flashes of light, and so on. Subjects tend to incorporate into the time interval these signs that themselves take an appreciable length of time. Wallace and Rabin (1960) noted that this criticism is particularly pertinent when very brief intervals are under consideration. Allan (1979) concluded that judged duration is very much influenced by the way in which the temporal interval is defined or marked.

CONCLUSIONS

The major conclusion to be drawn is that subjective time is defined to a large extent by its measurement. Temporal experiences are a product of various types of processes that are context dependent and utilize various types and sources of temporal as well as nontemporal information.

Hicks et al. (1977) suggested the following processes as characteristic of any theory of the "time sense": "time base, which is responsible for subjective temporal units, a counter which stores these units until the conclusion of the interval, and a response translator which maps the contents of the counter onto the response surface" (p. 442). I suggest that under different conditions different processes are utilized by the cognitive system to serve as the time base, the counter, and the response translator, on the basis of availability and relevancy. This idea might serve as a starting point for a metatheory of psychological time.

There are some methodological lessons to be learned by time researchers.

1. Direct comparisons between temporal experiences obtained under different conditions cannot be made unless the different processes involved are taken into consideration.
2. The design of subjective time experiments should be done carefully and all contextual factors should be considered. Table 3.3 presents a methodological checklist that can serve that purpose.
3. Testing the validity of any specific model of subjective time should be done only by using a measurement design that activates temporal processes which are assumed to be compatible with those inferred by the tested model. The measurement design itself should certainly be internally compatible. When these rules are not kept, the external validity of the experiment is disrupted, and any obtained confirmation or disconfirmation is of doubtful significance except for demonstrating that indeed temporal processes are complex and depend on context.

Table 3.3
Methodological Checklist

Checked items	What should be checked
1. Objective duration	- Is the duration too short or too long? - Will its length interfere with the temporal process tested?
2. Estimation method	- Why is this estimation method used? - Analyze the judgmental type, memory role, subjects' activity or passivity involved, and so on.
3. Time-order error	- Is there any potential for a time-order error? If so, is it of theoretical interest?
4. Potential cognitive and perceptual biases	- In the experiment as designed, what are the cognitive and perceptual biases to which subjects are vulnerable?
5. Estimation paradigm	- Why is this estimation paradigm used? - Analyze the role of memory, sequence effects, subject's engagement with temporal processes, and so on.
6. Perceived paradigm	- Is there any potential discrepancy between perceived paradigm and declared paradigm? (Look for removal of watch, induced time stress, environmental tempo, expectations, etc.)
7. Presentation order	- Might presentation order interfere with assigned or tested temporal processes?
8. Response delay	- What is the actual response delay? What is the influence of it on time-related processes?
9. Internal compatibility	- Are the estimation paradigm, method and response delay internally compatible?
10. Control over estimation strategies	- Is it possible that subjects will utilize estimation strategies? - Should effective control measures be used to prevent this?
11. Instructions	- Do the instructions act as high priority events? - Do the instructions direct subjects' attention to or away from the passage of time or create demand characteristics?
12. Demarcation signals	- What is the length of the demarcation signals relative to the length of the target interval? - Do the demarcation signs act as high priority events?
13. Contextual distractions	- Are there any contextual or environmental distractions which can direct or attract subjects' attention to or away from the passage of time?
14. Task complexity	- What are the criteria for defining task complexity? - Should subjective ratings be used for testing the validity of the criteria employed?
15. External validity	- Are the tested model and the overall estimation design used compatible in regard to temporal processs?

4. Analyzing time experiments by averaging time estimates across subjects and comparing group data might be misleading. Because contextual variables are important and because there might be individual differences in the way context is perceived, each subject should be treated separately or subjects should be grouped according to the way they perceived the experimental situation. Methods for doing so need to be developed.

Time is a domain in which modern physics and psychology meet. The uncertainty principle, which was originally stated by Heisenberg in 1927, says that every measurement disturbs the measured system when the measurement tool is not essentially different from the measured phenomenon. This principle applies in the field of psychological time almost as well as it does in the domain of quantum physics. This might not be a coincidence.

ACKNOWLEDGMENTS

This research was supported by research grants given by the Israeli Academy of Sciences and by the basic research fund of Tel Aviv University.

REFERENCES

Allan, L. G. (1979). The perception of time. *Perception & Psychophysics, 26,* 340-354.

Aschoff, J. (1984). Circadian timing. In J. Gibbon & L. Allan (Eds.), *Timing and time perception* (pp. 442-468). New York: New York Academy of Sciences.

Aschoff, J. (1985). On the perception of time during prolonged temporal isolation. *Human Neurobiology, 4,* 41-52.

Avant, L. L., Lyman, P. J., & Antes, J. (1975). Effect of stimulus familiarity upon judged visual duration. *Perception & Psychophysics, 17,* 253-262.

Bindra, D., & Waksberg, H. (1956). Methods and terminology in the studies of time estimation. *Psychological Bulletin, 53,* 155-159.

Block, R. A. (1974). Memory and the experience of duration in retrospect. *Memory & Cognition, 2,* 153-160.

Block, R. A. (1978). Remembered duration: Effects of event and sequence complexity. *Memory & Cognition, 6,* 320-326.

Block, R. A. (1979). Time and consciousness. In G. Underwood & R. Stevens (Eds.), *Aspects of consciousness: Vol. 1. Psychological issues* (pp. 179-217). London: Academic Press.

Block, R. A. (1982). Temporal judgments and contextual change. *Journal of Experimental Psychology: Learning, Memory, and Cognition, 8,* 530-544.

Block, R. A. (1985). Contextual coding in memory: Studies of remembered duration. In J. A. Michon & J. L. Jackson (Eds.), *Time, mind, and behavior* (pp. 169-178). Berlin: Springer-Verlag.

Block, R. A. (1989). Experiencing and remembering time: Affordances, context, and cognition. In I. Levin & D. Zakay (Eds.), *Time and human cognition: A life span perspective* (pp. 333-363). Amsterdam: North-Holland.

Block, R. A., George, E. J., & Reed, M. A. (1980). A watched pot sometimes boils: A study of duration experience. *Acta Psychologica, 46*, 81-94.

Block, R. A., & Reed, M. A. (1978). Remembered duration: Evidence for a contextual-change hypothesis. *Journal of Experimental Psychology: Human Learning and Memory, 4*, 656-665.

Burnside, W. (1971). Judgment of short time intervals while performing mathematical tasks. *Perception & Psychophysics, 9*, 404-406.

Cahoon, D., & Edmonds, E. M. (1980). The watched pot still won't boil: Expectancy as a variable in estimating the passage of time. *Bulletin of the Psychonomic Society, 16*, 115-116.

Carlson, V. R., & Feinberg, Z. (1970). Time judgment as a function of method, practice, and sex. *Journal of Experimental Psychology, 85*, 171-180.

Clausen, J. (1950). An evaluation of experimental methods of time judgment. *Journal of Experimental Psychology, 40*, 756-761.

Coren, S., Porac, C., & Ward, L. M. (1984). *Sensation and perception* (2nd ed.). New York: Academic Press.

Curton, E. D., & Lordahl, D. S. (1974). Attentional focus and arousal in time estimation. *Journal of Experimental Psychology, 103*, 861-867.

Denner, B., Wapner, S., McFarland, J., & Werner, H. (1963). Rhythmic activity and the perception of time. *American Journal of Psychology, 76*, 287-292.

Devane, J. R. (1974). Word characteristics and judged duration for two response sequences. *Perceptual and Motor Skills, 38*, 525-526.

Doob, L. W. (1971). *Patterning of time.* New Haven, CT: Yale University Press.

Fraisse, P. (1963). *The psychology of time* (J. Leith, Trans.). New York: Harper & Row.

Fraisse, P. (1984). Perception and estimation of time. *Annual Review of Psychology, 35*, 1-36.

Frankenhaeuser, M. (1959). *Estimation of time: An experimental study.* Stockholm: Almqvist & Wiksell.

Hartley, A. A. (1977). Mental measurement in the magnitude estimation of length. *Journal of Experimental Psychology: Human Perception and Performance, 3*, 622-628.

Hawkes, G., Ray, W., & Hayes, R. L. (1974). Judgment of stimulus duration with a competing task requirement. *Journal of Auditory Research, 14*, 187-191.

Hawkes, G. R., Warshan, R. W., & Ray, W. S. (1973). Response delay effects on duration judgments for helicopter noise stimuli and vibration. *Journal of Auditory Research, 13*, 26-30.

Hawkins, N. E., & Meyer, M. E. (1965). Time perception of short intervals during finished, unfinished and empty task situations. *Psychonomic Science, 3*, 473.

Hicks, R. E., Miller, G. W., & Kinsbourne, M. (1976). Prospective and retrospective judgments of time as a function of amount of information processed. *American Journal of Psychology, 89*, 719-730.

Hicks, R. E., Miller, G. W., Gaes G., & Bierman, K. (1977). Concurrent processing demands and the experience of time-in-passing. *American Journal of Psychology, 90*, 431-446.

Hornik, J. (1981). Time cue and time perception effect on response to mail survey. *Journal of Marketing Research, 18*, 243-248.

Hornik, J. (1984). Subjective vs. objective time measures: A note on the perception of time in consumer behavior. *The Journal of Consumer Research, 11*, 615-618.

Jackson, J. L. (1985). Is the processing of temporal information automatic or controlled? In J. A. Michon & J. L. Jackson (Eds.), *Time, mind, and behavior* (pp. 179-190). Berlin: Springer-Verlag.

Levin, I. (1989). Principles underlying time measurement: A developmental analysis of children's conception of counting time. In I. Levin & D. Zakay (Eds.), *Time and human cognition: A life span perspective* (pp. 145-183). Amsterdam: North-Holland.

Lordahl, D. S., & Berkowitz, S. (1975). The watched pot does boil: A case of the wrong control group. *Bulletin of the Psychonomic Society, 5*, 45-46.

Lyman, P. J., & Avant, L. L. (1975). Stimulus familiarity modifies perceived duration in precognition visual processing. *Journal of Experimental Psychology, 104*, 205-219.

McKay, T. D. (1977). Time estimation: Effects of attentional focus and a comparison of interval conditions. *Perceptual and Motor Skills, 45*, 584-586.

Michon, J. A. (1965). Studies on subjective duration: II. Subjective time measurement during tasks with different information content. *Acta Psychologica, 24*, 205-219.

Michon, J. A. (1966). Tapping regularity as a measure of perceptual-motor load. *Ergonomics, 9*, 401-412.

Michon, J. A. (1975). Time experience and memory processes. In J. T. Fraser & N. Lawrence (Eds.), *The study of time II* (pp. 302-313). New York: Springer-Verlag.

Michon, J. A. (1985). The compleat time experiencer. In J. A. Michon & J. L. Jackson (Eds.), *Time, mind, and behavior* (pp. 20-52). Berlin: Springer-Verlag.

Navon, D. (1978). On a conceptual hierarchy of time, space and other dimensions. *Cognition, 6*, 223-228.

Orne, M. T. (1962). On the social psychology of the psychological experiment: With particular reference to demand characteristics and their implications. *American Psychologist, 17*, 776-783.

Ornstein, R. E. (1969). *On the experience of time*. Harmondsworth, England: Penguin.

Poynter, D. G. (1983). Duration judgment and the segmentation of experience. *Memory & Cognition, 11*, 77-82.

Poynter, D. G. (1989). Inferring time's passage. In I. Levin & D. Zakay (Eds.), *Time and human cognition: A life-span perspective* (pp. 305-331). Amsterdam: North-Holland.

Poynter, D. G., & Homa, D. (1983). Duration judgment and the experience of change. *Perception & Psychophysics, 33*, 548-560.

Thomas, E. A. C., & Brown, I. (1974). Time perception and the filled duration illusion. *Perception & Psychophysics, 16*, 449-458.

Thomas, E. A. C., & Weaver, W. B. (1975). Cognitive processing and time perception. *Perception & Psychophysics, 17*, 363-367.

Treisman, M. (1963). Temporal discrimination and the indifference interval: Implications for the model of the "internal clock." *Psychological Monographs, 77* (Whole no. 576).

Tulga, M. K. (1978). *Dynamic decision making in multitask supervisory control: Comparison of an optimal algorithm to human behavior*. Cambridge, MA: MIT Man-Machine Systems Laboratory.

Tversky, A., & Kahneman, D. (1974). Judgment under uncertainty: Heuristics and biases. *Science, 185*, 1124-1137.

Vroon, P. A. (1970). Effects of presented and processed information on duration experience. *Acta Psychologica, 34*, 115-121.

Wallace, M., & Rabin, A. (1960). Temporal experience. *Psychological Bulletin, 57*, 213-235.

Ward, L. M. (1975). Sequential dependence range in cross modality matches of duration to loudness. *Perception & Psychophysics, 18*, 217-223.

Wickens, C. D. (1984). *Engineering psychology and human performance*. Columbus: Charles E. Merrill.

Zakay, D. (1989a). An integrated model of time estimation. In I. Levin & D. Zakay (Eds.), *Time and human cognition: A life-span perspective* (pp. 365-397). Amsterdam: North-Holland.

Zakay, D. (1989b). *A meta-analysis of time estimation research*. Unpublished manuscript, Tel Aviv University, Tel Aviv, Israel.

Zakay, D., & Fallach, E. (1984). Immediate and remote time estimation: A comparison. *Acta Psychologica, 57*, 69-81.

Zakay, D., Nitzan, D., & Glicksohn, J. (1983). The influence of task difficulty and external tempo on subjective time estimation. *Perception & Psychophysics, 34*, 451-456.

4 Perceptual Moment Models Revisited

Robert Patterson
Montana State University

Temporal integration in the visual system is the tendency for separate stimuli presented in close temporal proximity to be treated or perceived as one stimulus. Temporal integration is inversely related to the phenomenon of temporal resolution, the ability of the visual system to detect variation in stimulation over time. For example, consider visual masking, a phenomenon possibly involving temporal integration. Of several types of masking (for recent review, see Breitmeyer, 1984), one type — masking by structure — involves perceptual interference between spatially overlapping patterns. On some trials, one pattern — the target — is briefly presented to an observer closely followed by presentation of the other pattern — the mask. On other trials, the order of target and mask is reversed. On still other trials, target and mask are presented simultaneously. When the two stimuli are presented in close temporal proximity, the presence of the mask degrades or interferes with the visibility of the target. Under certain conditions, this interference may be produced by temporal integration (Breitmeyer, 1984).

Perceptual moment models are a once popular class of model concerning temporal integration. The early research, which was often interpreted in terms of these models, has been reviewed by Block (1979) and Fraisse (1984). This chapter considers more recent research that, although it has generally not been framed in terms of a test of the perceptual moment models, is relevant to those models. The chapter also discusses the reasons why most writers believe the models are no longer tenable, if they ever were. I argue that these models have never been adequately tested. In an effort to remedy that problem, I assess the likelihood of evidence bearing on the notion of a perceptual moment using results from studies investigating visual persistence. First, I introduce the models.

PERCEPTUAL MOMENT MODELS

Perceptual moment models (e.g., Harter, 1967; Shallice, 1964; Stroud, 1955; White, 1963) assume that perceptual information is processed in temporally discrete, fixed intervals or moments. Stroud (1955) is usually credited with the original perceptual moment model. Although Stroud's model was vague in that he did not state whether the moments are free-running or initiated by the onset of stimulation, I am interpreting his (and others) model as proposing the existence of moments that are of fixed duration and uninfluenced by stimulus variables; within each moment, temporal-order information is lost due to temporal integration. According to these models, the moments are produced by the operation of a central (cortical) intermittency or scanning mechanism, and the period of oscillation of this mechanism determines the duration of the moment. This is an idea derived, in part, from cybernetics (e.g., Wiener, 1948). Some authors (see Harter, 1967, for review) have suggested that the central intermittency is related to the alpha rhythm of the brain, but this specific idea has gained little empirical support (see Block, 1979, chapter 1, this volume).

General support for perceptual moment models comes from the results of studies by Stroud (1955), White (1963), Shallice (1964), and possibly Efron (1970a, 1970b). Stroud, for example, showed that the brightness of a brief flash of light increases with exposure duration up to 90 ms. This finding provides evidence of temporal integration, suggesting that the maximum duration of integration is about 90 ms. This is consistent with the perceptual moment models. In a later study using a perceived simultaneity technique (in which the subject adjusts the onset of a visual probe stimulus so that it appears to be simultaneous with the offset of a visual test stimulus), Efron (1970b) showed that the perceived duration of a test stimulus exposed for 130 ms or less is always about 230 ms. This finding suggests that there is a fixed duration of perception for brief stimuli. Although Efron did not discuss the perceptual moment models at all, his results would seem to be consistent with those models.

Despite these results, more recent studies by Allport (1968), Efron and Lee (1971), Westheimer and McKee (1977), and DiLollo and Wilson (1978) have obtained evidence against the perceptual moment models.

In a perceived simultaneity experiment, Allport (1968) found that 12 thin, horizontal lines presented sequentially appeared to flash on and off simultaneously when presented within a brief interval of time (e.g., 90 ms). This duration of perceived simultaneity was influenced by stimulus luminance, with the duration lengthening as luminance decreased. Also using a perceived simultaneity paradigm, Efron and Lee (1971) found that stroboscopic illuminations of a line appeared simultaneous when the illuminations occurred within a brief period of time (e.g., 140 ms). In this case also, the duration of perceived simultaneity was influenced by luminance. They concluded that perceived simultaneity is influenced by stimulus variables such as intensity, and that this is inconsistent with the idea that a central mechanism produces moments of fixed duration.

Westheimer and McKee (1977) showed that the temporal order of visual stimuli can be correctly identified (i.e., 75% threshold identification) at stimulus onset asynchrony values of only several milliseconds. Because such durations are much briefer than those assumed for perceptual moments, this result is inconsistent with the idea that temporal-order information is lost for the entire duration of the moment (e.g., in vision, 90-100 ms). DiLollo and Wilson (1978) directly tested predictions derived from the perceptual moment models. They presented three sets of sequential dots produced on an oscilloscope screen to observers such that the interval between the first and second set of dots was shorter than the interval between the second and third set of dots. The duration of the first set of dots was manipulated over trials. DiLollo and Wilson found that, at long durations, temporal integration between the first and second set was impaired relative to integration between the second and third set, even though the interval in the former case was shorter. Yet, if the perceptual moment models are correct, with a shorter interval it should be more likely that the two sets of dots would fall within one moment and be integrated; a shorter interval should lead to greater, not less, integration. DiLollo and Wilson's results are inconsistent with the models.

Taken together, the results of these studies seem to provide compelling evidence against the perceptual moment models. In the spirit of these results, contemporary authors (Breitmeyer, 1984; Coltheart, 1980; DiLollo & Wilson, 1978; Long, 1980) have argued that such models are no longer tenable.

However, the studies from which these results derive may not really be relevant to perceptual moment models. This is because those studies (and also studies supporting the models) investigated peripheral, sensory mechanisms, whereas the models propose the operation of a central intermittency mechanism. The idea that evidence against the perceptual moment models derives from studies of only sensory mechanisms was proposed by Breitmeyer (1984). Because no studies have examined the models using an experimental paradigm that investigates higher, central (cortical) mechanisms, it seems that the perceptual moment models have yet to be adequately tested.

A USEFUL PARADIGM

It is interesting to speculate on the possibility of applying the perceptual moment models to higher, cortical levels of the visual system. One way to indirectly investigate the models at higher levels of visual processing is to consider research on visual persistence, a process also thought to underlie temporal integration. The term *visual persistence* refers to the perceived image or trace of stimulation immediately following the physical offset of a stimulus. Visual persistence, which has been extensively studied for hundreds of years (for reviews, see Boyton, 1972; Breitmeyer, 1984; Coltheart, 1980; Long, 1980), may be subdivided into five different kinds. One kind, involving a peripheral form of persistence, was investigated in the context of the perceptual moment models by Allport (1968) and Efron and Lee (1971), for example. A second kind, also involving a peripheral form of persistence, occurs with the induction of retinal afterimages. But three other kinds of persistence are most likely of cortical origin, and so their properties may be more relevant to the perceptual moment models.

I discuss the properties of various kinds of visual persistence here in the context of those models. Research on persistence is used to examine one principal assumption of the models—namely, that the duration of a moment is fixed and uninfluenced by stimulus variables (e.g., intensity). This hypothesis of fixed moments derives directly from the idea of central intermittency; thus, a fundamental property of the models is examined. The question naturally arises as to how to compare durations of persistence to durations of moments. To do so, I rely on a paradigm employed by Efron (1970b).

This paradigm involves obtaining from observers judgments of perceived onset and offset of a visual test stimulus. The test stimulus is presented for durations ranging from 10 to 500 ms, and a visual probe stimulus is presented for a duration of 500 ms. The observer's task is to adjust the onset of the probe so that it appears simultaneous with either the onset or the offset of the test stimulus; thus, the probe serves as a marker of perceived onset and offset of the test stimulus. Efron found that perceived onset of the test stimulus occurs within 5 to 10 ms of the physical onset of the test stimulus. Its perceived offset, however, occurs much later than its physical offset. The interval between its physical offset and its perceived offset (measured by the probe) provides an estimate of visual persistence. The duration of persistence depends on stimulus duration. With stimulus durations longer than about 130 ms, visual persistence is constant at about 100 ms (e.g., a 130-ms stimulus appears to last for about 230 ms and a 180-ms stimulus appears to last for about 280 ms). For briefer stimuli, persistence is inversely related to stimulus duration: As stimulus duration is decreased, persistence increases, so that the perceived duration of stimulation (from perceived onset to perceived offset) remains constant at 230 ms. (This is true when test and probe stimuli are in the same sense modality; for discussion, see Coltheart, 1980.) This led Efron to propose the idea that all brief stimuli appear as one fixed duration (i.e., there is a fixed duration of perception).

I apply Efron's paradigm to investigate whether stimulus duration and persistence duration are inversely related (i.e., whether there is a constant duration of perception at higher levels of the visual system). To do so, I examine the literature on different kinds of visual persistence. Like Efron, it is assumed that the duration of perception is the sum of stimulus duration and estimated persistence duration (less about 5-10 ms; see Figure 4.1). Further, because I explore different kinds of persistence, there is no basis for assuming that the inverse relationship between stimulus duration and persistence duration will hold only for stimulus durations of up to about 130 ms; it is possible that the inverse

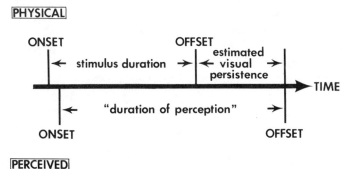

Figure 4.1. The relationship between physical onset and offset of a stimulus and perceived onset and offset. It is assumed that stimulus duration plus estimated visual persistence is equivalent to the duration of a perception, less about 5-10 ms.

relationship could obtain for stimuli of longer durations. Finally, equating the beginning of a perception with stimulus onset is appropriate, because Efron found that perceived onset and physical onset are closely coupled in time.

Evidence for a fixed duration of perception (stimulus and persistence duration inversely related) will be taken as prima facie evidence supporting the idea of a fixed moment. Moreover, if the duration of perception is indeed fixed, then that duration will serve as an estimate of the duration of a moment. For this interpretation to be correct, it is important that the duration of perception be uninfluenced by stimulus variables such as intensity. However, evidence for a variable duration of perception will be taken as evidence against a fixed moment, and thus evidence against one principal assumption of the perceptual moment models.

One can raise objections to this approach. Most importantly, this approach may be too simplistic because it assumes that the beginning of stimulation always coincides with the beginning of a perception or of a moment. But what if the onset of a moment is independent of the onset of stimulation; what if the onset of stimulation can occur at any time during the course of a moment? This would mean that, over trials, estimates of the duration of a moment would be highly variable; sometimes the onsets of stimulation and moment would coincide and sometimes the onset of stimulation would occur late relative to that of a moment. In this case, for briefly exposed stimuli, the average estimate of the duration of a moment would be an underestimate of its true value by about 50%. Such criticism, however, is not fatal to the present approach because the average duration of a perception or moment should not systematically vary with changes in stimulus parameters if the moment is truly governed only by a central mechanism. Any systematic influence of stimulus variables on the duration of the perception or "moment" seriously undercuts the validity of the perceptual moment models (Efron & Lee, 1971).

The following examines the evidence pertaining to this notion.

VISUAL PERSISTENCE

The current literature on visual persistence (for reviews, see Boyton, 1972; Breitmeyer, 1984; Coltheart, 1980; DiLollo, 1984; Long, 1980) suggests that there are five different types of persistence. Although the number five is quite speculative, based on their properties these kinds of persistence can be ordered along an assumed hierarchy of levels or stages of visual processing. This hierarchy provides the context within which the different types of persistence are examined. After discussing each type of persistence, its relationship to the perceptual moment models is considered.

It should be pointed out that several authors (e.g., Coltheart, 1980; Long, 1980) have distinguished between visual persistence and neural persistence. *Visual persistence* refers to the perceived image or trace that follows the physical offset of stimulation, lasting on the order of milliseconds or seconds; the different varieties of visual persistence are the topic of this chapter. *Neural persistence* refers to persistence in the response of the neural substrate hypothesized to underlie visual persistence. Although for some kinds of visual persistence direct physiological evidence for the corresponding neural persistence is lacking, there is good evidence of neural persistence at peripheral levels of the visual system. Breitmeyer (1984) provided a good discussion of this research.

The following are five different kinds of visual persistence: retinal afterimages, pattern persistence, cortical persistence, stereoscopic persistence, and informational persistence. I describe each of these five kinds of persistence.

Retinal Afterimages

When a very bright stimulus is briefly presented to an observer, a visual "image" of the stimulus persists for hundreds of milliseconds following its offset. Interestingly, the phenomenal quality and strength (e.g., color, brightness) of the persistence usually fluctuates over time, giving rise to several distinct phases involving images having contrast of the same polarity as the induction stimulus (positive afterimages) and images having contrast of the opposite polarity (negative afterimages) (Brown, 1965). This kind of visual persistence is produced by the induction of retinal afterimages (Coltheart, 1980), a topic that has had a long history of investigation (see Brown, 1965). To investigate this kind of persistence, methods involving the use of stimuli of high illuminance (above 3.0-5.0 log trolands), typically obtained by flashing bright stimuli to dark-adapted observers, are used. Many studies (for a review, see Coltheart, 1980) have shown that the energic properties (e.g., intensity) of stimulation govern the duration of retinal afterimages, with increases in energy producing increases in persistence. This type of persistence has been related to activity in the retinal receptors (Brown, 1965; Coltheart, 1980). (The prolongation of afterimages that can be achieved by employing temporally modulated backgrounds involves post-receptoral processes; see Gerling & Spillman, 1987.) It is interesting that many writers (e.g.,

Breitmeyer, 1984; Coltheart, 1980; Yeomans & Irwin, 1985) have argued that retinal afterimages should be considered a phenomenon distinctly different from visual persistence, which possibly reflects a desire to keep separate phenomena involving photochemical processes and those involving neural processes (see also DiLollo, Clark, & Hogben, 1988).

Because this kind of persistence is produced by activity in retinal receptors, it is a phenomenon too peripheral in origin with respect to the visual system to be considered relevant to the perceptual moment models.

Pattern Persistence

When a stimulus of intermediate brightness is briefly presented to an observer, an image of the stimulus will persist for about 100 ms or more following stimulus offset; the image will have relatively high fidelity and quality. This form of persistence is a phenomenon that has also had a long history of study (for reviews, see Boyton, 1972; Breitmeyer, 1984; Coltheart, 1980). Judging from descriptions of the methods used in the original investigations of the perceptual moment models (e.g., Allport, 1968; Efron, 1970b; Efron & Lee, 1971), it is this type of persistence that was studied. To examine this kind of persistence, researchers use methods involving stimuli of lower illuminance (below 2.5 to 3.0 log troland), such as those employed in much of contemporary psychophysics. Many studies (see Coltheart, 1980) have shown that, for stimulus exposures of up to about 100-130 ms, stimulus variables such as intensity and duration govern the duration of this kind of persistence, with increases in either variable typically producing decreases in persistence. (Recall that for exposures longer than about 130 ms, persistence duration is a constant 100 ms. This may be a different form of persistence and it is discussed later.) This type of persistence has been related to the response properties of neural mechanisms encoding the pattern characteristics of stimuli, so-called *sustained mechanisms* (located at peripheral and intermediate stages of the visual pathway; see later). This idea is developed in the following section.

There is psychophysical and neurophysiological evidence for the existence of two classes of neural mechanisms or channels within the visual system, one with sustained and the other with transient properties. The results of psychophysical studies (Burbeck & Kelly, 1981; Green, 1981, 1984; Keesey, 1972; Kulikowski & Tolhurst, 1973; Legge, 1978; Tolhurst, 1973) indicate the existence of two classes of visual mechanisms that can be distinguished on the basis of their spatial and temporal properties. The sustained mechanisms are more sensitive to fine or narrow stimulus features (high spatial frequencies) and slow temporal variation in luminance, whereas the transient mechanisms are more sensitive to coarse or wide features (low spatial frequencies) and faster temporal variation. It is believed that the sustained mechanisms encode predominantly pattern information about stimuli, whereas the transient mechanisms encode predominantly information about stimulus change (e.g., Breitmeyer, 1984; Breitmeyer & Ganz, 1976; Burbeck & Kelly, 1981; Green, 1981; Kulikowski & Tolhurst, 1973; Tolhurst, 1973).   However, a strict dichotomy may not exist (see Green, 1981; Lennie, 1980).

Unlike transient mechanisms, one property of sustained mechanisms is that they exhibit visual persistence, termed *pattern persistence*. Recall that with this type of persistence, persistence duration and stimulus duration (or intensity) are inversely related. This is thought to be the case because inhibition arising from the transient mechanisms (called transient-on-sustained inhibition), which are activated at stimulus offset, is what terminates pattern persistence; and the response latency of the transient mechanisms is inversely related to those stimulus variables (Breitmeyer, 1984; Breitmeyer & Ganz, 1976; Coltheart, 1980; DiLollo, 1984).   Thus, the latency of interchannel inhibition determines the duration of pattern persistence.   The idea of transient mechanisms inhibiting sustained mechanisms forms the basis of explanations of other phenomena as well, such as saccadic suppression (e.g., Matin, 1974).

The results of neurophysiological studies (for reviews, see DeYoe & Van Essen, 1988; Livingstone & Hubel, 1987, 1988) suggest possible neural substrates for separate sustained and transient pathways in the primate visual system, the parvocellular and magnocellular pathways. The parvocellular pathway begins with Type B retinal ganglion cells and projects, via four parvocellular layers of the lateral geniculate nucleus (LGN), to areas in temporal cortex (e.g., V4).   Neurons of this system have small axons, small receptive fields, slow conduction velocity, and are activated by sustained stimuli; many parvocellular neurons are sensitive to wavelength. The magnocellular pathway begins with Type A ganglion cells and projects, via two magnocellular layers of the LGN, to areas in parietal cortex (e.g., MT).   Neurons of this system have large axons, large receptive fields, fast conduction velocity, and at cortical levels many neurons are activated by moving stimuli and retinal disparity (the cue for stereoscopic depth perception); magnocellular neurons are not sensitive to wavelength.   (As previously mentioned, physiological evidence for interchannel, transient-on-sustained, inhibition has been reviewed by Breitmeyer, 1984.)

It should be pointed out that, for pattern persistence, the inverse relationship between persistence duration and stimulus duration or intensity has not always been obtained. In some studies, a positive relationship has been reported (see Coltheart, 1980). Hawkins and Shulman (1979) attempted to explain this difference in results by proposing that studies of pattern persistence should be subdivided into two different kinds (i.e., Type I and Type II persistence) based on differences in methodology. Unfortunately, DiLollo (1984) pointed out that many studies reviewed by Hawkins and Shulman were misrepresented by them. For example, some studies of Type I persistence had actually employed Type II methods. Thus, it is currently not known why most studies show an inverse relationship, whereas others show a positive relationship between persistence duration and stimulus duration or intensity.

Consider the implications of findings on pattern persistence for the notion of a fixed duration of perception. The inverse relationship between persistence duration and stimulus duration usually found in studies of pattern persistence suggests, at first glance, that perception duration is constant. But because variation in stimulus intensity produces changes in the duration of pattern persistence, and thus changes in the duration of perception (stimulus duration plus persistence duration), it might be concluded that pattern persistence provides no evidence for a fixed duration of perception. Indeed, it was the finding of stimulus intensity effects on the estimate of the "moment" that led previous researchers (e.g., Allport, 1968; Efron & Lee, 1971) to argue against the notion of a fixed perceptual moment. Yet, as discussed earlier, because this kind of persistence is produced by activity of mechanisms located at peripheral and intermediate stages (e.g., LGN of thalamus) of the visual system, it is a phenomenon relatively too peripheral in origin to be considered relevant to the perceptual moment models (Breitmeyer, 1984).

Consider now three kinds of visual persistence which may provide evidence for a fixed duration of perception at higher (cortical) levels of visual processing.

Cortical Persistence

Recall that if a stimulus of intermediate brightness is briefly exposed to an observer, a visual image of the stimulus persists following stimulus offset, which is referred to as *pattern persistence*. Recall also that for stimulus exposures of up to about 130 ms, the duration of pattern persistence is inversely related to stimulus duration. Yet, for stimulus exposures longer than about 130 ms, persistence duration is almost constant at about 100 ms (Efron, 1970b). Bowling and Lovegrove (1980, 1981) argued that although pattern persistence obtained with stimulus exposures under about 130 ms may be peripheral in origin, the persistence obtained with longer exposures is cortical in origin. Evidence supporting this idea comes from studies in which both stimulus duration and stimulus orientation are manipulated and persistence duration is measured. Bowling and Lovegrove (1981) found that stimulus orientation influences the persistence duration obtained with the longer exposures but not the persistence duration obtained with the shorter exposures. Because orientation sensitivity in the primate visual system is a property of cortical neurons (Hubel & Wiesel, 1977), Bowling and Lovegrove took these results as evidence for a cortical persistence separate from the visual persistence obtained with brief exposures. In a sense, this idea could be termed a *two-process theory* of pattern persistence, with the origin of the first process located peripherally and that of the second process located in visual cortex.

With respect to evidence of a fixed duration of perception, the constant duration of persistence obtained with stimuli of longer duration means that as stimulus duration varies so does the duration of perception. Further, changes in the duration of persistence produced by variation in stimulus orientation also means that the duration of perception may change. (There may also be intensity effects; see Bowling & Lovegrove, 1981.) In short, these results argue against a fixed duration of perception. Finally, because this kind of persistence seems to be produced by activity of mechanisms located at cortical levels of the visual system, it is a phenomenon that could potentially be relevant to the perceptual moment models; it is therefore noteworthy that we do not find evidence supporting the models.

Stereoscopic Persistence

When a purely stereoscopic stimulus is briefly and repetitively exposed to an observer, and the interstimulus interval between successive presentations is systematically varied, the interval at which stereopsis appears continuous can be taken as a measure of stereoscopic persistence (Engel, 1970). In a study investigating this kind of persistence, Engel found that stereopsis appears continuous for interstimulus intervals of at least 300 ms (i.e., the duration of stereoscopic persistence is on the order of 300 ms). To investigate this kind of persistence, Engel employed methods involving the use of stimuli created from random-dot stereograms. Random-dot stereograms, developed by Julesz (1971), consist of a pair of random-dot textures, with one texture presented to each eye of an observer. Retinal disparity is created by shifting laterally a subset of dots in one eye's view relative to corresponding dots in the other eye's view, a shift camouflaged by the surrounding dots in each view. The stereoscopic form defined by disparity cannot be seen in a monocular view or by someone who lacks stereopsis; it is purely stereoscopic. In someone with stereopsis, the textures of the two eyes are perceptually fused into one, and the shifted subset of dots is perceived in a depth plane different from that of the background dots. Employing these stimuli, Engel found that the duration of stereoscopic persistence, in addition to being relatively long, is positively related to stimulus duration and intensity; persistence duration increases as either stimulus duration is lengthened or intensity is increased. Because in the primate visual system only cortical mechanisms are activated by retinal disparity, the origin of stereoscopic persistence must be cortical (Coltheart, 1980).

Lehmkuhle and Fox (1980) investigated stereoscopic persistence in a visual masking experiment that involved stereoscopic stimuli created from random-dot stereograms. They found that masking occurs for target-mask onset asynchronies on the order of hundreds of milliseconds. If it is assumed that the basis of this kind of masking is visual persistence (the persistence of the mask interferes with visibility of the target; see Breitmeyer, 1984), these results are consistent with those of Engel (1970).

Interestingly, stereoscopic persistence as investigated by Engel appears to be different from the so-called cortical persistence studied by Bowling and Lovegrove (1981). On this point, stereoscopic persistence may be similar to what Wolfe (1986) termed the *purely binocular process*. On this idea, the purely binocular process represents a level of processing in which both eyes must be stimulated for activation of this process (equivalent to a logical "AND" process). The cortical persistence studied by Bowling and Lovegrove, however, may be related to a different binocular process activated through either one or both eyes (equivalent to a logical "OR" process). Regardless of the validity of this specific proposal, this analysis suggests that there may be several different varieties of cortical persistence.

With respect to evidence of a fixed duration of perception, the positive relationship between persistence duration and stimulus duration means that as stimulus duration increases so does the duration of perception. Further, changes in the duration of persistence produced by variation in stimulus intensity also means that the duration of perception can change. In short, these results argue against a fixed duration of perception. Because this kind of persistence is produced by activity of mechanisms located at cortical levels of the visual system, it is a phenomenon that should be relevant to the perceptual moment models. Therefore, it is again noteworthy that we do not find evidence supporting the models.

Informational Persistence

If an array of letters containing three rows of four letters each is presented briefly (e.g., for 50 ms) to an observer, and he or she is asked to report as many letters as possible from the entire array (a full report), the number correct is usually four or five letters. If, however, the observer is asked to report items of only one row of the array at a time (a partial report), with the relevant row cued by a tone occurring shortly after the exposure of the array, the number correct is typically three letters. On the assumption that the same number of letters in each of the other rows would also be reported if they were cued, the estimated number of letters available at the time of the cue is nine letters (three letters per row times three rows). Sperling (1960), who performed the original investigation of this phenomenon, called the difference in performance between the full and partial report the *partial-report superiority effect*. Partial-report superiority has been found to decrease with increasing cue delay up to about 300 ms, beyond which performance under the two conditions is equal. Partial-report superiority has been taken as evidence supporting the idea that, under full-report conditions, about nine letters are originally encoded by the observer, but due to elapsed time between exposure of the array and the report some items are lost from memory. The 300-ms limit beyond which no superiority occurs is taken as an estimate of the duration of memory. Various kinds of visual information can serve as cues in the partial-report method, such as spatial location, color, brightness, shape, direction of motion, and flicker (Coltheart, 1980). Also, several studies (see Coltheart, 1980; Yeomans & Irwin, 1985) have shown that this type of memory is unrelated to stimulus variables such as intensity or duration. This kind of memory has been called *iconic memory*, and also *informational persistence*.

With respect to evidence of a fixed duration of perception, the constant duration of persistence that is obtained with arrays of letters of varying duration means that as the duration of the stimuli varies so does the duration of perception (defined here as the interval between onset of the array and the end of partial report superiority). Thus, even though informational persistence is independent of stimulus intensity, we find no overall support for the idea of a fixed duration of perception. Because the neural locus within the visual system or brain of this kind of persistence remains unknown (for reviews of the controversy surrounding this issue, see Coltheart, 1980; Long, 1980), it is difficult to know how relevant this type of persistence is to the perceptual moment models. Nevertheless, given the independence between the duration of informational persistence and stimulus variables such as intensity and duration, it can be postulated that the origin of this kind of persistence may occur at relatively high levels of the visual system. If this is the case, then this evidence also fails to support the perceptual moment models.

SUMMARY AND CONCLUSIONS

Despite the original successes of the perceptual moment models, most current theorists (e.g., Coltheart, 1980; Long, 1980) believe that they are no longer tenable. Interestingly, the studies (e.g., Allport, 1968; Efron & Lee, 1971) that originally tested the models are not relevant to these models because the studies involved the investigation of peripheral, sensory mechanisms whereas the models propose the operation of a central intermittency (Breitmeyer, 1984). Because no studies have examined the models at the level of central (cortical) mechanisms, I attempted to review the models at that level by considering research on visual persistence. I used research on persistence to examine one crucial assumption of the models—namely, that the duration of a moment is fixed and uninfluenced by stimulus variables such as intensity.

To compare durations of persistence and durations of moments, I adopted a paradigm employed by Efron (1970b): For briefly exposed stimuli, I determined whether stimulus duration and persistence duration are inversely related, that is, whether there is a constant duration of perception when the latter is defined as beginning at stimulus onset and ending at perceived offset. Evidence for a fixed duration of perception would have been taken as evidence consistent with the idea of a fixed moment. Yet, for the five kinds of persistence examined here, variation in stimulus parameters did significantly influence the duration of perception; no evidence supported the perceptual moment models. Of course, this is consistent with the original arguments made against the models (e.g., Allport, 1968; Efron & Lee, 1971), but the original criticism was derived from studies of peripheral mechanisms. The present contribution to this argument comes from the effort to investigate the models at higher cortical levels of visual processing. Although it is still possible that evidence supporting the perceptual moment models may be obtained from empirical studies investigating even higher level mechanisms of the brain, at this point in time I am forced to conclude that the models clearly are not supported by any relevant evidence and just as clearly are rejected by abundant evidence. We are left with the view that the perception of brief stimuli is significantly influenced by stimulus variables—a bottom-up, rather than top-down, view of information processing.

REFERENCES

Allport, D. A. (1968). Phenomenal simultaneity and the perceptual moment hypothesis. *British Journal of Psychology, 59*, 395-406.

Block, R. A. (1979). Time and consciousness. In G. Underwood & R. Stevens (Eds.), *Aspects of consciousness: Vol. 1. Psychological issues* (pp. 179-217). London: Academic Press.

Bowling, A., & Lovegrove, W. (1980). The effect of stimulus duration on the persistence of gratings. *Perception & Psychophysics, 27*, 574-578.

Bowling, A., & Lovegrove, W. (1981). Two components to visible persistence: Effects of orientation and contrast. *Vision Research, 21*, 1241-1251.

Boyton, R. M. (1972). Discrimination of homogeneous double pulses of light: In D. Jameson & L. M. Hurvich (Eds.), *Handbook of sensory physiology: Vol. 7. Visual psychophysics* (pp. 202-232). Berlin: Springer.

Breitmeyer, B. G. (1984). *Visual masking: An integrative approach*. New York: Oxford University Press.

Breitmeyer, B. G., & Ganz, L. (1976). Implications of sustained and transient channels for theories of visual pattern masking, saccadic suppression and information processing. *Psychological Review, 83*, 1-36.

Brown, J. L. (1965). Afterimages. In C. H. Graham (Ed.), *Vision and visual perception* (pp. 479-503). New York: Wiley.

Burbeck, C. A., & Kelly, D. H. (1981). Contrast gain measurements and the sustained/transient dichotomy. *Journal of the Optical Society of America, 71*, 1335.

Coltheart, M. (1980). Iconic memory and visible persistence. *Perception & Psychophysics, 27*, 183-228.

DeYoe, E. A., & Van Essen, D. C. (1988). Concurrent processing streams in monkey visual cortex. *Trends in Neuroscience, 11*, 219-226.

DiLollo, V. (1984). On the relationship between stimulus intensity and duration of visible persistence. *Journal of Experimental Psychology: Human Perception and Performance, 10*, 144-151.

DiLollo, V., Clark, C. D., & Hogben, J. H. (1988). Separating visible persistence from retinal afterimages. *Perception & Psychophysics, 44*, 363-368.

DiLollo, V., & Wilson, A. E. (1978). Iconic persistence and perceptual moment as determinants of temporal integration in vision. *Vision Research, 18*, 1607-1610.

Efron, R. (1970a). Effect of stimulus duration on perceptual onset and offset latencies. *Perception & Psychophysics, 8*, 231-234.

Efron, R. (1970b). The relationship between the duration of a stimulus and the duration of a perception. *Neuropsychologia, 8*, 37-55.

Efron, R., & Lee, D. N. (1971). The visual persistence of a moving stroboscopically illuminated object. *American Journal of Psychology, 84*, 365-375.

Fraisse, P. (1984). Perception and estimation of time. *Annual Review of Psychology, 35*, 1-36.

Engel, G. R. (1970). An investigation of visual responses to brief stereoscopic stimuli. *Quarterly Journal of Experimental Psychology, 22*, 148-160.

Gerling, J., & Spillman, L. (1987). Duration of visual afterimages on modulated backgrounds: Post-receptoral processes. *Vision Research, 27*, 521-527.

Green, M. (1981). Psychophysical relationships among mechanisms sensitive to pattern, motion, and flicker. *Vision Research, 21*, 971-983.

Green, M. (1984). Masking by light and the sustained-transient dichotomy. *Perception & Psychophysics, 35*, 519-535.

Harter, M. R. (1967). Excitability cycles and cortical scanning: A review of two hypotheses of central intermittency in perception. *Psychological Bulletin, 68*, 47-58.

Hawkins, H. L., & Shulman, G. L. (1979). Two definitions of persistence in visual perception. *Perception & Psychophysics, 25*, 348-350.

Hubel, D. H., & Wiesel, T. N. (1977). Ferrier lecture: Functional architecture of macaque monkey visual cortex. *Proceedings of the Royal Society of London B, 198*, 1-59.

Julesz, B. (1971). *Foundations of cyclopean perception.* Chicago: University of Chicago Press.

Keesey, V. T. (1972). Flicker and pattern detection: A comparison of thresholds. *Journal of the Optical Society of America, 62*, 446-448.

Kulikowski, J. J., & Tolhurst, D. J. (1973). Psychophysical evidence for sustained and transient detectors in human vision. *Journal of Physiology, 232*, 149-162.

Legge, G. E. (1978). Sustained and transient mechanisms in human vision: Temporal and spatial properties. *Vision Research, 18*, 69-81.

Lehmkuhle, S. W., & Fox, R. (1980). Effect of depth separation on metacontrast masking. *Journal of Experimental Psychology: Human Perception and Performance, 6*, 605-615.

Lennie, P. (1980). Parallel visual pathways: A review. *Vision Research, 20*, 561-594.

Livingstone, M. S., & Hubel, D. H. (1987). Psychophysical evidence for separate channels for the perception of form, color, movement, and depth. *Journal of Neuroscience, 7*, 3416-3468.

Livingstone, M. S., & Hubel, D. H. (1988). Segregation of form, color, movement, and depth: Anatomy, physiology, and perception. *Science, 240*, 740-749.

Long, G. M. (1980). Iconic memory: A review and critique of the study of short-term visual storage. *Psychological Bulletin, 88*, 785-820.

Matin, E. (1974). Saccadic suppression: A review and analysis. *Psychological Bulletin, 81*, 899-917.

Shallice, T. (1964). The detection of change and the perceptual moment hypothesis. *British Journal of Statistical Psychology, 17*, 113-135.

Sperling, G. (1960). The information available in brief visual presentations. *Psychological Monographs, 74*, 1-29.

Stroud, J. M. (1955). The fine structure of psychological time: In H. Quastler (Ed.), *Information theory in psychology: Problems and methods* (pp. 174-205). Glencoe, IL: The Free Press.

Tolhurst, D. J. (1973). Separate channels for the analysis of the shape and the movement of a moving visual stimulus. *Journal of Physiology (London), 231*, 385-402.

Westheimer, G., & McKee, S. P. (1977). Perception of temporal order in adjacent visual stimuli. *Vision Research, 17*, 887-892.

White, C. T. (1963). Temporal numerosity and the psychological unit of duration. *Psychological Monographs, 77* (Whole no. 575).

Wiener, N. (1948). *Cybernetics.* New York: Wiley.

Wolfe, J. M. (1986). Stereopsis and binocular rivalry. *Psychological Review, 93*, 269-282.

Yeomans, J. M., & Irwin, D. E. (1985). Stimulus duration and partial report performance. *Perception & Psychophysics, 37*, 163-169.

5 Circadian Rhythms and Human Temporal Experience

Scott S. Campbell
Institute for Circadian Physiology

We doubt that we could live with a clock that was always right, any more than with a person who was always right.   — E. B. White (1934)

Modern society is grounded in schedules and clocks. As such, time estimation is neither a well-reinforced behavior nor one for which there is much opportunity to practice. Yet, most of us are reasonably confident of our ability to at least roughly determine the proper intervals for eating, sleeping, rest, and activity. Many people are confident, for example, that they can awaken themselves at a preselected time following a night's sleep. And to a degree, this confidence is borne out by experimental results. Zung and Wilson (1971) found that a group of young adults were able to awaken themselves within 10 min of a preselected wake-up time more often than would be expected by chance alone. In absolute numbers, however, this meant that only 14 of 44 such attempts were successful.

In their discussion of the results, the authors noted that "the process by which subjects were able to perform this task is completely unknown" (p. 163). Yet, the very fact that humans show some capacity for estimating elapsed time, in the apparent absence of external time cues and even conscious awareness, suggests the existence of some type of endogenous time-keeping mechanism. This chapter examines some of the properties of this putative biological clock, particularly with respect to how it functions in the perception of relatively long time intervals— that is, on the order of hours.

As the evidence presented later in the chapter indicates, it is quite likely that the process by which humans estimate the passage of long time intervals is intimately related to the endogenous circadian system assumed to be responsible for the temporal regulation of numerous functions of the body and brain. Therefore, it seems useful to begin with a brief overview of this biological timing system.

THE NATURE OF CIRCADIAN RHYTHMS

Discovery of Circadian Principles

In response to the natural alternation in light and darkness, virtually all species have developed endogenously mediated rhythms with frequencies close to 24 hr. The pervasive nature of such rhythmic components in physiology and behavior suggests that this circadian (*circa* = about, *dies* = day; Halberg, 1959) temporal organization is vital to the overall well-being of the organism. Among the numerous systems and functions mediated by the circadian timing system are hormonal output, body core temperature, rest and activity, sleep and wakefulness, and motor and cognitive performance. In all, literally hundreds of circadian rhythms in mammalian species have been identified (see, for example, Aschoff, 1981; Conroy & Mills, 1970), and Aschoff (1965) has noted that "there is apparently no organ and no function in the body which does not exhibit a similar daily rhythmicity" (p. 1427).

The proof that such rhythms are governed by factors inherent to the organism, rather than by the environmental cues with which they are typically synchronized, can be derived only from studies of organisms living in the absence of external factors that may provide cues to time of day or, more generally, to the passage of time. The first published study to utilize such a methodology reported on the daily leaf movements in a plant, *Mimosa pudica* (de Mairan, 1729; cited in Bünning, 1960). Although the plant was kept in total darkness, its leaves continued to exhibit closure and unfolding at times roughly corresponding to dusk and dawn. The further discovery, a century later, that such leaf movements showed a periodicity distinctly different from the natural 24-hr cycle of light and darkness (de Candolle, 1832) provided perhaps the clearest indication that such rhythms were driven by endogenous mechanisms, rather than being the product of environmental stimuli. In the following decades, thousands of investigations established the existence of similar free-running rhythms in species ranging from single-celled organisms to a wide variety of laboratory species. However, another 130 years were to pass before the first attempts were made to study temporal components of human physiology and behavior under analogous experimental conditions.

Circadian Systems as Clocks

Meanwhile, studies primarily of insect and bird behavior provided the first clear evidence that the endogenous circadian system was utilized, by at least some organisms, as a chronometer with which to temporally interact with the environment. Specifically, investigations of food-gathering behavior in honeybees (Beling, 1929) revealed that these animals had a remarkable capacity to return to a rich food source 24 hr from a time deemed successful by prior experience. This time-keeping capacity was not altered even when experiments were conducted deep within a salt mine, where environmental time cues were eliminated. Further studies revealed that bees could be trained to visit the same feeding site not only at 24-hr intervals, but also at several specific times within a given circadian period.

Studies of navigation in various avian species (Kramer, 1952) also made it clear that so-called *time-compensated sun compass orientation* (von Frisch, 1950) required the capacity to measure the passage of time. Such orientation requires an animal to determine its location and intended direction based on the sun's position. Yet, the sun's celestial orientation changes not only as a function of the animal's own movement through space, but also as a function of elapsed time. In order to make the appropriate navigational corrections, the animal must be able to keep track of that passage of time. This time-keeping capacity allows certain insect and avian species to migrate thousands of miles with considerable precision.

It was long assumed that such memory for the passage of time may be restricted to migratory species and to those that naturally rely on periodically available food sources. However, increasing evidence suggests that similar time-keeping capacity may be fairly widespread across the animal kingdom (Daan, 1981). It has been demonstrated, for example, that numerous species (e.g., rats, finches, killifish, starlings) exhibit anticipatory behavior shortly before food is available, after having been maintained on restricted daily feeding schedules for several days. Moreover, several species show the capacity to respond with behaviors that have been differentially conditioned to be rewarded at various specific times of day. In the wild, some predator species return daily to hunting sites at a time previously associated with availability of prey.

Thus, it appears that many species are able to utilize the inherent temporal organization associated with circadian rhythms as a means of gauging the passage of time. This general time sense appears to be fine-tuned not only by temporal environmental factors, but also by the individual's prior experience. Do humans possess a similar mechanism by which to track the passage of time? Before examining the limited data that bear on this question, it is necessary to first return briefly to the nature of the circadian system, this time with respect to human behavior.

HUMAN CIRCADIAN RHYTHMS

Sleep and Temperature

In the early 1960s, Aschoff and co-workers initiated a series of studies that, over the next 20 years, would lay the groundwork for much of what is known today about the circadian system (for a comprehensive summary of much of this work, see Aschoff & Wever, 1981; Wever, 1979). All but a few pilot studies were conducted in an underground laboratory (see Figure 5.1) consisting of two studio apartments that were free of all environmental cues to time of day. The laboratory was heavily sound-dampened, and the timing and intensity of illumination could be controlled from outside the apartments by the experimenters. In addition, subjects were studied in isolation in order to eliminate possible time cues provided by social contact.

The first experiments conducted in this unique environment (Aschoff, 1965; Aschoff & Wever, 1962) established that adult humans exhibit free-running rhythms of rest and activity averaging slightly longer than 25 hr (see Figure 5.2). That is, a subject's average "day" continued for about an hour longer than the natural day, although in some people the subjective day continued for a substantially longer period (up to 50 hr). Further investigations of numerous other systems confirmed that in humans, endogenous daily rhythms tended to free-run at frequencies slightly longer than 24 hr, and that all such rhythms typically maintained stable phase relationships with one another.

This internal organization among rhythms is seen clearly in the usual relationship between the sleep/wake system and the rhythm of body temperature. In the time-free environment, major sleep episodes tend to be initiated several hours prior to the nadir of the temperature rhythm and are terminated several hours after the nadir (see Figure 5.2). Aschoff and Wever observed remarkable interindividual precision in the period length of the sleep/wake rhythm under these conditions (± .5 hr

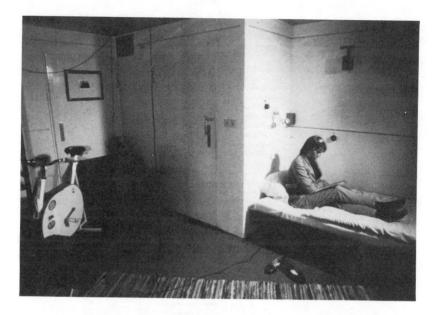

Figure 5.1. Photograph of the inside of an isolation apartment at the Max-Planck-Institute, Erling-Andechs, West Germany. The apartment is essentially soundproof and completely isolated from environmental cues to time of day. Similar settings have been employed for most studies of human biological rhythms.

for the 25-hr period averaged from a sample of 147 subjects; Wever, 1979).

Intraindividually, however, the extreme flexibility of the circadian sleep/wake rhythm is both obvious and well documented. We are not suddenly overcome with sleep at a particular temperature phase, nor are we startled awake each morning by a biological alarm clock tied to the temperature rhythm. In normal life, we routinely shift our bedtimes and wake-up times to accommodate changes in our daily schedules.

Likewise, in the time-free environment, subjects often advance or delay sleep times by several hours in relation to this "preferred" phase position for sleep. In fact, sleep may occur at virtually any phase of the temperature rhythm (see Campbell & Zulley, 1989, Figures 2 & 3; Zulley & Wever, 1982, Figure 2). Moreover, only minor changes (see later) are required in the usual experimental conditions under which subjects are studied, in order to obtain a profile of the human circadian system that is characterized by a considerably greater degree of "sloppiness."

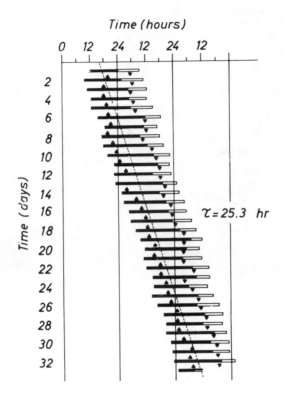

Figure 5.2. Representation of the free-running rhythm of a 26-year-old male living under constant conditions in a time-free environment (see Figure 5.1). Successive circadian periods are shown, one beneath the other, as a function of local time and days in isolation. The free-running period, in this case, was 25.3 hr. The black bars represent activity periods. The open bars represent rest. The maximum (▲) and minimum (▼) of each day's body core temperature is shown as well. (From Wever, 1979. Reprinted by permission.)

The Influence of Behavioral Controls

Traditionally, subjects entering the time-free environment have been instructed to lead a "regular" life—that is, to carry on with their normal daily activities, to eat three meals a day in normal sequence, and to avoid napping (i.e., to go to bed only when they are certain it is "for the night") (Aschoff, 1965; Wever, 1979). Thus, although time cues were eliminated from this environment, behavioral controls on the free-running rhythms certainly were not. The circadian system remained under the entraining influence of experimental instructions. The extent to which such controls provide structure and stability to the circadian sleep/wake rhythm is demonstrated by results of experiments in which subjects are instructed, instead, to eat and sleep whenever they are inclined to do so.

Webb and Agnew (1974) observed shorter and substantially more variable sleep/wake cycles in 14 subjects who lived in an otherwise typical time-free environment, but who were instructed to sleep "whenever you find this an acceptable response." In one extreme case, half of the subject's sleep onsets deviated from predicted sleep times (based on least-squares estimate of circadian period) by 3 hr or more. For all subjects, 56% of sleep onsets deviated from the line of best fit by more than 1 hr. Protocols that further reduce the influence of behavioral controls on the circadian system, by restricting the availability of behavioral options to sleep, evoke still more labile sleep/wake patterns (Campbell, 1984; Campbell & Zulley, 1985; Nakagawa, 1980). Under the most permissive experimental conditions, the sleep/wake system becomes virtually unrecognizable as a coherent circadian system; sleep occurs often and with extreme temporal variability (Campbell, 1984; Nakagawa, 1980).

In view of the considerable lability in the temporal organization of human behavior, and the apparent dependence on behavioral controls for the maintenance of circadian integrity, several questions regarding the adequacy of this system as the basis for an internal-clock mechanism become apparent. For example, is the "time sense" presumably mediated by this system also highly labile? Does the availability of behavioral controls in one's environment influence the accuracy with which the passage of time is measured? Relatively few studies have attempted to address such questions, but some clues are available. The next section examines the data germane to these issues.

TIME-KEEPING IN HUMANS

Although a great deal of work has focused on short-term time estimation in humans, there are relatively few studies that have examined the factors involved in the perception of longer time spans (see Table 5.1). In addition to the studies shown in Table 5.1, there are several studies (e.g., Zung & Wilson, 1971, referred to in the Introduction) which provide some insight into one specific aspect of such time perception, specifically, perception of elapsed time during sleep. Due to differences in methodology and focus, the results of the various studies are not

Table 5.1
Summary of Studies That Have Examined
Relatively Long-Term Time Estimation in Humans

Citation	N	Type of estimation	Duration of study	Mean "subjective hour"	Environment
Macleod & Roff (1936)	2	Time of day and intervals (17-56 min)	86 and 48 hr, respectively	1.22 hr[a]	Isolation unit with observation window
Vernon & McGill (1963)	33	Time of day and 1-hr intervals	8-96 hr	1.08 hr[a]	Sensory deprivation
Siffre (1964)	1	Time of day	2 months	2.14 hr[a]	Cave
Webb & Ross (1972)	28	Four consecutive 1-hr intervals	one trial (4 hr)	1.02-1.05 hr[a]	Soundproof room
Lavie & Webb (1975)	14	Time of day (interval derived)	14 days	1.12 hr[a]	Isolation unit
Aschoff (1985)	48	1-hr intervals	7 days- 1 month	1.47 hr	Isolation unit
Campbell (1986)	9	Time of day (interval derived)	60 hr	1.12 hr	Isolation unit with bed rest

Note. In addition to these, there are several reports that have investigated one aspect of time estimation, specifically, time estimation during sleep. The results of those studies are reviewed in the text.

[a] Calculated from data provided in the text.

always comparable. Yet, some general findings regarding certain properties of the human time-keeping system are remarkably consistent.

Lability of Time Estimation

Results of virtually all studies suggest that human time-keeping capacity is as labile, or more so, as the endogenous circadian system by which it is presumably mediated. In an early study of short interval estimation, von Skramlik (1934) concluded that the human physiological clock was approximately 400 times less accurate than the best mechanical clock (Macleod & Roff, 1936). Although this quantification of the "sloppiness" of the putative internal clock may be overstated, at least with respect to long-term time estimation, it is nevertheless clear that subjects are capable of judging the passage of time only in very general terms.

Aschoff (1985) identified "large intraindividual variability in consecutive estimates" (p. 42) as one of the most prominent features in the judgment of 1-hr intervals by subjects living for extended periods in isolation. In this experiment, subjects were required to press a designated button whenever they thought that an hour had elapsed. Such estimates were made throughout the time in isolation (ranging from 1 week to over 1 month), as long as the subject was awake. The consecutive productions of three subjects in that study are shown in Figure 5.3. The extreme variability in consecutive estimates is quite evident. For the entire group, standard deviations of subjects' estimates ranged from 25% to 49% of the 1-hr interval. Similar degrees of within-subject lability have been observed by other investigators, as well (Macleod & Roff, 1936; Webb & Ross, 1972).

The extent of lability in time estimation is also apparent in the low frequency with which subjects are accurate in their judgments. In two studies employing the same conditions and methodology, estimates of interval durations, ranging in length from 1 to 25 hr, were found to be "accurate" (i.e., within ±10% of the actual interval) in only about one fourth of total estimates made (Campbell, 1986; Lavie & Webb, 1975). Likewise, fewer than half of subjects asked to produce a judgment at each of four consecutive hours were accurate (±10%) in their estimations after the first hour, and only one-fourth of subjects were accurate following the fourth hour (Webb & Ross, 1972).

The general sloppiness that seems to characterize long-term time estimation is apparent not only to the experimenter. The haphazard nature of the estimation process is often recognized by subjects, as well, at the time a judgment is made. An excerpt from the diary of a subject (actually, Macleod himself) estimating various intervals during 48 hr in isolation, reflects a common feeling among subjects required to estimate the passage of relatively long intervals:

> The last few judgements I have made have been almost perfectly at random. I find that I have lost almost all interest in the problem of the estimation of time. When the signal comes I just make a wild guess (Macleod & Roff, 1936, p. 393).

In view of this hit-or-miss approach to the task and the resulting scatter of estimates, it may not be expected that a rather consistent trend would emerge in the way in which subjects perceive the passage of time; yet one does.

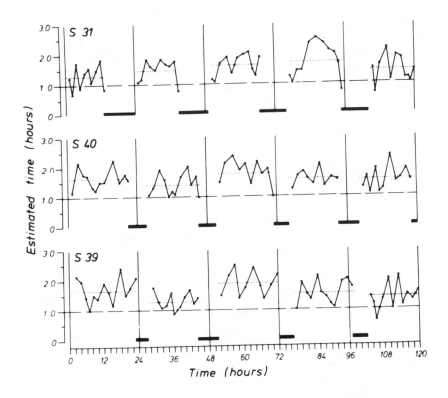

Figure 5.3. Consecutive 1-hr estimates of three subjects living in isolation for extended periods. Dotted lines represent mean "subjective hour." Black bars represent sleep periods. Note the extreme variability in consecutive estimates, and the strong tendency for "subjective hours" to continue for longer than 1 hr. (From Aschoff, 1985. Reprinted by permission.)

Underestimation of Time

The data presented in Figure 5.3 not only illustrate the considerable imprecision of the human "time sense," but they also reveal this second general property of long-term time estimation. In all three examples shown, the large majority of productions exceed the 1-hr target interval. That is, the "subjective hour" routinely continued for longer than an actual hour. Thus, a subject who emerges from a time-free environment after 14 days may believe that only 9 days have elapsed (see, for example, Webb & Agnew, 1974). As can be seen in Table 5.1, all studies have found this tendency for the underestimation of elapsed time, and the range in the duration of the average "subjective hour," across virtually all studies, is quite small, 1.08 to 1.47 hr.

The single investigation in which the hour estimate is clearly discrepant (but still underestimated) was conducted under notably different, and substantially more difficult, circumstances than the other studies (Siffre, 1964). In that study, a young French geologist named Michel Siffre lived for 2 months alone in a cave. His "isolation unit" was a nylon tent erected on a glacier, 375 ft below the surface of the earth. As a result of living on a floor of melting ice, in constant, near freezing conditions and 100% humidity, Siffre suffered from hypothermia ("a condition of semihibernation," p. 89) for most of the 2-month period. Under such conditions, it is little wonder that Siffre perceived time to pass so slowly!

Although there is good agreement across studies with respect to the lability and relative sluggishness of the human time-keeping system, there is considerably less consensus with regard to the factors that may be responsible for these properties. A number of factors have been suggested, and it seems likely that the characteristics of time estimation are the outgrowth of a combination of several of them. These factors may be separated into two general categories, as described here.

Effects of Physiological State. One factor that has long been hypothesized to influence the speed of the putative endogenous clock is metabolic rate. Hoagland (1933) postulated the existence of a temperature-modulated "chemical clock" to explain the finding that subjects with fever shortened their estimations of 1-s intervals. With respect to longer durations, the medical team that examined Siffre upon his emergence from the Scarasson Cavern believed that his drastic underestimation of time was related to the slowing of metabolism that accompanied his extended episode of hypothermia. Aschoff also hypothesized a link between metabolic rate and the degree to which elapsed time is underestimated (Aschoff, 1985; Aschoff, Goetz, Wildgruber, & Wever, 1986; Aschoff, Wever, Wildgruber, & Wirz-Justice, 1984). This conclusion was based on the findings that both the timing of inter-meal intervals (presumably reflecting metabolic processes) and subjective estimation of 1-hr intervals lengthened with the lengthening of free-running rest/activity periods of subjects living in isolation. Although Macleod and Roff (1936) rejected the possible influence of metabolism on the speed of the endogenous clock, they, nevertheless, reported that a subject tended to overestimate the duration of those intervals during which exercise was the principal activity.

Results of studies that have examined time-keeping capacity during sleep may also bear on the question of whether metabolic rate is associated with the speed at which the endogenous clock runs.   Daily metabolic rate is at its lowest during sleep, even when compared to bed rest without sleep (Shapiro & Moore, 1981). Thus, one might expect a corresponding slowing in the passage of subjective time during periods of sleep.   Such results have been reported in a number of studies (Campbell, 1986; Lavie & Webb, 1975; Tart, 1970; Vernon & McGill, 1963; Zepelin, 1968), although not all (Boring & Boring, 1917; Noble & Lundie, 1974; Zung & Wilson, 1971). These findings notwithstanding, Pittendrigh (1960) made a convincing argument against any significant influence of changes in temperature (or any other perturbations likely to be normally encountered by the organism) on the inherent frequency of biological clocks. That is, the frequency of circadian oscillations is subject to "general homeostatic control." His argument was based on the quite logical premise that a temperature-sensitive clock mechanism would be of little adaptive value. "For unless the spontaneous frequency of a sense organ is compensated for temperature . . . it will be useless for anything except temperature sensing" (p. 179). Quite simply, if a biological clock is to be of utility as a time-keeping device, it must be impervious to the daily temperature excursions that characterize both the internal milieu and the environmental milieu in which it functions.

Of course, metabolic rate is not the only physiological alteration occurring during sleep that may affect time-keeping capacity. Consciousness is also dramatically altered in certain sleep states and lost entirely in others. It is quite likely that time estimation is affected by such changes, independent of any metabolic component.

Subjects may employ physiological factors as cues to gauge their estimates of the passage of time, as well. For example, Vernon and McGill (1963) found that 82% of their subjects used "observable bodily processes" to judge elapsed time. These cues, listed in the order of frequency of use, included hunger, beard growth, urination, defecation, and sleepiness. Boring and Boring (1917) also found that temporal judgments after sleep were based most frequently on "general bodily state," such as, restedness versus sleepiness. In direct contrast, however, Macleod and Roff (1936) concluded that they had "no basis for assuming that the subjects read the time of day from any observable bodily processes" (p. 407).

Effects of Behavioral Factors.   Considerable additional evidence suggests that behavioral factors may also play an important role in the manner in which we perceive the passage of time. Perhaps the most basic illustration of this notion is reflected in the common expression that "time flies when you're having fun." It has generally been acknowledged that an interval filled with some activity, for example, solving anagrams or working problems in long division, is perceived to pass more quickly than an "empty" interval of the same duration, during which subjects simply sit. This result has been found in virtually all studies investigating the perception of short intervals. However, the finding by Aschoff (1985) that short-term and long-term time estimations are probably mediated by different mechanisms, and therefore, not necessarily subject to influence by the same factors, raises the possibility that the latter may not be influenced in the same way by the nature of the interval to be estimated.

A comparison of the results of two studies conducted in the same laboratory, but under very different conditions, suggests that in the case of long-term estimation, the degree to which an interval is "filled" or "unfilled" does not directly affect the manner in which it is perceived. In the first study (Lavie & Webb, 1975), subjects lived for 14 days in a time-free environment, during which they were permitted to continue their daily schedules and a subgroup was, in addition, maintained on a daily exercise regimen. In the second study (Campbell 1986), subjects lived in the same time-free environment for 60 consecutive hours, but they were confined to bed for the entire period and were prohibited from reading, writing, listening to music, and so on. Thus, subjects in the first condition could be considered to be estimating filled time, whereas those in the bed rest condition were clearly judging the passage of empty time.

In both cases, subjects were asked to estimate the time of day at irregular intervals throughout the study. Under the assumption that filled time passes more quickly than empty time, it would be expected that subjects in the extremely monotonous bed rest condition would underestimate the passage of time to a much greater extent than those studied by Lavie and Webb. This was not the case, however. The average subjective hour in empty time continued for precisely the same duration − 1.12 hr − as that in filled time (see Table 5.1). Moreover, time estimates of subjects living under the more drastic conditions of sensory deprivation resulted in an average subjective hour of a similar duration (Vernon & McGill, 1963; Table 5.1, this chapter).

Whereas the content of an interval appears to have little direct influence on its perceived length, the degree to which a subject's behavior during that interval deviates from prior experience (i.e., what he or she is used to) seems to be critically related to the accuracy with which time is estimated. As an illustration, consider the bed rest study just described (Campbell, 1984). Under normal circumstances, the natural photoperiod, regular meal times, and many other routine activities serve to partition the day into relatively uniform and consistent intervals. However, during the bed rest study, sleep and waking episodes occurred throughout the 24-hr day, with a single episode rarely exceeding 4 hr in length. In addition, meals were served at irregular intervals and control of light and darkness was at the discretion of each subject. As such, the background against which subjects judged the passage of time differed in significant ways from that experienced in normal daily life. The accuracy with which subjects judged the passage of time under these conditions was directly related to the extent of behavioral deviation from the typical day. Such deviation may be best reflected in altered sleep/wake patterns.

Lavie and Webb (1975) reached a similar conclusion, based on the finding that errors in time estimation were greater for the group of subjects who carried out a daily exercise regimen than for those who did not. The authors attributed this difference to the more disrupted sleep/wake rhythm of the exercise group.

Subjects often attribute their reduced time-keeping capacity to behavioral changes, as well. For example, in contrast to the conclusions of his medical team, Siffre (1964) believed that his time estimation capacity suffered primarily from his disinclination to continue with a normal daily routine. Within several days of entering the cave he chose to dispense with the usual three-meals-a-day schedule in favor of irregular snacking. At the same time, napping became a frequent occurrence. As with physiological processes, subjects may use behavioral factors as cues upon which to base their estimation of the passage of time. Subjects required to estimate the passage of four consecutive hours frequently gauged the passage of time by the amount of material they had read (Webb & Ross, 1972). Similarly, one subject studied by Macleod and Roff (1936) often based his judgments on the amount he had written since the previous estimate. Environmental observations such as towels drying and soup cooling have also been cited as providing cues to the passage of time (Vernon & McGill, 1963). It should be noted, however, that in none of these studies were there any indications that the use of such strategies resulted in greater accuracy of estimation.

SUMMARY AND CONCLUSIONS

One of the early studies of human time estimation concluded that "it is clear that when the normal cues for clock time were removed, what was left was not a temporal vacuum but rather an organized temporal system, a personal time" (Macleod & Roff, 1936, p. 405). Taken together, the findings reviewed in this chapter support that conclusion. Although, on occasion, estimates bear little resemblance to reality, and even subjects sometimes have little confidence in their own judgments, the body of evidence indicates that humans do possess some degree of time-keeping ability. The data further suggest that this personal temporal system is characterized by two properties not typically associated with clocks—sloppiness and sluggishness.

Whether "personal time" is directly related to physiological factors such as metabolic rate, or more generally tied to the changes in behavior that characterize life in the time-free environment, it seems quite likely that the consistently observed slowing in subjective time is closely related to the slowing of the human circadian system, which is typically reflected in free-running rhythms with periods slightly longer than 24 hr. For example, Aschoff (1985) showed that long-term time estimation was strongly related to the free-running period of sleep and waking—the longer the subjective day, the longer the subjective perception of an hour. He concluded from these findings that the estimation of 1-hr intervals was "coupled in some way to the circadian system, or more precisely, to the sleep/wake cycle" (p. 49). In contrast, it was concluded that the estimation of short intervals (on the order of minutes) was not related to sleep/wakefulness or any other aspect of the circadian timing system.

If it is indeed the case that "personal time" is coupled to the sleep/wake cycle, then it is not surprising that human time estimation is not only sluggish, but also sloppy. In the absence of the structuring influence of behavioral controls, the human sleep/wake system becomes remarkably labile. In the time-free environment, sleep can occur at any time of day. Only when the system is structured by the presence of social and occupational pressures, or by experimental instructions, does it take on the precise monophasic character of daily experience.

In the same way, when the human time-keeping system functions in the presence of social and behavioral cues that temporally structure one's environment, it serves as a reasonably accurate mechanism for tracking the passage of time. Most of us are reasonably proficient at tracking the passage of a normal day without reference to celestial cues or human-made chronometers. Yet, if required to function without the benefit of cues derived from an environment well-grounded in prior experience, the human "clock" becomes unrecognizable as such. Long-term time estimation frequently becomes a guessing game.

The functional role of such a "personal time," which is mediated through endogenous mechanisms but is highly dependent on prior experience, remains unclear. It is important to keep in mind, in this regard, that the study of human long-term time estimation is still in its infancy. Although the human investigations reviewed here span over 50 years, the actual number of subjects studied is remarkably small, and the approach of most studies has been largely descriptive. Further, more critical study is required in order to arrive at meaningful conclusions concerning the role of human time-keeping capacity.

Nevertheless, the utility of this imperfect, sloppy "clock" is probably best understood within the context of human evolution. Until very recently in our history, temporal precision has not been viewed as an important requisite of human behavior. The ability to only roughly estimate appropriate times for eating, sleeping, working, and socializing has been quite adequate for the successful completion of daily routines, at least until the last few centuries. Viewed in this way, the seemingly paradoxical properties of the human "clock" seem considerably less restrictive. As Aldous Huxley has observed:

> To us, the moment 8:17 AM means something—something very important, if it happens to be the starting time of our daily train. To our ancestors, such an odd eccentric instant was without significance—did not even exist. In inventing the locomotive, Watt and Stevenson were part inventors of time.

REFERENCES

Aschoff, J. (1965). Circadian rhythms in man. *Science, 148*, 1427-1432.

Aschoff, J. (Ed.). (1981). *Handbook of behavioral neurobiology: Vol. 4. Biological rhythms.* New York: Plenum Press.

Aschoff, J. (1985). On the perception of time during prolonged temporal isolation. *Human Neurobiology, 4*, 41-52.

Aschoff, J., & Wever, R. (1962). Spontanperiodik des Menschen bei Ausschluss aller Zeitgeber [Spontaneous periodicity of humans when excluded from all time cues]. *Naturwissenschaften, 49*, 337-342.

Aschoff, J., & Wever, R. (1981). The circadian system of man. In J. Aschoff (Ed.), *Handbook of behavioral neurobiology: Vol. 4. Biological rhythms* (pp. 311-331). New York: Plenum Press.

Aschoff, J., Goetz, C. von, Wildgruber, C., & Wever, R. (1986). Meal timing in humans during isolation without time cues. *Journal of Biological Rhythms, 1*, 151-162.

Aschoff, J., Wever, R., Wildgruber, C., & Wirz-Justice, A. (1984). Circadian control of meal timing during temporal isolation. *Naturwissenschaften, 71*, 534-535.

Beling, I. (1929). Über das Zeitgedächtnis der Bienen [On the memory of time in bees]. *Zeitschrift für Vergleichende Physiologie, 9*, 259-338.

Boring, L. D., & Boring, E. G. (1917). Temporal judgements after sleep. In *Studies in psychology: Contributions to the E. B. Titchener commemorative volume* (pp. 225-279). Worcester, MA: Louis N. Wilson.

Bünning, E. (1960). Opening address: Biological clocks. In *Cold Springs Harbor Symposia on Quantitative Biology, Biological Clocks* (Vol. 25, pp. 1-9). Baltimore: Waverly Press.

Campbell, S. S. (1984). Duration and placement of sleep in a "disentrained" environment. *Psychophysiology, 21*, 106-113.

Campbell, S. S. (1986). Estimation of empty time. *Human Neurobiology, 5*, 205-207.

Campbell, S. S., & Zulley, J. (1985). Ultradian components of human sleep/wake patterns during disentrainment. In H. Schulz & P. Lavie (Eds.), *Ultradian rhythms in physiology and behavior* (pp. 234-255). Berlin: Springer-Verlag.

Campbell, S. S., & Zulley, J. (1989). Napping in time-free environments. In D. Dinges & R. Broughton (Eds.), *Sleep and alertness* (pp. 121-138). New York: Raven Press.

Conroy, R. T., & Mills, J. N. (1970). *Human circadian rhythms.* Baltimore: Williams & Wilkins.

Daan, S. (1981). Adaptive daily strategies in behavior. In J. Aschoff (Ed.), *Handbook of behavioral neurobiology, biological rhythms* (Vol. 4, pp. 275-298). New York: Plenum Press.

De Candolle, A. (1832). *Physiologie Vegetale* [Physiology of vegetation] (Vol. 2). Paris: Bechet Jeune.

De Mairan, J. (1729). Observation botanique [Observation on botany]. In *Histoire de l'Academie Royale des Sciences* (p. 35). Paris.

Halberg, F. (1959). Physiologic 24-hour periodicity: General and procedural considerations with reference to the adrenal cycle. *Zeitschrift für Vitamin-, Mormon- und Fermentforschung, 10*, 225-296.

Hoagland, H. (1933). The physiological control of judgements of duration: Evidence for a chemical clock. *Journal of General Psychology, 9*, 267-287.

Frisch, K. von (1950). Die Sonne als Kompass in Leben die Bienen [The sun as a compass in the life of bees]. *Experientia, 6*, 210-221.

Kramer, G. (1952). Experiments on bird orientation. *Naturwissenschaften, 94*, 265-285.

Lavie, P., & Webb, W. B. (1975). Time estimates in a long-term time-free environment. *American Journal of Psychology, 88*, 177-186.

Macleod, R. B., & Roff, M. F. (1936). An experiment in temporal disorientation. *Acta Psychologica, 1*, 381-423.

Nakagawa, Y. (1980). Continuous observation of EEG patterns at night and in daytime of normal subjects under restrained conditions: I. Quiescent state when lying down. *Electroencephalography and Clinical Neurophysiology, 49*, 524-537.

Noble, W. G., & Lundie, R. E. (1974). Temporal discrimination of short intervals of dreamless sleep. *Perceptual and Motor Skills, 38*, 445-446.

Pittendrigh, C. (1960). Circadian rhythms and the circadian organization of living systems: In *Cold Springs Harbor Symposia on Quantitative Biology, Biological Clocks* (Vol. 25, pp. 159-184). Baltimore, MD: Waverly Press.

Shapiro, C. M., & Moore, A. T. (1981). Circadian heat transfer. In W. P. Koella (Ed.), *Sleep 1980* (pp. 340-343). Basel: Karger.

Siffre, M. (1964). *Beyond time* (H. Briffault, Ed. & Trans.). New York: McGraw-Hill.

Skramlik, E. von (1934). Die Angleichung der Subjektiven Zeitauffassung an Astronomische Vorgänge: Die Physiologische Uhr [Adaptation to astronomical events of subjective time estimation: The physiological clock]. *Naturwissenschaften, 22,* 98-105.

Tart, C. T. (1970). Waking from sleep at a preselected time. *Journal of the American Society of Psychosomatic Dentistry and Medicine, 17,* 3-16.

Vernon, J. A., & McGill, T. E. (1963). Time estimations during sensory deprivation. *Journal of General Psychology, 69,* 11-18.

Webb, W. B., & Agnew, H. W. (1974). Sleep and waking in a time-free environment. *Aerospace Medicine, 45,* 617-622.

Webb, W. B., & Ross, W. (1972). Estimation of the passing of four consecutive hours. *Perceptual and Motor Skills, 35,* 768-770.

Wever, R. A. (1979). *The circadian system of man: Results of experiments under temporal isolation.* New York: Springer-Verlag.

White, E. B. (1934). *Every day is Saturday.* New York: Harper & Brothers.

Zepelin, H. (1968). Self-awakening and the sleep cycle. *Psychophysiology, 4,* 370.

Zulley, J., & Wever, R. (1982). Interaction between the sleep-wake cycle and the rhythm of rectal temperature. In J. Aschoff, S. Daan, & G. Groos (Eds.), *Vertebrate circadian systems* (pp. 253-261). Berlin: Springer-Verlag.

Zung, W. W. K., & Wilson, W. P. (1971). Time estimation during sleep. *Biological Psychiatry, 3,* 159-164.

6 Time and Order: A Comparative Perspective

H. L. Roitblat
K. N. J. Young
University of Hawaii at Manoa

Time and its effects have been particularly sticky problems in the history of behavioral analysis. As any visitor to a zoo probably knows, animals are quite good at anticipating the impending delivery of their food. By some accounts this anticipation is nothing more than the animal's sensitivity to events preceding the food delivery. For example, the animal may smell, hear, or see its caretaker. Alternatively, the animal may be responding to particular levels of ambient light or sound changes associated with the time of day (e.g., of zoo visitors arriving in the area). Finally, its anticipation may be the product of a timing ability, which it uses to predict the occurrence of a regular event.

Animals' ability to respond temporally presented a problem to traditional forms of behavioral analysis because animals were thought to behave in response to specific stimulus events, and no specific stimulus could be identified to explain temporal anticipation. Attributing responding to the passage of time, and not directly to stimuli that change with time, would be equivalent to showing that the animal was responding to something that could not be observed, but had to be inferred from changing experience. Such inferences were thought to be incompatible with a straightforward stimulus-response account of behavior and, therefore, beyond the ability of animals.

For example, in delay conditioning, the animal is trained with a fairly long interval between the beginning of the presentation of the conditional stimulus (CS) and the presentation of the unconditional stimulus (US). Early in training the animal performs the conditional response

119

immediately following the presentation of the CS. Later in training, the animal delays its production of the conditional response until late in the interval, just before the presentation of the US. This delay in the occurrence of the conditional response is called *inhibition of delay*. Pavlov (1927) and later Hull (1943) attributed inhibition of delay to changes in the effective CS as the animal perceives it. This explanation requires that we distinguish between the nominal CS as the experimenter presents it, and the effective CS as the animal perceives it. Sensory adaptation, for example, would cause changes in the perceived magnitude of the effective CS. The animal could then selectively associate the conditional response with the particular effective stimulus that preceded the US and extinguish the response to the slightly different effective stimuli occurring earlier in the trial. Although the use of effective stimuli as the cause of inhibition of delay also required the use of unobservable stimuli, these stimuli were thought to be more firmly grounded in the events of the trial and, although unobservable, they could be made observable, at least in principle, with the development of an appropriate apparatus, and they did not require the animal to make any inferences. Inhibition of delay and its implications for timing are described in greater detail later.

The discovery of circadian rhythms (see e.g., Saunders, 1977; Silver & Bittman, 1984) in, for example, body temperature, sleep/wakefulness, activity level, and feeding, and the discovery that these rhythms persist in the absence of external environmental variations provided a model timing phenomenon in animals that was sensitive to changing environmental events, but not dependent on them. For example, the daily activity cycle of most animals is correlated with the daily changes in light and dark. The temporal pattern of these activities (e.g., the common rodent pattern of high activity at night and low activity during the day) continues even under conditions of constant illumination.

These rhythms are controlled by pacemaker oscillators located in certain areas of the animal's brain (e.g., the suprachiasmatic nucleus). The pacemaker is disrupted by certain chemicals such as lithium chloride and deuterium, but is generally unaffected by other factors that ordinarily modify the functioning of neurons. These endogenous oscillators function as models for the time of day. They allow the animal to take advantage of regularities in the day/night cycle and thereby anticipate important daily events (see Terman, Gibbon, Fairhurst, & Waring, 1984).

Time as a Dimension

Time has ordinal and interval properties. Given a sequence of events, each event either precedes or follows another event. The order in which two events occur is often a significant variable in determining the importance or success of behavior. For example, digger wasps (*Vespula* spp) visit their nests at one time and then provision them later in the day, with the amount of food determined by the number of grubs in the nest and the amount of available food. Once the nest has been provisioned, the mother wasp need not return there until at least the next day. Clearly, the order of the two visits is important. There is a significant difference between having visited the nest, finding it in need of food, and having provisioned it, versus provisioning the nest, then visiting it and finding it in need of food. Mistakes of one sort regarding the order of the visits mean that the mother wasp spends too much time revisiting the nest (perhaps she could be a compulsive wasp), mistakes of the other sort mean that the grubs go without provisions for a while.

Maintaining the order of these events, however, probably presents no significant difficulty for the digger wasp. Presumably mother digger wasps have evolved a scheme for keeping these events in the proper order. For example, the need to visit a nest could be high, conditional on the mother's own hunger state, or on the occurrence of waking up for the day, and so forth, and then become low, conditional on having provisioned the nest. Whatever the factors that do actually control nest visiting, this scheme illustrates one possible solution to problems of temporal order. At least some temporal order problems can be solved by associating behaviors (drives, intentions, motivations) with some environmental or behavioral event.

Research on timing with animals has been very much concerned with identifying the basis for the animal's temporal behavior. Part of this concern comes from a strong behaviorist tradition that viewed behavior as the response to circumscribable, objectively observable external stimuli. Timing presented a serious problem to this perspective because time is more abstract. There is no specific stimulus to which one can point as the stimulus for timing. The animal times the duration of an event, but there is no ostensible event or item that is time. This theme of identifying or ruling out potential external mediators as explanations for timing recurs in the field and in the pages that follow.

As previously mentioned, an animal could appear to be timing the duration of some event or sequence of events if it could respond to some properties of that event that vary regularly with time. Although animals are not unresponsive to environmental events, every animal that has been studied has shown evidence of circadian timing and most animals have shown evidence of internal clocks that can be used to time many different events.

EVENT DURATION

Delay and Temporal Conditioning as Paradigm Timing Procedures

Optimal CS-US Interval. In classical conditioning studies, the findings of optimal CS-US intervals, inhibition of delay, and temporal conditioning suggest that animals can use elapsed time as a variable affecting their performance. Early investigators of these phenomena explained them in terms of the animals' response to changes in the environment rather than the utilization of temporal representations. Recent evidence, however, is more supportive of an explanation in terms of direct temporal discrimination. As in circadian rhythms, animals respond on the basis of an internal clock and measured duration; they do not respond simply to changes in external stimuli. These internal clocks are accessible for timing a wide range of events.

For conditioning, the optimal interval between the presentation of the CS and the start of the US falls within a distinct range, depending on the unconditional stimulus and the response being measured. The limited range of this interval may indicate that animals time the interval, perhaps because some amount of time is optimal for the animal to prepare for the presentation of the US. Conditioning is poorer with shorter CS-US intervals because the animal does not have adequate time to prepare for the presentation of the US. Conditioning is poorer with longer CS-US intervals because the contiguity between the CS and the US is reduced or because there is increased variability in the judged duration of longer than of shorter intervals (see later).

Another explanation of the optimal interval (Hull, 1943; Pavlov, 1927) is that a minimal time is necessary for the neural activity produced by the apprehension of the CS to rise to sufficient levels that it can be associated with the US. Conditioning is poor with short CS-US intervals because the trace representation of the CS does not have time to achieve its optimum strength before the US is presented. Conditioning is poorer with longer CS-US intervals because the trace of the CS has time to decay before the presentation of the US.

Inhibition of Delay. As mentioned earlier, inhibition of delay (Pavlov, 1927) occurs when the interval between the CS and the US is relatively long and the animal learns to delay the production of its conditional response (CR) until just before the presentation of the US. Pavlov (1927) and Hull (1943) argued that the delay in producing the response results from differential conditioning of two sets of neural or sensory elements. Elements activated early in the presentation of the CS come to be conditioned inhibitors of responding, whereas those elements activated later in the CS (different because of sensory adaptation) come to elicit the conditional response. What appears to be timing of the CS-US interval is really, according to this explanation, simply differential conditioning to items that are contiguous versus those that are not contiguous with the presentation of the US. Changes in the perceived sensory situation, not timing, are the basis for the phenomenon in this analysis.

Temporal Conditioning.   Temporal conditioning is another phenomenon that would appear to indicate that animals can time events. In temporal conditioning there is no explicit CS other than the passage of time, the US is presented repeatedly, at regular intervals. Eventually, the animals make the conditional response just before the US. Pavlov (1927) attributed this phenomenon to timing (hence the name *temporal conditioning*). In contrast to his explanation of other apparent timing phenomena, he argued that the passage of time itself functions as the CS in temporal conditioning. In principle, however, even temporal conditioning could be explainable in terms of responses to specific stimulus or perceptual changes. For example, if a dog were to close its eyes every time it received some food, then it could briefly dark-adapt its visual system and use sensory adaptation to time the interval.

In every case of classical conditioning, at least two hypotheses are available to explain why the animal behaves regularly with the passage of time. The first explains instances of timing as a result of the discrimination of changes in the properties or effectiveness of external stimuli. According to this hypothesis, the apparent timing of an event is simply the product of responding directly to properties of that event. The second hypothesis presumes that animals have the ability to discriminate the duration of intervals, possibly using an internal clock. According to this class of hypothesis, the apparent timing of an event is the product of some generalized timer that can be separated from the events it is measuring and can be used to time several different kinds of events. For example, when we use a clock to time the baking of a cake or to anticipate the presentation of an interesting television show, we are responding to an external stimulus that varies with the passage of time. Variations in the clock (e.g., the position of its hands) control our response to the event we are timing, not variations in the event itself. Unlike sensory adaptation, however, we can use the same clock that we use to determine cooking times also to measure other durations (e.g., telephone conversations). It is not tied to the specific events. Timing based on sensory adaptation is a direct response to the stimulus that is being timed. Although the kitchen clock is also a stimulus, we are not typically interested in the clock, rather we tend to use the clock to time other events.

Animals do not generally have access to kitchen clocks. They do, however, appear to time events using an internal clock with many of the features of a kitchen clock or timer. This internal clock varies systematically with the passage of time and can be used to time different events. The question is whether they use this internal timer to measure the durations of events or whether they only respond to the properties of the events themselves.

In most cases in which it has been studied, the evidence is actually quite poor that apparent timing effects are the result of direct responses to changes in the effective stimulus. For example, if the optimal CS-US interval was due to the time necessary for optimal stimulus effectiveness, then the optimal interval would depend on the type of CS, and the processing involved for that type of stimulus; the optimal CS-US interval employing tones as the CS might be longer than one utilizing a CS of lights. This however, does not seem to be the case. Vandercar and Schneiderman (1967) simultaneously recorded rabbits' nictitating-membrane blink CRs and heart-rate CRs. They found that the optimal CS-US interval for the nictitating-membrane response was about .5 s, whereas that for the heart rate response was 6.75 s, despite using identical conditional and unconditional stimuli. The conditioning of a nictitating membrane response with a .5-s CS-US interval indicates that the CS was fully effective within .5 s and that the animal was capable of processing the CS in time to associate it with the US. Effectiveness cannot, therefore, explain the long CS-US interval that was optimal for heartrate conditioning. A better explanation is that the variance of the optimal CS-US interval depends on the CR being measured. Slow behaviors, such as heart rate responses, require longer CS-US intervals, whereas behaviors that occur quickly, such as a rabbit's nictitating membrane response, require shorter CS-US intervals. It seems that the optimal CS-US interval is not a simple product of the stimuli presented but relates directly to the behavioral system involved in the conditional response.

Dews' Experiments.   Dews (1962) examined directly the hypothesis that animals in tasks like delay conditioning respond directly to stimulus changes. His experiment was designed to remove the confound between such factors as sensory adaptation and the passage of time. Dews trained pigeons on a fixed-interval 500-s schedule (FI-500). Food was delivered for the first response to occur after 500 s had elapsed. On this schedule, the birds produced the typical fixed-interval scallop: They responded slowly at the beginning of an interval, and then increased their rate of response as the time of reinforcement approached. Dews then modified the experiment by turning the house light on and off in successive 50-s intervals during the FI period. The reward was still presented during a lighted interval after a total duration of 500 s. Under these conditions, the birds decreased responding while the light was off, but continued to respond at rates comparable to those observed in the standard 500-s interval when the light was on.

Turning the light off and on changes the effective visual stimuli significantly from the standard uninterruptedly lit interval. In the standard schedule, the birds had 500 s of sensory adaptation to the light, whereas in the alternating schedule, they had only 50 s to adapt to the light, followed by 50 s to readapt to the dark, followed by 50-s light adaptation, and so on. If the birds had regulated their response rate based on sensory effects, then we would expect them always to respond as if they were within the first 50 s of the fixed-interval schedule when tested with the alternating light/dark period. Instead, the birds continued to increase their rate of response correspondent to the time until reinforcement, not to the presence of the sensory stimulus. This experiment also illustrates that the animals could not have been using their own movements to time the duration of the interreinforcement interval. The pigeons decreased their response rates during the dark intervals, but kept response rate comparable to the standard interval during the light. Therefore, if the birds had been using something like total number of emitted pecks to judge the interval they would have judged the elapsed time with alternating light/dark intervals to be shorter (i.e., more time remaining until reinforcement) than the comparable elapsed time in the standard lit interval because fewer total responses were made. Dews' experiment suggests that these animals responded to the passage of time, not merely to changes in the effective properties of a stimulus situation or to perhaps ballistic properties of their own responses.

Some Techniques for Studying Timing

The experiments showing that timing is important in conditioning are consistent with other experiments that study animal timing more directly (see Church, 1978, 1984; Gibbon & Church, 1981, 1984; Roberts, 1981, 1983). Many of the same psychophysical techniques that have been used to study other stimulus dimensions in animals have been adapted to the study of timing in animals with similar results.

Temporal Matching.   One technique used to study animal timing directly is a variant of delayed matching-to-sample.   Animals are required to make a conditional discrimination between two alternatives on the basis of the duration of a preceding "sample" or "timing stimulus." One response is correct following "short" timing stimuli, and the other is the correct choice following "long" timing stimuli. Short stimuli are those that are shorter than a criterion duration and long stimuli are those that are longer than the criterion.   A trial begins with the presentation of a timing stimulus, typically a light or a tone, followed by a presentation of two choice stimuli (e.g., two different levers or two alternative stimulus patterns).

When the durations are plotted on a log scale, the result is an ogive, similar to that observed in many other psychophysical procedures relating choice probability to a stimulus dimension (e.g., brightness). The cumulative probability of reporting a "long" interval increases as the duration of the interval increases.   In addition, when pigeons are initially trained with only the shortest and longest durations and then tested with intermediate durations, the duration at which they are equally likely to respond short as long (the indifference point or the temporal bisection point) is the geometric mean of the two durations (Church & Deluty, 1977; Meck, 1984; Stubbs, 1976).   The bisection point is the duration that is judged by the animal as halfway between the shortest and longest durations.   This point is the midpoint between the two durations when measured on a log scale.   That the indifference point is the geometric mean (rather than the arithmetic mean) has important implications for the kind of clock animals use to time the duration of the timing stimulus. These implications are considered later.

Peak Procedure.   The *peak procedure* is another technique widely used to study temporal discrimination in rats (Meck, 1984; Roberts, 1981, 1983; cf. Wearden & McShane, 1988, for related data from human subjects). Two types of trials are randomly intermixed—fixed-interval (FI) trials and "empty" trials. Each trial begins with the presentation of a signal.   On FI-reinforced trials, a reinforcer is presented for the first response to occur at the end of the FI interval.   On empty trials, the signal is presented for twice as long as the reinforced interval, and no food is presented for any response.   The animal shows a typical FI scallop on reinforced FI trials.   Response rate is low at the start of the interval and increases until the reinforcer is delivered.   The informative data come from the empty trials.   Because at first the rat cannot discriminate FI from empty trials, the animal's response rate during the first half of the trial increases and reaches a peak at about the time that a reinforcer would have been given on a FI trial. The rate of response then decreases in a nearly symmetrical pattern for the rest of the trial.

The maximum response rate is called the *peak rate* and the time at which the peak rate occurs is called the *peak time*. The peak time indicates the point at which the animal maximally expects food.

The peak rate and the peak time can be dissociated. Increasing the proportion of empty trials decreases the peak rate of responding, but does not affect when that peak rate is produced. In contrast, prefeeding rats with lecithin or protein snacks shifts the peak time earlier, whereas prefeeding rats with carbohydrate snacks postpones the peak time (Meck & Church, 1987) without affecting peak rate. Other kinds of treatments have also been found to change the peak time. For example, injection of methamphetamine shortens the peak time, presumably because it speeds the operation of the clock (Maricq, Roberts, & Church, 1981). Additionally, the injection of certain drugs such as physostigmine or haloperidol, which modify brain neurotransmitter levels (Meck & Church, 1987), and brain lesions to the fimbria fornix (Meck, 1988), frontal cortex (Olton, 1989), medial septal area, or nucleus basalis magnocellularis (Meck, Church, Wenk, & Olton, 1987; Olton, 1989) of rats have been found to alter the peak time. These findings suggest that an increase in the effective levels of brain dopamine (e.g., due to methamphetamine or L-dopa) increases clock speed, and decreases in brain dopamine (e.g., due to haloperidol) decreases clock speed. Further, studies suggest that increases in the effective level of brain acetylcholine (e.g., due to carbohydrate snacks or lecithin loading) increases the memory-storage speed, thereby decreasing the remembered time of reinforcement; whereas decreases in the brain levels of acetylcholine (e.g., due to atropine) decreases memory-storage speed, increasing the remembered time of reinforcement (Meck & Church, 1987; Olton, 1989).

Properties of an Internal Clock

The data from these timing tasks lead to the conclusion that animals have access to internal clocks, which they can use to time events. Gibbon, Church, and their associates (e.g., Gibbon, 1977; Gibbon, & Church, 1981, 1984; Gibbon, Church, Fairhurst, & Kacelnik, 1988; Meck, 1984) have developed a theory, called *scalar timing theory*, based on the kind of timing mechanism shown in Figure 1.3 (see Grossberg & Schmajuk, 1989, for a related timing mechanism; and chapter 1, this volume). The system is composed of four major parts—a clock, a working memory, a reference memory, and an accumulator. This system detects the presence of a timing stimulus and measures its duration with a clock. It stores the measured duration in a working memory and can compare the value of the clock or the value of the working memory with some standard value stored in reference memory. The clock consists of a pacemaker, which produces pulses at regular intervals; a switch, which gates the pulses to the rest of the system; and an accumulator, which counts the pulses. When the switch is "on" (closed) pulses are allowed to pass from the pacemaker to the accumulator and the animal is timing some event. The value in the accumulator is then either passed to or combined with (depending on task demands) the value in working memory. The comparator can compare the value in the accumulator or the value in working memory with a standard value stored in reference memory and can decide whether the value in the accumulator is close enough to this standard to enable some response. When a response is made and a reinforcer is delivered, the information in the accumulator and working memory is transferred to reference memory for later use.

According to this model, the timing signal in the peak procedure causes the switch to "close" and thereby allows pulses to pass from the pacemaker to the accumulator. The total number of pulses in the accumulator is a measure of the time that has passed since the start of the timing signal. After some amount of training, reference memory contains the number of pulses that have in the past been followed by reinforcement. As the number of pulses totaled in the accumulator increases during the timing signal, their total approaches the value stored in reference memory and the comparator becomes increasingly likely to decide that the value of the accumulator is close enough to that stored in reference memory to enable a response. The animal becomes increasingly likely to respond. On empty trials, the timing signal increases beyond the time of reinforcement expected in the reference memory. As the difference between the total number of pulses and the value stored in reference memory grows, the animal becomes less and less likely to respond. Its peak response rate will, thus, occur at the time when the total number of pulses counted by the accumulator most closely matches the value in reference memory, that is the time at which reinforcers had been delivered in the past.

The clock in this timing system is similar to a human-made stopwatch. The pacemaker in an electronic stopwatch is an oscillating crystal that produces pulses at regular intervals. When the watch is timing, impulses from the crystal are counted by an electronic counter analogous to the accumulator and displayed on the face of the watch. The display can be continuously consulted to determine the current time and perhaps compare it with some criterion time. The watch can be stopped at the end of the event or a time can be stored in a kind of working memory (lap time) while continuing to accumulate time in the accumulator. Both the electronic and the animal's internal clock begin timing from 0 up to some value. Both scale time linearly. Both can be stopped temporarily, and both can be used to time different events. These similarities are considered in turn.

Clock Times Up. In order for an internal clock to be useful in performing temporal discriminations, animals must be able to compare the time elapsed with the value of remembered times. There are two ways such a comparison could be made. A countdown timer would start with the critical value in the accumulator and with each pulse decrease the count. When the accumulator reaches 0, the interval is judged to be complete. A kitchen timer is an example of a countdown timer. If you want to boil an egg for 5 min, you set the timer for 5 min. When the timer reaches 0, the bell rings, and you take the egg out of the pot. In contrast, the animal could use a countup timer, which starts with 0 in the accumulator, and increments the count with each pulse from the pacemaker. When the value in the accumulator matches the criterion value in reference memory, the interval is judged to be complete. A stopwatch is an example of a countup timer.

Shift experiments use a variant of the peak procedure. These experiments suggest that rats use a countup timer to compare the current time to a criterion value in reference memory. In shift experiments, rats begin an interval timing in the presence of one stimulus, then must shift to finish timing in the presence of another stimulus. The rat is trained such that each stimulus predicts different times of reinforcement. For example, in the presence of a light, food is presented after 20 s, whereas in the presence of a tone, food is presented after 40 s. A shift trial starts with the light for 5, 10, or 15 s, then shifts to the tone for a combined duration of 80 s. No food is presented during these trials.

A countdown timer would read "5 s left" if the shift from light to tone occurred after 15 s, "10 s left" if the shift occurred after 10 s, and "15 s left" if the shift occurred after 5 s. If the animal does not reset its countdown timer to the criterion value appropriate to the tone at the time of the switch then it should expect food at the time appropriate for the light (i.e., after 5 s on 15-s shift trials, after 10 s on 10-s shift trials, and after 15 s on 5-s shift trials). The peak time (i.e., the time of the peak rate) for an animal using a countdown timer that does not reset is predicted to be 20 s after the start of the trial. In contrast, if the animal does reset its timer, then the timer would read 40 s left when the tone is presented, regardless of when the shift occurs. The peak time for an animal using a countdown timer that resets is predicted to be 40 s after the switch (i.e., either 45, 50, or 55 s after the start of the trial, when the switch occurs after 5, 10, or 15 s, respectively).

Alternatively, the animal could use a countup timer. This timer begins the trial with a count of 0. The animal expects food when the value of the accumulator matches the criterion value in reference memory. An animal that uses a countup timer that does not reset would continue timing during the switch from the light to the tone, it would only change the criterion it uses for comparison. The peak time for an animal using a countup timer that does not reset is predicted to be 40 s after the start of the trial. Finally, an animal that uses a countup timer and resets the counter to 0 when the switch from light to tone occurs is predicted to produce its peak rate 40 s following the switch (i.e., either 45, 50, or 55 s after the start of the trial). These predictions are outlined in Table 6.1.

Roberts (1981) found that rats in this shift experiment showed a peak response rate 40 s after the start of the trial, as predicted by a timer that counts up continuously from the start of the trial. Apparently, rats continued timing from the start of the trial and compared the accumulated values with the value appropriate to the current stimulus.

Clock Can Be Stopped. Roberts (1981) trained rats on another version of the peak procedure task. Trials were signaled by a light. On standard trials food was delivered on a FI-40 s schedule. As is typical of this procedure no food was presented on empty trials. On occasional probe trials the light was interrupted for a 5- or 10-s gap. Except for the gap, these trials were identical to the ordinary empty trials. Rats delayed their peak time on the gap trials. Compared with the empty trials, the peak time of a gap trial was delayed 7.2 s if the blackout had lasted 5 s, and was 13.3 s if the gap had been 10 s. Only the peak times were changed by the blackouts; in all other respects responding was identical to that observed on empty trials.

It is interesting to note that the rats' peak times were consistently later when the timing signal was interrupted than when it ran continuously. This discrepancy may be attributable to differences in the time it takes the switch in the clock to open and close. While the light is on the animal closes the switch, presumably with some latency, and begins timing the signal. Similarly, there will presumably be some latency between the time the signal ends and the time the switch opens. These latencies present no difficulties on the standard and empty trials because the same latencies were present during training as during testing. Hence, the animal represents the duration of the interval including the latencies, and therefore has no difficulty measuring intervals including these

Table 6.1
Predictions of Peak Response Times with Four Types of Timers

Time of shift	Clock reading	Predicted peak time
	Clock times down, no reset	
5	15 s left	20 s
10	10 s left	20 s
15	5 s left	20 s
	Clock times down, reset	
5	40 s left	45 s
10	40 s left	50 s
15	40 s left	55 s
	Clock times up, continuous timing	
5	5 s	40 s
10	10 s	40 s
15	15 s	40 s
	Clock times up, reset	
5	0 s	45 s
10	0 s	50 s
15	0 s	55 s

Note. Animals are trained to expect food after 20 s in the presence of light and after 40 s in the presence of tone. Time of shift is the time at which the light is replaced with a tone. Clock reading is the value in the accumulator immediately following the presentation of the tone. For a countdown timer it shows the time left, for a countup timer it shows the time elapsed. The predicted peak time is the time since the start of a trial at which the peak response rate is expected to occur.

latencies. On the trials with the gap, however, the signal was stopped for a time and then restarted. Unlike the standard trials, therefore, the trials with the gap included two latencies associated with closing the switch—once at the start of the trial and once at the end of the gap, and one latency associated with opening the switch at the start of the gap. The decrease in the judged duration of the timing stimulus with the gap apparently reflects the difference between the time it takes the switch to close and the time it takes to open (see also Meck, Church, & Olton, 1984).

Linear Versus Logarithmic Time. In the timing system described earlier, the assumption that the pacemaker produces pulses at regular intervals implies that subjective time is a linear function of "real" time, as is measured by an electronic watch. Superficially, linear subjective time is difficult to reconcile with some of the known findings of animal timing, such as Weber's law (e.g., Yamashita, 1986) and the location of the midpoint between two durations at their geometric mean (Church & Deluty, 1977; Meck, 1984; Stubbs, 1968).

Weber's law holds that the judged difference between two intervals depends on the magnitude of the intervals being discriminated. In particular, the discriminability of two temporal intervals is equivalent when the ratios of these intervals is constant, independent of their absolute magnitude. For example, although one can discriminate fairly easily between 5 s and 10 s, one has difficulty discriminating between 1 hr and 1 hr plus 5 s without using a mechanical clock, although the difference between each of the two pairs of intervals is constant, the ratio of the longer to the shorter duration is smaller in the longer pair (2:1 vs. 3605:3600).

Both of these problems would be resolved if the animal's subjective time scale were the logarithm of real time instead of a linear function. Differences on a log scale correspond to ratios on a linear scale, and the mean of the logs of two durations is their geometric mean.

On a linear scale, the difference between two durations does not depend on the point at which they begin. When time is measured on a log scale, on the other hand, the difference does depend on the intervals starting point. Differences of a certain magnitude are larger on a log scale when they occur near the start of an interval than when they occur later in an interval, for example, the difference between 1 and 2 is much larger than the difference between 20 and 21 when measured on a log scale (.693 vs. .049). As a result, intervals in the future should be discounted relative to intervals in the present if the animal is using a log scale.

The available data, however, argue against a logarithmic subjective time scale (Gibbon, 1977; Gibbon & Church, 1981, 1984; Gibbon et al., 1988). For example, Gibbon and Church (1981) tested animals' comparisons of currently elapsing and future intervals to determine if, in fact, animals employed logarithmic differences and discounting in present and future intervals. In one experiment, rats were trained on two FI schedules. One removable lever in an operant chamber produced reinforcers on a fixed-interval 60-s schedule (FI-60), another produced reinforcers on a fixed-interval 30-s schedule (FI-30). The trial began with the presentation of the FI-60 lever. Then, either 15, 30, or 45 s later the FI-30 lever was inserted into the operant chamber. The animal was allowed either to continue responding on the FI-60 lever or to switch and begin responding on the FI-30 lever. Presumably, the rat will tend to choose the lever that offers the subjectively shorter time to reinforcement. One would expect the rat to switch from the FI-60 to the FI-30 lever if it judged the time left until reinforcement on the FI-60 lever to be greater than the time left on the FI-30 lever. Likewise, it would continue to respond on the FI-60 lever if it judged the time remaining until reinforcement on the FI-60 lever to be less than that of the FI-30 lever.

If the animal judges time on a logarithmic scale, then when comparing a partially elapsed interval (FI-60) with the newly presented duration (FI-30), the animal should judge the elapsing time on the FI-60 lever to be less than the fresh time on the FI-30 lever, no matter when the FI-30 lever is presented, because of the nature of future discounting. On a logarithmic scale, the time remaining until reinforcement on the FI-30 lever when it is inserted is proportional to 3.40. If 15 s has already elapsed on the FI-60 lever, then the time remaining until reinforcement on this lever is proportional to the log of the total 60-s interval minus the log of the already elapsed time, or 4.09 - 2.71 = 1.38. Hence, the animal should prefer the ongoing FI-60 lever at all times tested if its subjective time is logarithmic. On the other hand, if subjective time is linear, then the animal should prefer the FI-30 lever if the time remaining on the FI-60 lever is more than 30 s, should prefer the FI-60 lever if time remaining is less than 30 s, and should be indifferent if the two durations are equal. Animals in this experiment generally selected the response alternative with the shorter remaining time to reinforcement, thus indicating that they judged time along a linear rather than a logarithmic scale. Gibbon (1977) has developed a scalar timing theory to explain the data just discussed, which accommodates the apparent contradictions found by Weber's law and which explains why the midpoint of two durations is the geometric mean.

Scalar Timing Theory. Scalar timing theory proposes that the variability of judgments, not the scale along which these judgments are made, increases with the duration being judged. Subjective time is assumed to be a linear rather than a logarithmic function, but two times are compared according to their ratio rather than their arithmetic difference. The theory also assumes that the coefficient of variation of subjective time is constant: The standard deviation of a judged duration increases proportionally with the magnitude of the duration (e.g., due to variability in the rate of pulse production by the pacemaker). Scalar timing theory is consistent with the timing results just reviewed, without predicting the kind of future discounting required by the use of a log scale. Ratios in a linear scale correspond to differences on a log scale, and a constant coefficient of variation on a linear scale corresponds to a constant variance in a log scale. The appropriate conclusion from these experiments on animal timing is that subjective time for an animal is judged along a linear scale with a constant coefficient of variation as predicted by scalar timing theory.

In terms of the timing model depicted in Figure 1.3, these findings support the notion that timing is ultimately controlled by a pacemaker that produces pulses at a more or less steady rate (although with some variance in this rate). These findings also suggest that the comparator operates by computing the ratio between the current value in the accumulator and/or in working memory to that in reference memory. The decisions reported by the comparator depend on the value of this ratio, not on the absolute differences between the values.

SEQUENTIAL BEHAVIOR

In addition to representing the interval properties of time, animals also represent time's ordinal properties. Events not only occur with some measurable duration, they occur in a particular order relative to one another. As James (1890) noted, a succession of feelings is not sufficient to provide a feeling of succession. Representation of the ordinal properties of time requires more than an ordered set of representations, it requires that the items all be represented at the same time along with information about the order of their succession. A coherent representation of order is one in which the items and their order are represented explicitly and as a unit. Neither sequential behavior nor sequence discrimination demand that the animal employ coherent representations of the sequence; many alternative schemes are available that allow the animal to perform appropriately with other sorts of more disjoint representations.

Nonsequential Representations of Sequential Behavior

There are many schemes an animal could use to represent information about the order of a set of events. An animal can behave under certain conditions as if it had a representation of the order of a set of events without a coherent representation of the sequence if it has sufficient information to compute the ordering relation. For example, in classical conditioning, the order of the CS and US are very important in determining what kind if any conditioning occurs. If the CS occurs before the US, then conditioning occurs, if the CS occurs following the US, then no conditioning or inhibitory conditioning may occur. These facts of conditioning might imply that the animal has an explicit representation of the sequence of the CS and US (see earlier discussion). In the standard Pavlovian analysis of conditioning as well as in more recent analyses of conditioning (e.g., Wagner, 1981), the order of the CS and US are important to conditioning, but their order is not represented by the animal. Instead, the presentation of the CS is thought to activate a representation (or excitation, etc.) of the US that follows it. If the US does not follow the CS, then the CS cannot elicit or activate an appropriate representation and the animal does not respond. The requirement that the CS precede the US for conditioning is a product of the patterns of activation, not evidence for the explicit representation of the order of the two stimuli.

Similarly, an animal that has learned to traverse a multiunit maze always performs the correct responses in a particular order. It may be tempting to assume that the animal has a representation of the sequence of left and right turns it must execute at each choice point. Correct traversal of the maze, however, does not require a representation of the order of the choices. Each choice point is unique (i.e., it is in a unique location, and is associated with unique stimuli) and the animal need have no information about how it reached a choice point in order to make the correct response there (Bever, Straub, Terrace, & Townsend, 1980). The sequential order of the choices derives from the sequential order of the choice points, not from a coherent representation of the order of choices. As each response takes the animal to the next choice point, the stimuli associated with that point cue the animal to make a particular response, independent of the path or order by which the animal arrived at that choice point. The observed sequence of performance is due to an unordered representation of choice-point response pairs.

In both of these examples, the causal structure of the environment allows the animal to behave as if it had a coherent ordered representation of the sequence of events in the task. Earlier stimuli can only activate responses that follow, they cannot be cues for responses that precede them. The structure of the maze carries the animal from one choice point to the next when it makes the response appropriate to that choice point.

Animals can also use other heuristics to perform in sequentially structured tasks. For example, a pigeon could discriminate a two-color sequence AB (where A and B stand for different colors) from BA, either on the basis of the first stimulus in the sequence (a primacy heuristic) or on the basis of the final stimulus in the sequence (a recency heuristic; see Weisman, Wasserman, Dodd, & Larew, 1980). In order to rule out a primacy explanation, one must show that the animal performs differentially as a function of the later stimulus. For example, if the animal responds differently to the sequences AB and AA, then the animal is sensitive to the identity of the second stimulus in the sequence, and cannot, therefore, be using a simple primacy heuristic. Similarly, if the animal discriminates between the sequence AB and BB, then the animal cannot be using a strict recency heuristic. The general principle is that the animal can be expected to be indifferent to stimulus changes along dimensions not included in its representation; the animal will treat as equivalent stimuli that are represented identically, even if they differ along nominal dimensions that are not represented.

Other behaviors seem to require the presence of a coherent representation of the sequence. Certain kinds of skilled movements, such as typewriting or piano playing require finger movements that are so rapid that there is insufficient time for the information about a preceding response to travel to the brain and then to the finger in time to make the next movement (Lashley, 1951). Therefore, the performance of one note in an arpeggio cannot serve as a cue for the next note in the same way that the presence at a choice point can serve as a cue for the next choice. Speed of response in other situations also suggests explicit representation of ordered information. Some young piano players find it very difficult to play a piece of music without starting at the beginning of the unit or of the piece. The latency to respond with the next letter in the alphabet (e.g., given D the correct response is E) depends on the location of those letters in the alphabet. More particularly, the latency depends on the distance of the letters from the start of one of the phrases in the alphabet song most North Americans learn as children (Klahr, Chase, & Lovelace, 1983). The first few phrases are ABCD-EFG-HIJK-LMNOP. Latency increases within phrases and decreases at the start of a new phrase. Similar investigations, so far as we are aware, have not been conducted with animals.

Serial Anticipation Learning

Both human and nonhuman animals find learning complex sequences to be more difficult than simple sequences (Hulse & Dorsky, 1977; Jones, 1974; Restle & Brown, 1970). For example, a human subject might be shown the following sequence, 4 5 1 2 3 4 4 5 1 3 4 5 4 5, and asked to produce the next five elements in the sequence. Anticipation of this sequence is more difficult than anticipation of the following simpler sequence, 4 5 1 2 3 4 5 1 2 3 4 5 1 2. Animals show similar sensitivity to the complexity of the sequence. Two patterns consisting of exactly the same elements can be either difficult or simple for the animal to learn depending on the structural properties of that sequence.

Animal serial-anticipation tasks typically employ sequences constructed from an alphabet of food rewards of different sizes. Rats, for example, are trained to run down an alley in anticipation of a food reward. The size of the food reward (number of food pellets) changes from one run to the next in some regular pattern, and the rat's running speed is taken as an index of its expectation for the size of the food reward. Provided the pattern is sufficiently simple, rats learn to run quickly in anticipation of large rewards and slowly in anticipation of small rewards.

In one set of experiments (Hulse & Dorsky, 1977, 1979), rats were trained either with a monotonic sequence or with a nonmonotonic sequence. Each run in the monotonic sequence was rewarded with decreasing numbers of food pellets (14-7-3-1-0). The first run of the sequence was rewarded with 14 pellets, the second with 7, and so on, until the final run of the sequence, which was not rewarded (the 0-pellet element). The same elements were presented in the nonmonotonic sequence, but in a different order (14-1-3-7-0). Like the monotonic sequence, the nonmonotonic sequence began with a 14-pellet element and ended with a 0-pellet element. Rats trained with the monotonic sequence learned to anticipate, that is run slowly to, the terminal 0-pellet element, but rats trained with the nonmonotonic sequence ran equally quickly to all of the elements.

Both the monotonic and the nonmonotonic sequences are made of the same elements. They differ only in the relation between successive elements. The monotonic sequence can be described by a simple rule according to which each element is less than the preceding elements, whereas the nonmonotonic sequence cannot be described by the same kind of rule. The difference in the ease with which each sequence is learned suggests that the rats are sensitive to the abstract relational properties of the sequence.

Alternative Representations

Although the difference in ease of learning between the monotonic and the nonmonotonic sequences is consistent with a coherent sequence representation, animals could use a number of other strategies to solve the anticipation problem. Several dimensions are correlated in the standard experiment (Hulse & Dorsky, 1977, 1979) and the rats could use representations of one of these correlated dimensions instead of a coherent sequence representation. For example, as rats receive successive elements in the sequence they eat cumulatively greater numbers of food pellets (14 after the first run, a total of 21 after the second run, etc. in the monotonic sequence). Rats may run more slowly to later elements in the decreasing series because of increasing satiety rather than as a result of a coherent representation of the sequence. Alternatively, rats may anticipate the terminal 0-pellet element on the basis of the passage of time or on the basis of the cumulative number of previous elements in the series.

Although satiety, temporal anticipation, and counting are logically possible accounts of serial-anticipation learning in rats, in fact, none of them provides an adequate account, because all three variables are equally good predictors of the terminal 0-pellet element in both the monotonic and the nonmonotonic sequences. Animals in both groups have received four elements containing 25 food pellets prior to the presentation of the terminal 0-pellet element. Therefore, rats in both groups should be equally sated and should have counted the same number of preceding elements. Additionally, rats learn equally well to anticipate (run slowly to) the 0-pellet element whether it comes at the end of a monotonically decreasing sequence or at the beginning of a monotonically increasing sequence (Hulse & Campbell, 1975). Finally, rats can be run on multiple trials in a day without any obvious correlation between running speed and the cumulative number of food pellets eaten that day. These correlated variables, therefore, do not provide an adequate account of serial-anticipation learning.

Rats' representations of the serial-anticipation task apparently include information about the items in the sequence. There are at least three hypotheses for how animals use this information. According to the association-generalization hypothesis, rats represent the sequence as sets of paired associates. Receipt of the 14-pellet element cues an expectation of the 7-pellet element. Presentation of the 1-pellet element cues the presentation of the 0-pellet element, and so forth. Like the rats in a multiunit maze, the sequential performance of the rats in the serial-anticipation task may be the result of a direct association between a stimulus situation (receipt of an element of a particular size) and a response (running at a certain speed). A model of this sort has been suggested by Capaldi and his associates (e.g., Capaldi, Verry, & Davidson, 1980, see also Roitblat, 1982).

A rule-based model proposes that the animal learns a rule like item $i + 1$ < item i. Hulse and Dorsky (1977, 1979) proposed a representation of this sort. According to this model, the animal represents the sequence in terms of the rule. A strong version of the model denies that animals have any specific information about the items in the sequence. A weaker version of the model assumes that the primary representation of the sequence is in terms of the monotonic rule, but the animal may also have information about the specific values that appear in the sequence. The relative difficulty of the nonmonotonic sequence, however, suggests that rats have very little knowledge about the specific items (or the knowledge that they do have is not particularly useful) and rely instead on their relationship, because the very same items appear in both sequences, differing only by their order. Like the association-generalization view of serial-anticipation learning, the rule-based view implies that the animal responds to successive items in the sequence on the basis of the preceding items. The association-generalization model attributes this response to learned associations between successive items and the rule-based model attributes this response to employment of the rule. A third possibility is that the rats employ a coherent representation of the sequence.

Rule Encoding. According to the rule-encoding hypothesis, the animal's primary representation of the sequence is in terms of the rule relating successive items in the sequence to previous items in the sequence. Monotonic sequences are, thus, easier to learn because they can be described by a single very simple rule. Nonmonotonic sequences are more difficult to learn because they require a more complex rule (e.g., a U-shaped function of serial position).

There is considerable support for the use of rules in rats' representations of the serial-anticipation task. For example, Hulse and Dorsky (1979) trained rats with sequences of variable length between two and four elements (e.g. 10-5-3-1, 10-3-1-0, 10-3-0, 5-1-0, 5-3, 10-0). In this experiment there was no reliable pairing between successive elements, so learning of a paired association between successive elements was very difficult. For example, the 10-pellet element could be followed by a 5-pellet element in the four-item sequences, by either a 5-pellet or a 3-pellet element in the three item sequence, and by any element in the 2-element sequence. A control group was trained with sequences of the same elements presented in a scrambled order.

After training with these sequences for 70 trials (each trial consists of a presentation of the complete series), the rats were tested on new five-element sequences (16-9-3-1-0 or 16-1-3-9-0). Rats that had initially been trained on the variable length monotonic sequences learned the new monotonic sequence very quickly relative to the other groups, and learned the nonmonotonic sequence more slowly than did the other groups.   Previous training with the monotonic rule thus facilitated learning a new monotonic sequence and interfered with learning a new nonmonotonic sequence, suggesting that the animals represented the *monotonicity* of the sequence.

Association-Generalization Model.   In addition to representing the rule relation between successive elements, rats also appear to represent information about the specific magnitudes.   The strong rule-encoding hypothesis argues that the magnitude of the stimuli in the sequence is irrelevant because the animal uses only the rule to reduce its expectancy for the value of the succeeding element.   In contrast, the association-generalization model emphasizes the relationship among specific items in the sequence.   The model assumes that running speed is controlled by the excitatory potential associated with each element.   An item's excitatory potential, in turn, depends on the magnitude of the item it cues (the following item in the sequence) and on its similarity to other items.   In a 14-7-3-1-0 sequence, for example, the 7-pellet element gains some excitatory potential from its similarity to the 14-pellet element and from the fact that the 14-pellet element signals the 7-pellet element.   It gains weaker excitatory potential from its similarity to the 3-pellet element and its signalling of the 1-pellet element.   The animal uses the receipt of the 7-pellet element to control its running speed to the next element in the sequence.   According to this model, monotonic sequences are easier to learn because they present consistent patterns of association and generalization.   Nonmonotonic sequences are more difficult to learn because they present inconsistent patterns of association and generalization.   For example, in the sequence, 14-1-3-7-0, the expectancy cued by the 7-pellet element is inconsistent because it directly cues the 0-pellet element, but it is similar to the 3-pellet element, which signals the 7-pellet element and is similar to the 14-pellet element, which signals the 1-pellet element.

The importance of the association-generalization model is not in its ability to explain the data obtained by Hulse and his associates.   In general it cannot do so (see Roitblat, 1982).   Instead, the hypothesis is important for the attention it calls to the similarity among the elements in the sequence.   It seems clear that animals know something about the particular items in the sequence in addition to knowing about the relationship among items (see Capaldi, Nawrocki, & Verry, 1982; Capaldi, Verry, & Davidson, 1980; Capaldi, Verry, & Nawrocki, 1982).

The rule-based and the association-generalization models differ in the type of representations they attribute to the animals.   The rule-based model emphasizes the relations among the items and the representation of this relation as an abstract rule. In contrast, the association-general-ization model emphasizes the particular items in the sequence, represented as paired associates between items accompanied by generalization among similar items.

Coherent Sequence Representations. A third alternative is that the animal employs a coherent representation of the sequence, containing information about the order of the events and their magnitude, as well as some more abstract information about their relationship. In one experiment (Roitblat, Pologe & Scopatz, 1983) rats were trained to anticipate the sequence 14-7-3-1-0. Following acquisition they were tested on occasional probe trials in which one of the elements in the sequence was replaced by a 0-pellet element (i.e., either 0-7-3-1-0, 14-0-3-1-0, 14-7-0-1-0, or 14-7-3-0-0). If the rats were using paired associates to represent the sequence, then performance should be disrupted on the run following the 0-pellet element because the 0-pellet element has always been at the end of the sequence and no element has been learned to follow it. On the other hand, if the rats were using a strong version of the rule-based hypothesis, then performance following the 0-pellet probe element should be disrupted because the rats had learned a less-than rule and no value is less than this probe item. In contrast to both of these predictions, the rats' running speeds to the item following the probe 0-pellet element was indistinguishable from their speeds on comparable runs in the standard sequence. These results show clearly that rats use more information than the preceding element to determine their running speed in the serial-anticipation task (see also Capaldi et al., 1980). Animals appear to form coherent representations of these kinds of sequences that contain more global and abstract information about the sequence. These representations are not disrupted when a novel element occasionally replaces one of the elements in the sequence.

SEQUENCE DISCRIMINATION

Animals have also been trained in sequence recognition tasks. The serial-anticipation task tests animals' ability to anticipate a sequence that is consistent from trial to trial and that provides feedback at each point in the sequence. In contrast, experiments on sequence discrimination test the animals' ability to discriminate one sequence of elements from other sequences of the same events. Feedback is delayed until the end of the trial.

One example of this procedure has already been described (Weisman et al., 1980). The pigeons in that experiment were trained to discriminate a sequence of two colors, designated AB, from other sequences made from the same two colors (AA, BA, and BB) and from sequences containing a third element, X (XA, XB, AX, BX, and XX), which was actually a dark, unfilled interval. Pecks to a test stimulus, presented following the sequence, were reinforced if the sequence had been AB but not if any other sequence had been presented. Discrimination was indicated by the difference in response rates following the positive relative to the negative sequences.

Negative sequences AA, XA, and those ending in X were the easiest for the animals to learn to discriminate from the positive sequence, AB. In contrast, sequences ending with B (BB and XB) were the most difficult, and the sequence BA was intermediate. These results indicate that pigeons can discriminate sequences on the basis of the order of the elements. They use both elements in the sequence in making their discrimination (AX and XB are discriminated from AB), but the final element is particularly important in that negative sequences that end with the same final element as the positive sequence are the most difficult to discriminate from the positive sequence.

Schemes for Sequence Discrimination

The birds must compare each sequence that is presented with some representation of the positive sequence in order to discriminate them. There are a number of different schemes animals could use to represent and discriminate these sequences. These include retrospective scanning, prospective conditional discriminations, and coherent hierarchical sequence representations. As the term is used here, a *scheme* is a combination of a class of representations and a set of processes for operating on those representations.

Retrospective Scanning. Using a retrospective-scanning scheme, the animal would hold each stimulus in working memory and then compare the remembered list of stimuli with an analogous list of the positive sequence (represented in reference memory; see Honig, 1978). This scheme is retrospective in that it assumes that the pigeon postpones its decision until the test stimulus is presented. It then "scans backward" over its list of remembered stimuli and compares the scanned list with its permanent representation of the positive sequence. As previously noted, the animal must have some means not only of identifying the stimuli that had been presented in the sequence, but also of identifying the order of their appearance. One possibility for representing order would be to use the strength of the representation of each stimulus as an analog of its time of arrival. If each stimulus generates a "trace" of a certain strength, which then begins to weaken with time, the relative strengths of the stimuli could provide a cue for the time of presentation of each stimulus. In this case, sequence discrimination becomes a problem of trace-strength discrimination.   Alternatively, the animal could directly represent the time of arrival of each stimulus (e.g., by reference to an ongoing clock) and keep track of order on that basis.   In this case, sequence discrimination becomes a problem of temporal discrimination.

Prospective Conditional Discrimination.   Using a prospective conditional discrimination scheme, an animal would compare each element as it is presented with the corresponding element in the positive sequence. For example, in the two-element sequence discrimination described earlier, the presence of the B stimulus at the start of a trial is sufficient to reject the sequence because the positive sequence begins with A. The use of this scheme provides an opportunity for the bird to minimize its working memory load because it need only remember the most recently presented stimulus and whether the sequence has yet been rejected or not.   On this view, the animal processes a sequence until it reaches a stimulus that does not match the corresponding stimulus in the positive sequence and then stops processing further stimuli.

This prospective scheme employs an unordered set of production rules. A production rule is a conditional instruction, containing a set of criterion conditions and an action. When the conditions for the rule have been met, the production "fires" and the specified action is taken. The action can be almost anything, in this case, it is a modification of the contents of memory or a decision to peck or not peck at the test stimulus. The conditions in this case are specified combinations of a working memory state and a stimulus. Table 6.2 shows an example production system that is adequate to perform the two-item sequence discrimination, described earlier.

The animal must discriminate the start of the trial and each of the stimuli. It begins the trial with its memory in a starting state. The combination of start state and the presentation of the green stimulus causes a change to the peck state. The combination of the start state and any other stimulus causes the animal to enter a reject state. The combination of a peck state and the presentation of the red stimulus causes the animal to stay in the peck state. Other combinations cause it to either enter or remain in the reject state. The combination of the peck state and the presentation of the test stimulus causes the pigeon to

Table 6.2
A Production System for Sequence Discrimination

Memory	Stimulus	Memory production	Action production
Start	Green	Peck	
Start	Red	Reject	
Peck	Red	Peck	
Peck	Green	Reject	
Peck	Test		Pecking
Reject	Any stimulus	Reject	No pecking

Note. After Roitblat, 1987. Adapted by permission.

peck at the test stimulus. Otherwise the pigeon does not peck. This scheme is analogous to that described earlier for the solution of a maze on the basis of associations between choice points and responses. The rules are not represented in any particular order, they do not specify explicit information about the sequence other than the information embodied in the conditional structure of the individual rules. As in the maze, the serial structure of the discrimination derives from the structure imposed by the sequentially presented stimuli.

There are several important differences between the retrospective scanning and prospective schemes. According to the prospective scheme the bird makes its decisions during the course of the presentation of the stimuli rather than at the end of the sequence. This scheme assumes that the contents of working memory is a decision whether to peck or reject the sequence. In contrast, the retrospective model assumes that the contents of working memory include the stimuli that were presented along with information concerning the time of their presentation.

The same kind of prospective production system can be extended to longer sequences. With only two stimuli in the sequence, three memory states are necessary. At the start of the trial the bird's memory is in state "Start." After the first stimulus is presented the bird's memory is either in state "Peck" or in state "Reject." As noted in Table 6.2, all decisions can be made unambiguously given these memory states and no other information about the sequence. An additional memory state is necessary for a three-item sequence. In another experiment Weisman et al. (1980) trained pigeons to discriminate three-item sequences consisting of two colors followed by a line orientation. The sequences green-red-horizontal (designated ABC) and red-green-vertical (designated BAD) were positive, other sequences (AAC, BAC, BBC, AAD, ABD, BBD) were negative. The line-orientation stimuli served as both the third element in the sequence and the test stimulus.

The use of ABC and BAD as positive sequences meant that there was no fixed relation between the serial position of the stimulus and whether it was positive or negative. The animal could no longer reject a sequence that began with B because one of the positive sequences did begin with B. The bird could not make a final determination about whether the sequence was positive or negative until either the second (in sequences starting BB or AA) or third stimulus (in sequences BAC and ABD) had been presented and identified. Nevertheless, the birds learned this discrimination about as rapidly as the simple two-item sequence discrimination.

Although there was no fixed relation between serial position and item identity, a prospective production system could still be used to perform this discrimination. Three memory states are required. These can be labeled "Null," "Green," and "Red." The animal starts in state "Null" at the start of a trial. The combination of the "Null" state and the presentation of red places the memory in state "Red." The combination of the "Null" state and the presentation of green puts the memory in state "Green." The combination of state "Red" and the presentation of green puts the memory in state "Green." The presentation of red and the memory state "Green" puts the memory in state "Red." Other combinations of memory states and colors put the memory in state "Null." The combination of memory state Red and the presentation of the vertical line produces pecking as does the combination of memory state "Green" and the presentation of the horizontal line. The "Null" state in combination with either line-orientation stimulus produces no pecking.

This scheme, like the one for discriminating two-item sequences, allows the animal to perform a sequence discrimination without a coherent, ordered representation of the sequence. An unordered set of transition rules provides the animal with sufficient information to properly discriminate the sequences. In general, a prospective production system will require one memory state more than the number of stimuli in the sequence, assuming that negative sequences can contain any combination of the stimuli. If stimuli are constrained so that some stimuli can appear in only a limited range of serial positions (e.g., the line orientation stimuli appeared only in the third position), then a production system with fewer memory states will often be sufficient.

In support of a prospective conditional discrimination scheme, some experiments have found that pigeons are capable of deciding and reporting that a particular sequence is negative even before the sequence ends. These experiments employed a variation of the standard sequence discrimination procedure in which the pigeon is allowed to indicate a decision before the end of the sequence. For example, Weisman, Gibson, and Rochford (1984) provided their pigeons with an "advance" key. The advance key was available throughout a trial. A peck to this key terminated the trial and advanced immediately to the next trial. Weisman and his associates found that pigeons frequently responded to terminate the presentation of a negative sequence before the sequence was complete. Termination of the trial before its completion indicates that the birds could identify the sequence as a negative exemplar before its presentation was complete. Hence, these data are inconsistent with the notion that the pigeons wait until the end of the sequence to make their decision.

Terrace (1986) trained pigeons on another variant of this task. He provided two keys. Pecks to the positive key were reinforced if the positive (ABC) sequence had been presented and pecks to the negative key were reinforced if the negative sequence had been presented. The positive and negative keys were always presented in a consistent location. Although they were not illuminated until the end of the sequence, Terrace discovered that the pigeons were responding to the locations of these two keys on a substantial number of trials, prior to the end of the sequence.

Both of these experiments (Terrace, 1986; Weisman, et al., 1984) show that animals do not always need to wait for the end of the sequence to make a decision about its identity. Terrace interpreted these results as evidence for a purely prospective scheme and as evidence against the use of higher-order sequence representations.

Hierarchical Sequence Representations. In contrast to the predictions of the prospective production system scheme, Roitblat, Scopatz, and Bever (1987) found evidence that pigeons use hierarchical representations in three-item sequence discriminations. Roitblat et al. tested three-element sequences in which a single test stimulus appeared following the sequence. The positive sequence consisted of a series of three colors (designated ABC corresponding to different colors for different birds), and the negative sequences consisted of the other 26 combinations of these same colors (e.g., AAA, BAC, BCA, CAC). Pecks to the test stimulus following the positive sequence were reinforced, and pecks following the negative sequences were not reinforced.

Roitblat and his associates investigated the patterns by which the elements of the sequence gained control over responding. They used a regression technique to estimate the degree to which seven discernable units in the sequence were controlling discriminative performance. One unit represented each of the three stimulus elements, one unit represented the combination of the first and second elements, one represented the combination of the first and third elements, one represented the combination of the second and third, and the final unit represented the combination of the first, second, and third elements. Each of these units took on a positive value if the corresponding elements in the sequence were identical to those in the same position in the positive sequence, and took on negative values otherwise.

Early in acquisition, the pigeon's performance was controlled largely by the final element in the sequence. If this final element matched the final element in the positive sequence (i.e., stimulus C), then the bird pecked at the test stimulus. If it did not match, then the bird did not peck. Later in training, the birds' performance was controlled by higher-order combinations of units, for example, by the combination of the first and the third elements. Control by this combination unit produced responding when the presented sequence contained the A stimulus in the first position and the C stimulus in the third position, but not when other combinations appeared in these two positions. Control by higher-order combination units indicates that pigeons represent the sequences they learn in a hierarchical fashion and base their decisions on the correspondence between the presented sequences and their representation of the positive sequence. The observation that some of these higher-order units involve nonadjacent stimuli (e.g., the combination of the first and third stimuli) is inconsistent with a number of list-processing schemes, including the prospective conditional discrimination scheme, that could be used to discriminate the sequences. It suggests that the birds wait until the end of the sequence, that is until all of the elements represented by the relevant higher-order unit are presented, to make decisions regarding the identity of the sequence.

These data raise serious questions about the adequacy of the prospective conditional discrimination scheme as a basis for sequence discrimination. For example, Terrace (1986) noted that on a substantial number of trials the bird changed its decision after more complete information was available. Because a response to the advance key terminated the trial, similar data are not available from the study by Weisman and his associates (1984). Terrace also found that discrimination was poorest when the sequences ended with stimulus C, regardless of the stimuli that preceded it. A prospective decision model would predict that 24 of the 26 negative sequences would be rejected before the third stimulus was even presented (see Roitblat et al., 1987), and therefore, easily discriminated from the positive sequence. Taken together, these results certainly weaken the claim that Terrace's pigeons employed a prospective rather than a hierarchical representational scheme.

Roitblat, Bever, Harley, and Helweg (1989) tested pigeons on a three-element sequence discrimination with dual test keys. Like Terrace's (1986) procedure, pecks to one key were reinforced following the positive sequence (ABC) and pecks to the other stimulus were reinforced following negative sequences (all other combinations of A, B, and C). Unlike, Terrace's procedure, however, the choice keys were distinguished by a visual pattern, rather than by their position. As a result, the bird could not know where to peck until the choice keys were presented. On some trials the choice keys were presented at the start of the sequence; on some trials they were presented along with the second stimulus or the third stimulus. On the remaining trials they were presented only following the sequence. Once presented, they remained illuminated and in the same location until the end of the trial. Pecks to the choice stimuli before the end of the sequence were recorded, but had no programmed consequences. The first peck to one of the choice stimuli following the sequence, however, terminated the trial and was either rewarded or not depending on its accuracy.

Analysis of the latencies to respond to the two choice stimuli following the different sequences yielded a pattern of results similar to that observed earlier in the single-test, three-item discrimination using response rates (Roitblat et al., 1987). Five of the nine birds in this study showed patterns of responding that were apparently controlled by higher-order combinations involving nonadjacent stimuli (e.g., the combination of the first and third stimuli considered as a unit). As a result, these data are inconsistent with a prospective conditional discrimination scheme that says that discrimination of each element in the sequence is conditional on the immediately preceding element. Presenting the choice keys during the presentation of the sequence, therefore, does not seem to compel a linear prospective analysis of the sequence of the sort described by Terrace (1986). One explanation for the inconsistency between the results obtained from this experiment and Terrace's analysis is the finer-grain analysis conducted in the present experiment. The effects of combinations of stimuli are obscured by Terrace's decision to give choice accuracies only for classes of sequences characterized by individual elements (e.g., sequences beginning with C), averaged over the various combinations of the remaining stimuli. The results of his experiment, may have been supportive of a role for combination units, but we cannot know how supportive.

Analysis of the responses made during the sequence presentation indicates that pigeons do not need to wait until the end of the sequence in order to make a decision. Although responses during the sequence had no programmed consequences, our birds, like Terrace's (1986) responded on a substantial number of trials and discriminated positive from negative sequences with greater than chance accuracy. Like responding at the end of the sequence, responding during the sequence showed a sensitivity to more features of the sequence than the current stimulus. For example, sequences in which both of the so-far presented elements were different from the positive sequence were discriminated better than when only the second stimulus was different from the positive sequence. These patterns of online choice reveal that even the choices made during the course of the sequence presentation reflect the complex interaction among stimuli. They are not merely the result of start-to-finish conditional discriminations. Hence, they suggest that pigeons employ a coherent representation of the sequence in making their discrimination.

CONCLUSION

A major concern in the study of animal timing has been the extent to which the animal's behavior is controlled by internal abstract mechanisms versus the extent to which it is controlled by external variables. The behaviorist tradition emphasized the control by external variables and attributed temporal patterns of responding to temporal patterns in stimuli. The data seem clear that animals have access to and that they use internal clocks to control many aspects of their performance, including circadian and event timing. The data also seem clear that animals form and use hierarchical coherent representations of serially structured events. Again, the behaviorist tradition suggested that the serially structured behavior is merely the simple response to serially structured stimuli. In contrast, the data reviewed in this chapter suggest that this performance is controlled by more abstract representations that include information about events and their order.

REFERENCES

Bever, T. G., Straub, R. O., Terrace, H. S., & Townsend, D. J. (1980). A comparative study of serially integrated behavior in humans and animals. In P. Jusczyk & R. Klein (Eds.), *The nature of thought: Essays in honor of D. O. Hebb* (pp. 51-93). Hillsdale, NJ: Lawrence Erlbaum Associates.

Capaldi, E. J., Nawrocki, T. M., & Verry, D. R. (1982). Difficult serial anticipation learning in rats: Rule encoding vs. memory. *Animal Learning and Behavior, 10,* 167-170.

Capaldi, E. J., Verry, D. R., & Davidson, T. L. (1980). Memory, serial anticipation pattern learning and transfer in rats. *Animal Learning and Behavior, 8,* 575-585.

Capaldi, E. J., Verry, D. R., & Nawrocki, T. M. (1982). Multiple hedonic memory: Memory for more than one hedonic event in rats. *Animal Learning and Behavior, 10,* 351-357.

Church, R. M., & Deluty, M. Z. (1977). Bisection of temporal intervals. *Journal of Experimental Psychology: Animal Behavior Processes, 3,* 216-228.

Church, R. M. (1978). The internal clock. In S. H. Hulse, H. Fowler, & W. K. Honig (Eds.), *Cognitive processes in animal behavior* (pp. 277-310). Hillsdale, NJ: Lawrence Erlbaum Associates.

Church, R. M. (1984). Properties of the internal clock. In J. Gibbon & L. Allan (Eds.), *Timing and time perception* (pp. 566-582). New York: New York Academy of Sciences.

Dews, P. B. (1962). The effect of multiple S^Δ periods on responding on a fixed-interval schedule. *Journal of the Experimental Analysis of Behavior, 5,* 369-374.

Gibbon, J. (1977). Scalar expectancy theory and Weber's law in animal timing. *Psychological Review, 84,* 279-325.

Gibbon, J., & Church, R. M. (1981). Time left: Linear vs. logarithmic subjective time. *Journal of Experimental Psychology: Animal Behavior Processes, 7,* 87-107.

Gibbon, J., & Church, R. M. (1984). Sources of variance in an information processing theory of timing. In H. L. Roitblat, T. G. Bever, & H. S. Terrace (Eds.), *Animal Cognition* (pp. 465-488). Hillsdale, NJ: Lawrence Erlbaum Associates.

Gibbon, J., Church, R. M., Fairhurst, S., & Kacelnik, A. (1988). Scalar expectancy theory and choice between delayed rewards. *Psychological Review, 95,* 102-114.

Grossberg, S., & Schmajuk, N. (1989). Neural dynamics of adaptive timing and temporal discrimination during associative learning. *Neural Networks, 2,* 79-102.

Honig, W. K. (1978). Studies of working memory in the pigeon. In S. H. Hulse, H. Fowler, & W. K. Honig (Eds.), *Cognitive processes in animal behavior* (pp. 211-248). Hillsdale, NJ: Lawrence Erlbaum Associates.

Hull, C. L. (1943). *Principles of behavior.* New York: Appleton-Century-Crofts.

Hulse, S. H., & Campbell, C. E. (1975). "Thinking ahead" in rat discrimination learning. *Animal Learning and Behavior, 3,* 305-311.

Hulse, S. H., & Dorsky, N. P. (1977). Structural complexity as a determinant of serial pattern learning. *Learning and Motivation, 8,* 488-506.

Hulse, S. H., & Dorsky, N. P. (1979). Serial pattern learning by rats: Transfer of a formally defined stimuli relationship and the significance of nonreinforcement. *Animal Learning and Behavior, 7,* 211-220.

James, W. (1890). *The principles of psychology* (2 vols.). New York: Henry Holt.

Jones, M. (1974). Cognitive representations of serial patterns. In B. Kantowitz (Ed.), *Human information processing: Tutorials in performance and cognition* (pp. 187-229). Hillsdale, NJ: Lawrence Erlbaum Associates.

Klahr, D., Chase, W. G., & Lovelace, E. A. (1983). Structure and process in alphabetic retrieval. *Journal of Experimental Psychology: Learning, Memory, and Cognition, 9*, 462-477.

Lashley, K. S. (1951). The problem of serial order in behavior. In L. A. Jeffress (Ed.), *Cerebral mechanisms in behavior: The Hixon symposium* (pp. 112-136). New York: Wiley.

Maricq, A. V., Roberts, S., & Church, R. M. (1981). Methamphetamine and time estimation. *Journal of Experimental Psychology: Animal Behavior Processes, 7*, 18-30.

Meck, W. H. (1984). Attentional bias between modalities: Effect of the internal clock, memory, and decision stages used in animal time discrimination. In J. Gibbon & L. Allen (Eds.) *Timing and time perception* (pp. 528-541). New York: New York Academy of Sciences.

Meck, W. H. (1988). Hippocampal function is required for feedback control of an internal clock's criterion. *Behavioral Neuroscience, 102*, 54-60.

Meck, W. H., & Church, R. M. (1987). Nutrients that modify the speed of internal clock and memory storage processes. *Behavioral Neuroscience, 101*, 465-475.

Meck, W. H., Church, R. M., & Olton, D. S. (1984). Hippocampus, time, and memory. *Behavioral Neuroscience, 98*, 3-22.

Meck, W. H., Church, R. M., Wenk, G. L., & Olton, D. S. (1987). Nucleus basalis magnocellularis and medial septal area lesions differentially impair temporal memory. *Journal of Neuroscience, 7*, 3605-3511.

Olton, D. S. (1989). Frontal cortex, timing and memory. *Neuropsychologia, 27*, 121-130.

Pavlov, I. P. (1927). *Conditioned reflexes*. Oxford: Oxford University Press.

Restle, F. & Brown, E. R. (1970). Organization of serial pattern learning. In G. H. Bower (Ed.), *Psychology of learning and motivation* (Vol. 4, pp. 249-331). New York: Academic Press.

Roberts, S. (1981). Isolation of an internal clock. *Journal of Experimental Psychology: Animal Behavior Processes, 7*, 242-268.

Roberts, S. (1983). Properties and function of an internal clock. In R. L. Mellgren (Ed.), *Animal cognition and behavior* (pp. 345-398). Amsterdam: North-Holland.

Roitblat, H. L. (1982). The meaning of representation in animal memory. *The Behavioral and Brain Sciences, 5*, 353-406.

Roitblat, H. L. (1987). *Introduction to comparative cognition*. New York: Freeman.

Roitblat, H. L., Bever, T. G., Harley, H. E., & Helweg, D. A. (1989). *Online choice and the representation of serially structured stimuli*. Manuscript submitted for publication.

Roitblat, H. L., Pologe, B., & Scopatz, R. A. (1983). The representation of items in serial position. *Animal Learning and Behavior, 11*, 489-498.

Roitblat, H. L., Scopatz, R. A., & Bever, T. G. (1987). The hierarchical representation of three-item sequences. *Animal Learning and Behavior, 15*, 179-192.

Saunders, D. S. (1977). *An introduction to biological rhythms*. Glasgow: Blackie.

Silver, R., & Bittman, E. L. (1984). Reproductive mechanisms: Interaction of circadian and interval timing. In J. Gibbon & L. Allan (Eds.) *Timing and time perception* (pp. 488-514). New York: New York Academy of Sciences.

Stubbs, A. (1968). The discrimination of stimulus duration by pigeons. *Journal of the Experimental Analysis of Behavior, 11*, 223-238.

Stubbs, A. (1976). Response bias and the discrimination of stimulus duration. *Journal of the Experimental Analysis of Behavior, 25,* 243-250.

Terman, M., Gibbon, J., Fairhurst, S., & Waring, A. (1984). Daily meal anticipation: Interaction of circadian and interval timing. In J. Gibbon & L. Allan (Eds.), *Timing and time perception* (pp. 470-487). New York: New York Academy of Sciences.

Terrace, H. S. (1986). Positive transfer from sequence production to sequence discrimination in a nonverbal organism. *Journal of Experimental Psychology: Animal Behavior Processes, 12,* 215-234.

Vandercar, D. H., & Schneiderman, N. (1967). Interstimulus interval functions in different response systems during classical discrimination conditioning of rabbits. *Psychonomic Science, 9,* 9-10.

Wagner, A. R. (1981). SOP: A model of automatic memory processing in animal behavior. In N. E. Spear & R. R. Miller (Eds.), *Information processing in animals: Memory mechanisms* (pp. 5-47). Hillsdale, NJ: Lawrence Erlbaum Associates.

Wearden, J. H., & McShane, B. (1988). Interval production as an analogue of the peak procedure: Evidence for similarity of human and animal timing processes. *Quarterly Journal of Experimental Psychology, 40B,* 363-375.

Weisman, R. G., Gibson, M., & Rochford, J. (1984). Testing models of delayed sequence discrimination in pigeons: The advance key procedure. *Canadian Journal of Psychology, 38,* 256-268.

Weisman, R. G., Wasserman, E. A., Dodd, P. W., & Larew, M. B. (1980). Representation and retention of two-event sequences in pigeons. *Journal of Experimental Psychology: Animal Behavior Processes, 6,* 312-325.

Yamashita, H. (1986). Temporal discrimination of visual stimuli in pigeons. *Perception & Psychophysics, 40,* 119-122.

7

A Cognitive Approach to Temporal Information Processing

Janet L. Jackson
University of Groningen

TIME: BOTH A DEPENDENT
AND AN INDEPENDENT VARIABLE?

In the 19th century, psychology evolved into an experimental science and very quickly the introduction of the *use of time* and more specifically, the measurement of reaction time, became a standard experimental technique. An important contributor to this development was the Dutch scholar F. C. Donders, who in 1868 was professor of physiology in Utrecht. Donders (1868-1869/1969) devised methods for studying what he called "the speed of mental operations." His main hypothesis was that mental processes are embedded in *real time* and that reaction times could be used to estimate the speed of internal cognitive processes. His work is interesting because it offers a means of describing what is going on "inside our heads" by analyzing cognitive activity into separate stages. The underlying assumption arising from Donders' work—namely the assumption that mental operations can be measured in terms of the time they require—is a central feature of modern cognitive psychology. In fact, to paraphrase Ben Franklin who said "Time is Money," it may be more apt for experimental psychologists to say "Time is Cognition."

And so, in modern experimental psychology, the use and measurement of reaction time has continued to evolve steadily into a research methodology of great generality. However, in such research on mental chronometry, it is clear that time is viewed as a dependent variable, that is, as some property of a subject that can be observed and measured by

153

an experimenter. But what about the study of time as an independent variable, that is, as a psychological phenomenon in its own right?

The study of temporal phenomena in human experience was initially considered within the framework of classical time psychology that dealt mainly with the perception, estimation or reproduction of intervals, with the rate of flow of subjective time and with the experience of the so-called *specious present*.

The rise in prominence of time psychology until roughly 1910, its decline over the following decades, followed by a distinct revival of interest in the topic in the 1960s, has been mapped out in some detail by Block and Michon (chapters 1 and 2, this volume). This revival can best be highlighted by considering the large number of studies that have appeared in the experimental psychology literature since the 1960s. Although the main thrust of these studies is often still aimed at answering many of the classical questions, there has been a definite change in emphasis, and time as an independent variable—as information in its own right—is being studied not only by contemporary time psychologists but now also by those working within more traditional cognitive research areas such as memory and attention. This change in emphasis means that time is no longer seen as simply a homogeneous, continuous parameter of input/output relations, but as important information that requires to be processed. How such temporal information is actually processed and represented has become one of the most important research questions facing both groups of researchers. In fact, as has been pointed out elsewhere (e.g., Michon, 1967, 1972; Michon & Jackson, 1984, 1985), the types of questions both groups are asking are beginning to bear a strong resemblance to each other, with the result that the two traditions are beginning to merge into one. Time psychologists whose main interest had been in studying, for example, psychophysical scaling in which subjects were required to judge the durations of brief intervals by means of magnitude and ratio estimation, began to concentrate their attention on questions that ask how "real" order is coded and represented, what mechanisms are involved in the process, and how these produce the phenomenology of time experience. A number of psychologists working within more traditional fields of cognitive psychology where they had been exploring topics such as encoding and retrieval of item information from short-term memory also became interested in understanding the variables that govern our ability, or lack of it, to distinguish by memory the ordering of events in time.

The validity of both approaches, however, depends on the legitimacy of the assumption that temporal relations between events are indeed treated by the human organism as information in the same way as size, intensity, or color. In other words, on the assumption that time is explicitly represented in the mind. This assumption was explicitly stated in the equivalence postulate formulated by Michon (1972) and has also been voiced in similar ways by other authors such as Shiffrin (1968), Estes (1980, 1985), Hasher and Zacks (1979), Macar (1980), and Underwood (1969, 1977). More recently, Michon (1985) restated his "equivalence postulate," giving more emphasis to the role of representation. Although stimuli were thought of as possessing an explicit temporal attribute similar to a color or size attribute in his earlier formulation, in his more recent version he has taken an even stronger line. Now he argued for a more independent status for temporal information. He suggested "that temporal information corresponds to a representational system of its own, and that the encoding of sequential (or temporal) patterns takes place in a separate representational code . . ." (Michon, 1985, p. 32).

As cognitive psychologists, therefore, if we accept the assumption that temporal relations between events are treated by the human organism as information and that this information is represented in memory (perhaps as a separate code) and is used to guide behavior, then it should be possible to use general theories of human information processing to study how information about the temporal attributes of events or sequences are encoded and retained.

A GENERAL INFORMATION-PROCESSING MODEL

Current thinking and theorizing in cognitive psychology has been dominated by the metaphor that likens the human brain to a computer. Although a "functionalist" approach (Fodor, 1981) treats the mind as a device for manipulating symbols, the computational metaphor sets out a detailed account of the rules and processes required for instrumenting such manipulations. A framework that distinguishes between *process* and *structure* has been defined in various ways in the cognitive literature—for example, strategy and structure; software and hardware; cognitive penetrability and cognitive impenetrability (Pylyshyn, 1980); and performance and competence (Chomsky, 1967). Although these distinctions are not identical, they do resemble each other in that they all share the view that some aspects of the cognitive system are fixed, whereas others are flexible, dynamic, and variable. Any adequate cognitive theory must therefore distinguish between the fixed capacities of the mind (often referred to as the *functional architecture*) and the particular representations used in specific tasks. This is an important point, and I return to it later in the chapter. Although many sophisticated information-processing

Control Processes

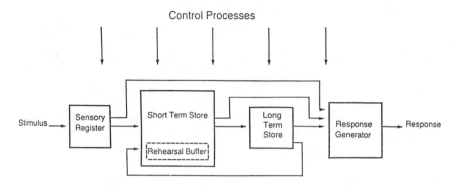

Figure 7.1. A conceptual model of human information-processing.

models now exist, it is sufficient for our purposes to describe a very general model that encompasses most of the basic features of the more specific and detailed varieties (Figure 7.1).

An important assumption in such a model is that while information is being processed it is stored in several memory stores each having different capacities and accessing characteristics. Incoming signals from the senses are held first for a second or two in one of several sensory information stores. These signals are registered in a fairly raw, sensory form that can easily be disturbed by further signals in the same sensory channel. Information is then transferred to a short-term or working memory store where it is processed further. According to several modern theorists (e.g., Anderson, 1983; Shiffrin & Schneider, 1977), this is not a separate, specialized store, but simply the portion of long-term memory that is currently and temporarily activated. The amount of information that can be held in this store is limited and, if not kept in its active state through some form of rehearsal, will fade away or be supplanted by new information within 20 to 30 s. However, well-processed information from working memory can be fixated in the long-term store and can be reactivated at a future date. This store has a very large capacity and relatively permanent storage. Most current models of human information processing also make a distinction between two basic processing modes, namely automatic and controlled processing. Automatic processing is viewed as a fast process that accepts many inputs simultaneously and produces outputs almost instantaneously. It requires no "effort" and there appears to be no upper limit to the structural complexity of the inputs it can handle. Because, by contrast, the deliberate (or controlled) processing mode can only treat inputs in a sequential fashion, it is a comparatively slow process that is limited in its capacity and requires conscious mental effort. Deliberate processing, in other words, requires attention. The focus of attention can be determined by the nature of the task, or by external or internal instructions. Also, if for one reason or another the progress of automatic information processing is interrupted, the deliberate mode will take over in an attempt to reinstate the normal processing routines.

EXPERIMENTAL APPROACHES

How have cognitive psychologists used such a model to explore the processing of temporal information?

In humans, memory for temporal information relating to everyday events can frequently entail either, simply, the remembering of explicit information relating to clock times or calendar dates, or other types of propositional information that permits the inference of clock times or calendar dates. In a recent review, however, Estes (1985) argued that such instances should also be interpretable in terms of general principles of factual memory. Moreover, in most laboratory research, and also in much everyday life experience, temporal memory does not involve explicit verbal encodings of times or dates, but may instead be interpreted in terms of the encoding and retention of information about the temporal attribute of events or sequences of events. The next step must therefore be to identify measures to index temporal coding of such discrete memories. From the experimental literature we find that empirical studies that aim to explore the encoding and retention of temporal information have been approached from several distinct standpoints. The types of tasks that have been employed include: judgments of duration, order judgments, lag estimates, position judgments, and dating of autobiographical memories. (Because the first of these, duration judgments, has been well covered in chapter 1 by Block, they are not discussed further in this chapter.)

Order Judgments[1]

Reference to this particular type of order judgment first appeared in the literature in 1963 when Yntema and Trask, departing from the tradition-

---

[1] Tasks that require relative order judgments are often referred to in the literature as *judgments of recency*. Because this term can lead to some uncertainty, often being confused with primacy/recency effects, the term *order judgments* is used in this chapter.

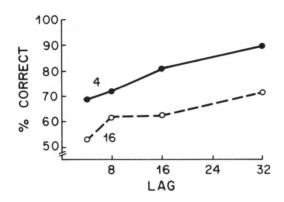

Figure 7.2. Percentage of correct judgments of relative recency as a function of the lag between the members of the pair of test items. The parameters (4 and 16) indicate the lag of the later item of the test pair from the end of the list. (From Estes, 1985. Reprinted by permission.)

al serial-learning paradigm, chose to study the temporal location of items by using a continuous task and several two-alternative forced choices. They presented subjects with a long series of common nouns, shown one at a time. These series were interleaved at various intervals with test cards on which appeared a pair of words. The subjects' task was to designate the word that they believed had occurred later (more recently) in the list as presented on the study trial. Later studies using order judgments (e.g., Jackson, Michon, Boonstra, De Jonge, & De Velde Harsenhorst, 1986; Underwood, 1977) have used shorter lists and subjects are asked to make their judgments after completion of the study trial. The most common result found in the various experiments that study such relative order judgments shows a negatively accelerated increasing function that relates the percentage of correct order judgments to the lag between the items of the test pair (for example, see studies by Brown, 1973; Fozard, 1970; Lockhart, 1969; Underwood, 1977). This result is schematized in Figure 7.2. A further robust result, found originally by Yntema and Trask (1963), shows that the number of correct order judgments decreases as the lag between the test and the position in the original sequence of the more recent member of the test pair increases (that is, *b* in the pair *a-b* occurs earlier in the sequence). This result is also indicated in Figure 7.2.

Spacing Judgments

Early researchers (e.g., Hinrichs & Buschke, 1968) used a procedure that consisted of presenting a sequence of items—usually letters, pictures, or words—to subjects and requiring them to make a numerical estimate of the number of items presented between successive occurrences of the test item (often termed *lag* in the experimental literature).   Later researchers (e.g., Hintzman, Summers & Block, 1975; Underwood, 1977) required subjects to estimate the number of items presented between two different items from the list.

The measures of lag that appear most frequently in the literature (e.g., Hintzman & Block, 1973; Hintzman et al., 1975; Underwood & Malmi, 1978) is simply a mean lag judgment across subjects. As can be seen in Figure 7.3, these mean judgments are often plotted separately for short and long lags. Evidence resulting from such measures suggests not only that the task is difficult, as can be seen by the rather small effect of learning in Figure 7.3, but also that results reflect a bias to give high lag judgments when guessing (Hintzman et al., 1975), and that subjects exhibit a central tendency within which no consistent difference is found between the judgments they make for long lags and those they make for short lags. As a result of this tendency to give a similar mean score to both short and long lags, subjects consistently overestimate short lags and underestimate long lags (Underwood, 1977). This idea is consistent with the well-known overestimation of short intervals versus under-estimation of long intervals, which is probably the oldest experimental result in time psychology (Vierordt, 1868).

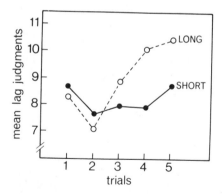

Figure 7.3. Lag judgments as a function of lag (long and short) and trials. The mean true lag for the short lag category was 6, that for the long lag category 16. (From Underwood & Malmi, 1978. Reprinted by permission.)

Position Judgments

As Hintzman and Block (1971) pointed out, the judgment of position is not a new invention, but instead involves a well-researched procedure. As early as 1955, Shultz asked his subjects to make judgments of the serial positions of input items after standard serial learning. Although this remains a useful technique, it is important to distinguish it from the more common task of simple ordered recall. Positional tasks explicitly require the recall of positional or temporal information about the occurrence of an item (Conrad, 1964; Jackson & Michon, 1984; Shiffrin & Cook, 1978; Tzeng, Lee, & Wetzel, 1979).

A number of investigators have shown that position judgments have validity (e.g., Jackson et al., 1986; Toglia & Kimble, 1976; Tzeng et al., 1979; Underwood, 1977) and as we see later, this type of positional recall has perhaps been the most fruitful source of information about the way in which memory for temporal attributes of items changes during retention intervals.

Dating of Autobiographical Memories

Autobiographical memory refers to the memories a person has of his or her own life experiences. It is not a new empirical research topic, investigations into his own recollections having been made as early as 1879 by Galton, but until very recently, it has been one of the least well-developed areas in the study of human memory (Rubin, 1986). Such naturalistic studies are, however, important to researchers in temporal processing because they offer the opportunity of investigating whether the functional relationships found in laboratory studies can be extended to such real-life situations.

One technique that has been used to explore such long-term memories is the method originally developed by Galton (1879) in which a subject is presented with a word and asked to find a memory relating to that word (Baddeley & Wilson, 1986; Crovitz & Schiffman, 1974; Zola-Morgan, Cohen, & Squire, 1983). A second technique is one pioneered by Linton (1975). Over a period of seven years she systematically recorded events from her daily life and then, at different retention intervals, she attempted to recall these events. Typically she would present herself with a full description of an event, attempting to recall the date on which it took place. More recently, White (1982) and Wagenaar (1986) have carried out similar studies. A further group of empirical studies have attempted to establish the nature and extent of temporal reference systems such as public events or school year (Brown, Shevell, & Rips, 1986; Robinson, 1986).

FURTHER EXPERIMENTAL DIMENSIONS

The description of the various experimental tasks used in studying memory for temporal information highlights one further difference, namely that the duration of the interval over which temporal information has to be retained can vary considerably. Such retention intervals, as well as the complexity of the items or events about which memory is tested, may impose important constraints on the processes that contribute to temporal judgments. Several studies (e.g., Conrad, 1964; Healy, 1974; Lee & Estes, 1977, 1981; Shiffrin & Cook, 1978) have used retention intervals within the short-term memory range and have employed digits and letters as stimuli. The focus of such studies has been mainly directed toward creating a model for short-term memory based on the encoding and perturbation of positional information about items of a memory set.

Although a few observational studies (e.g., Brown et al., 1986; Linton, 1975, 1978; Robinson, 1986; Squire, Chase, & Slater, 1975; Underwood, 1977; Wagenaar, 1986) have explored memory for complex real-life events for retention intervals ranging from days to years, the great majority of research on temporal memory has been carried out using more moderate retention intervals of minutes or hours. The stimuli employed in these studies are usually words, although a few (e.g., Fozard & Yntema, 1966; Lassen, Daniel, & Bartlett, 1974) have compared words and pictures.

THREE IMPORTANT ISSUES

Before examining the actual results of various studies that have investigated memory for temporal information within an information-processing framework, there are three important questions that should be raised in relation to the way(s) in which temporal information is processed (Michon & Jackson, 1984).

The Quest for the Temporal Attribute

Tulving and Madigan (1970) suggested that when a relatively discrete event (such as presentation of a word or picture) occurs, the memory for that event may carry information that reflects the point in time at which the memory was established. Thus, they argued that memories may be temporally coded and that temporal information is the stored information that allows us to make absolute or relative judgments concerning the time of storage of some other event. Such a statement highlights the first basic question that we as cognitive psychologists should be asking, namely: *What* is it that is encoded? *What* in a sequential stimulus configuration actually constitutes the functional stimulus or temporal attribute that serves as the input for temporal judgments? Although this may appear to be an obvious basic question to be tackled, definitive answers have been slow in appearing. As late as 1976, Galbraith was still forced to conclude that, in spite of a reasonable amount of consensus among researchers that it is in one way or another related to the content and complexity of the associative context, "there remains a prominent lack of understanding of exactly what constitutes the temporal attribute" (p. 525).

Is the Temporal Attribute Coded upon Acquisition or Constructed During Retrieval?

The second question, the *when* issue, asks whether the temporal attribute, once identified, is encoded upon acquisition or, instead, constructed during retrieval. Because this issue relates directly to the type of theories that have arisen to account for serial order performance, let us first consider a number of these.

Trace Strength Theories. Strength theory maintains that subjects judge how recently an item has occurred by judging how strong the memory trace is along a single dimension. Provided that strength is a monotonically decreasing function of time, or the number of intervening items, then recency and strength are necessarily highly correlated.

Such ideas were put forward as early as 1883 by Lipps but have been restated more formally by Peterson (1967), Morton (1968), and Hinrichs (1970). These authors argue that subjects do not store temporal position in memory but instead infer the recency of items from their strength. The strength of a memory trace of an event is at a peak shortly after the event occurs and declines thereafter. At the time of test, the memory trace is somehow accessed and judgments of recency are then derived from this strength. A variation to this theory has been proposed by Wickelgren (1972, 1974) in his (simple mathematical) theory of storage in long-term memory. The basic assumption of this theory is that a long-term memory trace has two properties that are critical for its characterization in storage: its *strength* and its *resistance*. The susceptibility of a trace to decay in storage is assumed to depend on both properties. A further assumption is that trace resistance increases monotonically, strictly as a function of time. Wickelgren also hypothesized that if trace resistance were to some extent a retrievable property of the memory trace, it would automatically provide a certain degree of time tagging that could mediate recency judgments. His argument therefore stated that the judgment of recency is based on the resistance to decay of the traces of an event, where resistance to decay is assumed to increase over time.

Conveyor Belt Model. As early as 1890, Guyau proposed a theory suggesting that memory is structured on a temporal basis. "Every change which registers itself in consciousness leaves [in memory] as a residue, a series of representations arranged on a sort of line, from which the more remote representations gradually fade, making room for other increasingly sharper representations" (Guyau, 1890/1988, p. 106).

A more recent version of this theoretical approach has been proposed by Murdock (1974). He suggested that representation of events are added to memory in a fashion similar to that of adding suitcases to a conveyor belt. When a subject is required to make a recency judgment, he initiates a backward serial scan along the conveyor belt. Such a search is terminated when the subject arrives at the trace of the test item. A counter, which is incremented each time a new trace is examined, indicates the recency of the test item.

Time-Tag Theory. Yntema and Trask (1963) suggested that some representation of absolute or relative time is part of the memory representation stores when an item occurs (i.e., when a memory trace of a past event is accessed it includes a tag that directly indicates when the event occurred). The ideas of Berlyne (1966) follow somewhat similar lines although he did not use the term *time tagging*. He suggested that whenever any study item or event is presented a counter is incremented and that the value of this counter at the time of study becomes associated with that item.

Context Tagging Theory. Anderson and Bower (1972, 1974), Flexser and Bower (1974), and Hintzman et al. (1975) suggested that events become associated with other events that have been occurring contiguously in time. They argue that the relevant associations are not only between the item and a verbal representation but also with what they call *context information*: "physical characteristics of an item's presentation, implicit associations to the item, and some cognitive elements representing the list in question . . . the subject's general mood or attitude, his physical posture and his physiological state, as well as any conspicuous external cues prevailing during the presentation of list n" (Anderson & Bower, 1972, p. 101). It is because of such associations between items and cues that a subject can determine that an item has occurred in one particular time and place rather than in another.

Those who consider the strength of a memory trace (e.g., Hinrichs, 1970), or its resistance against further decay (e.g., Wickelgren, 1972), or a counter (e.g., Murdock, 1974) as the temporal attribute, necessarily embrace a retrieval theory. In contrast, associative theories (such as Yntema & Trask, 1963; or Anderson & Bower, 1972, 1974) assume that temporal tags are associated with incoming stimuli and this naturally implies some sort of coding process.

Research by proponents of both these types of theory (retrieval or encoding) has, however, tended to be predominantly descriptive, and so it is difficult to make any explicit conclusions as to whether the temporal attribute is coded upon acquisition or constructed during retrieval. As an example, consider again the memory trace-strength theory of Hinrichs (1970). Describing the probability of a correct recency judgment in terms of the decaying strength of a "memory trace" merely amounts to restating the observations in different terms, unless the processes by which trace strength can be evaluated by the subject are clearly explained.

Is Temporal Information Processing Deliberate or Automatic?

The third issue, the *how* question, asks whether temporal information is processed as an inevitable, automatic byproduct of information in general, or whether temporal information processing in itself requires specific cognitive effort.

This question highlights a gulf that exists at the present time between time psychology proper and more mainstream psychology. Although time psychologists (e.g., Michon, 1967, 1972, 1978; Thomas & Weaver, 1975) have for some time agreed that the processing of temporal information requires effort, several memory psychologists (e.g., Hasher & Zacks, 1979; Tzeng et al., 1979) have argued for the automaticity explanation.

Hasher and Zacks (1979) clearly stated several criteria that require to be fulfilled before a process can be described as being innately automatic. Although they suggested that frequency, spatial, and temporal information were prime examples of genetically endowed automatic processes, at the time of writing their paper very little convincing data were available to substantiate this point of view. To complicate matters further, the same group of researchers (Zacks, Hasher, Alba, Sanft, & Rose, 1984) later reported data that challenges two of their original criteria. Answers to the *how* question therefore remain somewhat confused and confusing.

CURRENT ANSWERS TO THE THREE ISSUES

I now turn to a sample of experimental results that go a long way toward revealing some of the answers to the *what*, *when* and *how* questions I have raised, looking first at results from short-retention intervals (intervals falling within the short-term memory range).

Short-Term Range

Studies within this short-term range have typically employed variations of the method used initially by Conrad (1964) in which six items (letters) are presented briefly, read silently by the subjects, and then recalled in order immediately after the visual display has disappeared. The variations to be found in various studies of short-term temporal judgments (e.g., Healy, 1974; Lee & Estes, 1977; Shiffrin & Cook 1978), are adopted in order to manipulate rehearsal processes. Estes (1972), Healy (1974), and Lee and Estes (1977) prevented rehearsal by using short exposure durations (2.0-2.5 letters/s) and a procedure whereby the subjects were required to pronounce the name of each letter as it appeared. The technique employed by Shiffrin and Cook (1978) required the subjects to attend primarily to a concurrent task (e.g., signal detection), and they were instructed not to rehearse the stimulus letters.

Why have researchers using short-retention intervals been at such pains to control rehearsal processes? Estes (1985) suggested the following: "It seems likely that short-term memory for temporal positions or intervals between them can be directly assessed only when rehearsal is precluded by a shadowing task or the equivalent" (p. 153). When such techniques preventing rehearsal are not used, Estes argued that subjects tend to rehearse the items, and they may do this in an order that does not necessarily follow the order of input. This nonsequential order of rehearsal may in turn lead to memory representations that include temporal relations that differ from the original.

Estes therefore removed rehearsal processes from his experiments on ordered recall and discovered item and order information to be forgotten at different rates. Data from such studies were scored in terms of

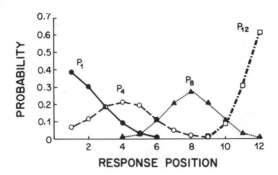

Figure 7.4. Observed uncertainty gradients for items presented in positions
1, 4, 8, 12 of a 12-item list. (From Estes, 1985. Reprinted by permission.)

two types of error: transposition and nontransposition errors. Transposition errors indicate loss of order information, but not item information. They occur when a subject correctly recalls the letters of a trial, but
transposes them (e.g., recalls G S T V P instead of G V T S P). Estes
found that, at very short-retention intervals, any errors that were made
tended to be of this transposition type. Results from studies that have
explored such errors in memory for temporal position information can be
most usefully summarized by looking at "uncertainty gradients" (Estes,
1972; Healy, 1974; Lee & Estes, 1977; Shiffrin & Cook, 1978). The
characteristic pattern of such gradients is illustrated schematically in
Figure 7.4. From the figure it can be seen that order information is fairly
accurate for the initial position and is extremely accurate for the final
position, with judgments in both cases clustering steeply around the
correct position. For the judgments of items from the center of the list,
the gradient no longer peaks so dramatically but instead, shows much
more variance or uncertainty about the correct position.

Let us now look at a particular model that has attempted to account
for and explain the orderliness of such gradients. This is the
encoding/perturbation model that was first proposed by Estes (1972) and
was later modified and extended by Lee and Estes (1981). The model
aims to explain dynamic changes in the encoding of temporal attributes
over time. It encompasses the idea that, because errors appear as a
matter of course in almost all studies of temporal memory, the encoding
of temporal information cannot be "unfailingly precise" (Estes, 1985).
The proposed model therefore sets out to describe how the position
information of items within a memorized list of letters or digits become
increasingly imprecise over time. This loss of precision is presumed to

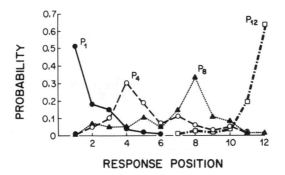

Figure 7.5. Predicted uncertainty gradients from the encoding/perturbation model for items presented at positions 1, 4, 8 and 12 of a 12-item list. (From Estes, 1985. Reprinted by permission.)

come about in the following way: A representation of an item or event, as well as its temporal position, is stored in memory; thereafter, it becomes periodically reactivated in a rehearsal-like mode, along with other events from the same episode or sequence of episodes. As a result of such automatic reactivation, the position information is re-encoded; furthermore, all items are subject to a two-directional random walk and as a result of such random perturbations, some of the items may move out of their proper positions in the memory representations; in other words, positional uncertainty occurs. At this stage, I do not describe the formal derivations of uncertainty gradients further (see Estes, 1972; Lee & Estes, 1977, 1981 for a detailed description), but simply acknowledge with the help of Figure 7.5, that the model yields a very satisfactory fit of the corresponding empirical functions.

A further development arising from the perturbation model has been the move to explore organizational factors similar to those found in hierarchical network models for semantic memory but now focusing on memory for temporal information. Estes (1982) said that time is information and that this information concerning memory for events or episodes is represented in an organized hierarchical system similar to other kinds of categorical information in semantic networks.

In the short-term recall experiments of Lee and Estes (1981), each trial was divided into segments that allowed locational information to be encoded and thus the possibility for perturbations to take place at three different levels: the relative position within a segment; relative position of segments within a trial; and relative position of the events of a trial within the trial sequence. Results suggested that information can indeed be represented by a hierarchical network in which information about the relative temporal position of items within a segment is encoded at the lowest level; information concerning the relative temporal positions of the segments at the next level in the hierarchy; and the relative temporal position of trials within the trial sequence at the highest level. Moreover, uncertainty gradients were shown to develop at each level in a manner similar to the original encoding/perturbation model.

Although the updated model of perturbation and hierarchical organization of temporal information has been shown to be viable for short-term memory, Estes suggested and I later look at studies that have used longer retention intervals but whose results also fit this model.

Let us for the moment, however, return to the three important issues I raised earlier in the chapter. First, *what* in such short-term memory studies is seen as the functional stimulus that serves as the input for temporal judgments? Within the perturbation model, it is assumed that, when an item is perceived, information relating to the interval between the event and others that serve as referents or markers is encoded. Estes (1985) proposed that when the experimental trial involves only a few items presented in a regular sequence, "the successively presented stimulus frames may provide adequate reference points, and then one speaks loosely of the memory representations or items being entered in slots (Conrad, 1964) or being given time tags (Flexser & Bower, 1974)" (p. 168). In other words, it appears that Estes is advocating a principle of intrinsic order (i.e., intrinsic old/new relations) as the functional stimulus and that this is encoded upon acquisition thereby answering the second, *when* question. However, relying on data from his empirical studies that preclude rehearsal, Estes suggested that intrinsic order may not be sufficient but instead distinctive markers that indicate the beginning and end of each sub-sequence or trial are used as reference points. This arises because of capacity limitations in the information-processing system that allow only a small number of item positions to be encoded accurately [between two and four positions at the beginning of a list (Drewnowski, 1980) and the last one or two items at the end of the list (Crowder & Morton, 1969)].

The discussion of capacity limitations leads directly to answers to the third *how* question. Estes argued that the reason why the encoding of intrinsic order relations between successive list items is not sufficient for accurate positional information is related to selective attention processes. Apart from the temporal relations between the beginning and end reference or anchor points and the adjacent items that he argued are encoded automatically, relations between items or events within a sequence are only encoded if they are explicitly attended to and rehearsed (Estes, 1972). In other words, apart from a few unique positions, veridical temporal judgments require deliberate processing. When, as in his experiments, deliberate processing such as rehearsal is prevented, temporal-information retention for all but the unique positions falls to a chance level.

Moderate Retention Intervals

Although there is abundant evidence to show that temporal coding does occur within such retention intervals (e.g., Underwood, 1977; Yntema & Trask, 1963; Zimmerman & Underwood, 1968) as I argued earlier in this chapter, the theories of temporal coding that arose from such research have been mainly descriptive. One of the first models in which the processes involved in temporal information are to some extent specified is that of Tzeng et al. (1979). The basic assumption underlying their model is that when subjects are memorizing (coding) a sequence of events such as successive words in a list, they will rehearse old items between the presentation of the last presented and the next item. This is called *study-phase rehearsal* or *study-phase retrieval* (Hintzman et al., 1975). Items in the rehearsal buffer constitute a context for ordered associations between old items and the current item.

Tzeng et al. therefore use the principle of intrinsic order as the functional stimulus: Intrinsic old/new relations, established through study-phase rehearsal, constitute the bases for temporal information judgments. Moreover, temporal-information processing within this model is clearly seen as a matter of coding (acquisition): The temporal order of items is contextually anchored at the input stage by means of the study-phase rehearsal process.

Our research group also holds similar views. We, too, believe that intrinsic order constitutes the functional stimulus for temporal judgments. This belief is supported by results from several of our experiments. For instance, within a directed forgetting paradigm similar to that used by Tzeng et al., words cued to be forgotten were found to exhibit very little temporal information (Jackson & Michon, 1984; see Table 7.1). Moreover, within a levels-of-processing approach, subjects who performed word-structure orienting tasks, which simply involve a perceptual scanning process, were very poor at making temporal judgments (Jackson et al., 1986). Taken together, these results suggest that being present in a rehearsal set (or, as we prefer to phrase it, being held in working memory for further processing) is a *necessary* condition for temporal coding to take place, allowing old/new relations to become established. The results are also clearly in agreement with the idea that the temporal attribute is encoded upon acquisition.

Table 7.1
Average Recognition, Recall, and Temporal-Order Retention (r^2)

	Concrete List		Abstract List	
	R-cued	F-cued	R-cued	F-cued
Recognition	19.2	15.0	18.6	16.2
r^2	.50	.03	.13	.01
Recall	13.5	2.25	7.5	1.1
r^2 (recalled)	.66	.02	.45	.43
r^2 (non-recalled)	.23	.03	.01	.00

Note. After Jackson and Michon, 1984. Adapted by permission.

Where our views differ from those of Tzeng et al. is in relation to the *how* question: Is the processing of temporal information automatic or controlled? The position adopted by Tzeng et al. (1979) and Tzeng and Cotton (1980) runs as follows: Quoting evidence from studies such as those of Underwood (1969) that stated that position judgment is unaffected by duration of stimulus presentation and by Toglia and Kimble (1976) in which intentional temporal judgment instructions failed to enhance temporal coding, they argue that "the robustness of temporal codes suggests that coding of temporal information of the stimulus events is an automatic process" (Tzeng et al., 1979, p. 53). In the same article, however, they state that because the "results of Experiment 1 showed that TBF (to-be-forgotten) items contain very little temporal information, this may be the first experiment which shows empirically that temporal coding is *not necessarily an automatic process*" (Tzeng et al., 1979, p. 63). However, in the same paragraph they introduce a different conception of the term *automatic*. Arguing in favor of a "contextual association theory" of temporal coding, they state that "since we remember prior items and we also rehearse previously encoded items while processing the current item, the temporal coding becomes an *inevitable* (or automatic) consequence of memory" (p. 63). In other words, although Tzeng and his colleagues claimed that their process model follows an automaticity view, it seems to incorporate some nonautomatic features—namely, rehearsal processes.

This is not the case with Hasher and Zacks (1979). These authors adopt an automatic stance stating that temporal information is automatically acquired and stored in memory as a byproduct of perceptual information. Hasher and Zacks view automatic processes as having the following characteristics: They do not improve with practice or feedback; they do not require awareness or intention; their operation cannot be willfully inhibited; they use minimal attentional capacity; knowledge gained by these processes is accessible to consciousness; and finally, although the focusing of attention on such processes does not improve their performance, it may reduce one's ability to engage in other, nonautomatic processing.

Hasher and Zacks consider two ways in which automatic processing can be achieved: heredity and learning.   Heredity implies that we are born with the ability to carry out some activities at an automatic level, and also that the nervous system is wired in such a way as to maximize the processing of certain types of information.   This type of processing should therefore require minimal experience and should not be influenced by either differences in age, culture, education, or early experience. Operations that fall within this category of "learning without effort" are thought to include the recording of frequency, spatial, and temporal information, processes that, Hasher and Zacks argued, allow us to "cognitively orient to the routine flow of events in our environment" (p. 360).

Having described the characteristics of automatic and effortful processes, Hasher and Zacks propose five criteria that they suggest distinguish between "innate" automatic and deliberate processing. These include intentional versus incidental learning; effects of instruction and practice; task interference; depression or high arousal; and developmental trends. They then reviewed the literature seeking either evidence or contradictions to substantiate their hypotheses.   The evidence collected by Hasher and Zacks in relation to temporal information is summarized in Table 7.2. As is evident from this table, the picture is far from complete: There are not yet sufficient data to evaluate all the criteria listed by Hasher and Zacks; only part of the evidence cited supports their framework (developmental trends); and finally, part of the evidence proves to be inadequate (in particular, a paper by Zimmerman and Underwood, 1968, discussed in Jackson & Michon, 1984). Notwithstanding the paucity of evidence, Hasher and Zacks reached the firm conclusion that temporal information is among the attributes of information that are indeed automatically encoded.

Although their view has been fairly widely accepted, we suggest that their argument is flawed because it fails to distinguish between the

Table 7.2
Evidence Relating to Temporal Information

Issue concerning temporal information	Evidence supporting framework	Evidence contradicting framework	No relevant evidence
1. Intentional versus incidental learning	Zimmerman & Underwood (1968); Miller et al. (1978)		
2. Effects of instruction and practice			0
3. Task interference	Zimmerman & Underwood (1968)		
4. Depression or high arousal			0
5. Developmental trends:			
(a) children	Brown (1973)	Mathews & Fozard (1970)	
(b) elderly			0

functional architecture of the mind and the particular representations and processes used in temporal judgments. Our view (Jackson, 1989; Michon, 1989) stresses the fact that events that are successive in physical reality and are also *perceived* in their correct order, should be seen as part of the hardware. In other words, it relates to the structure of the mind or to "timing your mind." According to Michon (1989) "timing your mind enables you to stay in tune with an intrinsically temporal world" (p. 20). Psychophysical necessity—that is, the fact that events that are successive in physical reality are also *perceived* in their correct order—should therefore be seen as relating to the structure of the mind. The particular representations and processes used in temporal judgments, however, should be viewed as flexible and variable, and we argue that these are affected by factors such as task demands, instructions, and goals.

Using criteria similar to those proposed by Hasher and Zacks (1979), we have collected results from many empirical studies (e.g., Jackson, 1985; Jackson & Michon, 1984) that directly challenge the automaticity stance and show that we do indeed "mind our time" (Jackson, 1989).

Minding our time has been described by Michon (1989) as "being primarily, if not exclusively, a consciously controlled way of coping with those aspects of the world that we cannot tune ourselves because we are not geared to those aspects by evolution or learning" (p. 21). To take an example of this "minding your time," let us look at one set of experiments (Jackson, 1985) that showed performance on order, lag, and position judgments to be related to subjects' strategy use, with those who used elaborative strategies achieving higher retention scores (see Figure 7.6). These experiments also revealed a considerable effect of level of practice. Both of these results indicate that making temporal judgments involves deliberate or controlled information processing.

Our disagreements with Tzeng et al., although less extreme, are still significant. Evidence from several of our studies support their view that being present in a rehearsal set is a *necessary* condition for intrinsic order relationships to be made. Data from the same experiments, however, also question whether this is a *sufficient* condition to produce adequate temporal retention in all tasks. For example, look again at Table 7.1. If being present in a rehearsal set is a sufficient condition, why should words that were cued to-be-remembered but that were *not* recalled exhibit so little temporal information retention? And why should abstract words that *are* recalled show so little retention? I suggest this is because being present in a rehearsal buffer is *not* sufficient but that something extra, either selective attention demands or processing strategies, play an

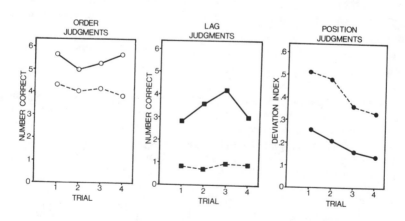

Figure 7.6. Mean judgment scores as a function of trial and strategy for order, lag, and position judgments (a score of 0 in the position judgments indicates perfect performance). Dotted lines represent simple rehearsal strategies; solid lines represent elaborative strategies. (From Jackson, 1985. Reprinted by permission.)

important role. For example, if concrete items encourage the use of more elaborate strategies such as incorporating words within a story context, this would lead to the storage of a very distinctive "context" that can be reinstated and used at retrieval time. Abstract items, on the other hand, may encourage less elaborative strategies, such as rote rehearsal, which would provide a less distinctive context at retrieval, perhaps simply the old current association. This, in turn, proves to be insufficient for efficient temporal coding.

Our answer as to the *how* question is therefore very similar to that of Estes, namely that, apart from a few unique positions which may indeed be encoded automatically, *"temporal information is not encoded unless noticed and not noticed unless meaningful"* (Michon & Jackson, 1984, p. 305).

Long-Term Retention Intervals

Although it would be useful to ask the same *what, when,* and *how* questions about temporal information retained over longer intervals, months or years, the state of the art does not yet lend itself to answering such questions successfully. In fact, it is only within the last decade that autobiographical memory has been studied within the framework of cognitive psychology. Perhaps part of the reason for this tardiness lay in the fact that most of the methods used previously to study autobiographical memory were highly subjective, relying on self reports that, in turn, were difficult to verify. Now other procedures are being used. In 1890, Guyau described autobiographical memory as being the effort to organize one's lifetime personal experiences into a coherent whole that is not at odds with one's presently held views and priorities.

> Time, in and of itself, is an artist idealizing the world. In fact, we remember only the prominent and characteristic aspects of past events. . . . We tend to embellish what has been pleasing to us and to deform what has displeased us, and this tendency, incessantly adding effect upon effect, finally reaches a point of maximum beauty or ugliness that constitutes the [ultimate] adaptation of a recollection to our personal inclinations. . . . This is necessarily an esthetic classification. Time is therefore a judgment based on the strength and the esthetic value of objects and events. (Guyau, 1890/1988, p. 140)

For Guyau, therefore, temporal order relies on the ability to store our memories in an organized fashion. It is precisely this topic, the organization of temporal memories, that has become one of the important current research topics.

In her diary studies, Linton (1982) looked at her retrieval strategies for all events occurring within a particular month. She found that many events were recalled by a temporally ordered search.   Others were organized in categories and were retrieved by searching through particular categories such as work or sporting activities.   A change in memory organization also became apparent: For events more than 2 years old, she found a shift away from chronological search toward a more consistent use of categorical search.   Her recall protocols also revealed events to be organized in terms of ongoing lifetime periods such as job, marriage, or place of residence.   Specific events were embedded within such timelines or periods and could be retrieved by cueing with the relevant period.

Wagenaar (1986) also used a diary procedure to record 2,400 events from his daily life over a period of 6 years.   His approach differed somewhat from that of Linton because he specifically recorded each event in terms of *who, what, where,* and *when.*   At retrieval time, he was therefore able to test himself using various of these cues.   When presented singly, the order of efficacy of the cues was *what, where, who,* and *when.*   *When* as a retrieval cue was found to be virtually useless! Chronological information was often missing from the memory of the event suggesting that, apart from a few landmark events such as birthdays and holidays that were dated precisely, memories for events are not filed by dates.

One further common experimental procedure has been to ask subjects to locate on a timeline various important public events.   From their results, Brown, Rips, and Shevell (1985) suggested that subjects very rarely have a precise memory record of the dates of such public events but instead estimate the dates from some other known autobiographical event, which often depends on some socially induced reference system such as school year (Robinson, 1986) and schooldays, time at college (Conway & Berkerian, 1987).   In other words, if a landmark event can be dated by some socially induced reference system, and the temporal relationship of landmark to the target is known, then the target date can be estimated.

A further result from the Brown, Rips, and Shevell study was that well-known events tended to be dated more recently than they had in fact occurred and, conversely, less well-known dates were dated more distantly.   Loftus and Marburger (1983) also explored the dating of events and found that subjects usually overestimate the *recency* of events; that is, they report a too recent date for an event, a bias that is known as *forward telescoping.*   When the same questions were posed but this time preceded by a temporal landmark (e.g., "Since last New Year's Day did you . . . ?"; or "Since the eruption of Mount St. Helens did you . . . ?"; or subjects were instructed to supply a personal landmark to use as a reference point), forward telescoping was reduced.

Very recently, Huttenlocher, Hedges, and Prohaska (1988) have proposed a model that goes some way toward explaining such reductions in biases. The model bears many resemblances to the hierarchical model proposed by Lee and Estes (1981) for short-term memory. It suggests that information is organized into multilevel structures involving successively larger divisions of a dimension or set of dimensions (e.g., last week, last month, last academic semester, last year, etc.) such that the higher level units provide "more coarsely grained division(s) than do units at lower levels" (Huttenlocher et al., 1988, p. 472). Biases are more likely to occur at the boundaries of such dimensions since they constrain estimates to a particular range. The model also holds that the level of precision of information retrieved by subjects depends on the type of question they have been asked, thus accounting well for the data of Loftus and Marburger (1983) where directing subjects to more particular, lower level units (e.g., Did X occur [a] in the last 6 months? [b] in the last 2 months?) reduced forward telescoping.

CONCLUSION

Over the last two decades we, as cognitive psychologists, have come a long way in our understanding of how temporal information is coded and represented. Unfortunately, as this and other chapters in the book show, there is still some way to go. Fortunately, the thread joining the various research directions is strong. Although the quotation is an old one, we as cognitive psychologists mainly agree that . . .

> Time is not a condition, but rather a simple product of consciousness. It is not an *a priori* form that we impose on phenomena, it is a set of relationships that experience establishes among them. Time as I see it, is nothing but a kind of systematic tendency, an organization of mental representations. And memory is nothing but the art of evoking and organizing these representations. Time, initially, is no more intrinsic to our mind than it is to an hourglass. (Guyau, 1890/1988, p. 145)

REFERENCES

Anderson, J. R. (1983). *The architecture of cognition*. Cambridge, MA: Harvard University Press.

Anderson, J. R., & Bower, G. H. (1972). Recognition and retrieval processes in free recall. *Psychological Review, 79*, 97-123.

Anderson, J. R., & Bower, G. H. (1974). A propositional theory of recognition memory. *Memory & Cognition, 2,* 406-412.

Baddeley, A. D., & Wilson, B. (1986). Amnesia, autobiographical memory, and confabulation. In D. C. Rubin (Ed.), *Autobiographical memory* (pp. 225-252). Cambridge: Cambridge University Press.

Berlyne, D. E. (1966). Effects of spatial order and inter-item interval on recall of temporal order. *Psychonomic Science, 6,* 375-376.

Brown, A. L. (1973). Judgments of recency for long sequences of pictures: The absence of a developmental trend. *Journal of Experimental Child Psychology, 15,* 473-480.

Brown, N. R., Rips, L. J., & Shevell, S. K. (1985). Subjective dates of natural events in very-long-term memory. *Cognitive Psychology, 17,* 139-177.

Brown, N. R., Shevell, S. K., & Rips, L. J. (1986). Public memories and their personal context. In D. C. Rubin (Ed.), *Autobiographical memory* (pp. 137-158). Cambridge: Cambridge University Press.

Chomsky, N. (1967). The general properties of language. In C. H. Millikan & F. L. Darley (Eds.), *Brain mechanisms underlying speech and language* (pp. 73-88). New York: Grune & Stratton.

Conrad, R. (1964). Acoustic confusions in immediate memory. *British Journal of Psychology, 55,* 75-84.

Conway, M. A., & Berkerian, D. A. (1987). Organization in autobiographical memory. *Memory & Cognition, 15,* 119-132.

Crovitz, H. F., & Schiffman, H. (1974). Frequency of episodic memories as a function of age. *Bulletin of the Psychonomic Society, 4,* 517-518.

Crowder, R. G., & Morton, J. (1969). Precategorical acoustic storage (PAS). *Perception & Psychophysics, 5,* 365-373.

Donders, F. C. (1969). On the speed of mental processes (W. G. Koster, Trans.). *Acta Psychologica, 30,* 412-431. (Originally published as "Over de snelheid van psychische processen." *Onderzoekingen gedaan in het Physiologisch Laboratorium der Utrechtsche Hoogeschool,* 1868-1869, Tweede Reeks II, 92-120.)

Drewnowski, A. (1980). Attributes and priorities in short-term recall: A new model of memory span. *Journal of Experimental Psychology: General, 109,* 208-250.

Estes, W. K. (1972). An associative basis for coding and organization in memory. In A. W. Melton & E. Martin (Eds.), *Coding processes in human memory* (pp. 161-190). Washington, DC: V. H. Winston & Sons.

Estes, W. K. (1980). Is human memory obsolete? *American Scientist, 68,* 62-69.

Estes, W. K. (1982). Multiple coding and processing stages: A review. In F. Klix, J. Hoffman, & E. van der Meer (Eds.), *Cognitive research in psychology* (pp. 14-21). Berlin: VEB Deutscher Verlag der Wissenschaften.

Estes, W. K. (1985). Memory for temporal information. In J. A. Michon & J. L. Jackson (Eds.), *Time, mind, and behavior* (pp. 151-168). Berlin: Springer-Verlag.

Flexser, A. J., & Bower, G. H. (1974). How frequency affects recency judgments: A model for recency discrimination. *Journal of Experimental Psychology, 103,* 706-716.

Fodor, J. A. (1981). The mind-body problem. *Scientific American, 244,* 124-132.

Fozard, J. L. (1970). Apparent recency of unrelated pictures and nouns presented in the same sequence. *Journal of Experimental Psychology, 86,* 137-143.

Fozard, J. L., & Yntema, D. B. (1966, April). *The effect of repetition on the apparent recency of pictures*. Paper presented at meeting of the Eastern Psychological Association, New York.

Galbraith, R. C. (1976). The effects of frequency and recency on judgments of frequency and recency. *American Journal of Psychology, 89*, 515-526.

Galton, F. (1879). Psychometric experiments. *Brain, 2*, 149-162.

Guyau, J.-M. (1988). *La genèse de l'idée de temps* [The origin of the idea of time]. In J. A. Michon, V. Pouthas, & J. L. Jackson (Eds.), *Guyau and the idea of time* (pp. 37-90; translation pp. 93-148). Amsterdam: North-Holland. (Original work published 1890)

Hasher, L., & Zacks, R. T. (1979). Automatic and effortful processes in memory. *Journal of Experimental Psychology: General, 108*, 356-388.

Healy, A. F. (1974). Separating item from order information in short-term memory. *Journal of Verbal Learning and Verbal Behavior, 13*, 644-655.

Hinrichs, J. V. (1970). A two-process memory strength theory for judgment of recency. *Psychological Review, 77*, 223-233.

Hinrichs, J. V., & Buschke, H. (1968). Judgment of recency under steady state conditions. *Journal of Experimental Psychology, 78*, 574-579.

Hintzman, D. L., & Block, R. A. (1971). Repetition and memory: Evidence for a multiple-trace hypothesis. *Journal of Experimental Psychology, 88*, 297-306.

Hintzman, D. L., & Block, R. A. (1973). Memory for the spacing of repetitions. *Journal of Experimental Psychology, 99*, 70-74.

Hintzman, D. L., Summers, J. J., & Block, R. A. (1975). Spacing judgments as an index of study-phase retrieval. *Journal of Experimental Psychology: Human Learning and Memory, 1*, 31-40.

Huttenlocher, J., Hedges, L., & Prohaska, V. (1988). Hierarchical organization in ordered domains: Estimating the dates of events. *Psychological Review, 95*, 471-484.

Jackson, J. L. (1985). Is the processing of temporal information automatic or controlled? In J. A. Michon & J. L. Jackson (Eds.), *Time, mind, and behavior* (pp. 179-190). Berlin: Springer-Verlag.

Jackson, J. L. (1989). The processing of temporal information: Do we indeed time our minds? In J. T. Fraser (Ed.), *Time and mind: Interdisciplinary issues* (pp. 43-57). Madison, CT: International Universities Press.

Jackson, J. L., & Michon, J. A. (1984). Effect of item concreteness on temporal coding. *Acta Psychologica, 57*, 83-95.

Jackson, J. L., Michon, J. A., Boonstra, H., De Jonge, D., & De Velde Harsenhorst, J. (1986). The effects of depth of processing on temporal judgment tasks. *Acta Psychologica, 62*, 199-210.

Lassen, G. L., Daniel, T. C., & Bartlett, N. R. (1974). Judgment of recency for pictures and words. *Journal of Experimental Psychology, 102*, 795-798.

Lee, C. L., & Estes, W. K. (1977). Order and position in primary memory for letter strings. *Journal of Verbal Learning and Verbal Behavior, 16*, 395-418.

Lee, C. L., & Estes, W. K. (1981). Item and order information in short-term memory: Evidence for multi-level perturbation processes. *Journal of Experimental Psychology: Human Learning and Memory, 7*, 149-169.

Linton, M. (1975). Memory for real-world events. In D. A. Norman & D. E. Rumelhart (Eds.), *Explorations in cognition* (pp. 376-404). San Francisco: Freeman.

Linton, M. (1978). Real world memory after six years: An in vivo study of very long memory. In M. M. Gruneberg, P. E. Morris, & R. N. Sykes (Eds.), *Practical aspects of memory* (pp. 69-76). London: Academic Press.

Linton, M. (1982). Transformations of memory in everyday life. In U. Neisser (Ed.), *Memory observed: Remembering in natural contexts* (pp. 77-91). San Francisco: Freeman.

Lipps, T. (1883). *Grundtatsachen des Seelenlebens* [Basic facts of inner life]. Bonn: Cohen.

Lockhart, R. S. (1969). Recency discrimination predicted from absolute lag judgments. *Perception & Psychophysics, 6*, 42-44.

Loftus, E. F., & Marburger, W. (1983). Since the eruption of Mt. St. Helens, has anyone beaten you up? Improving the accuracy of retrospective reports with landmark events. *Memory & Cognition, 11*, 114-120.

Macar, F. (1980). *Le temps: Perspectives psychophysiologiques* [Time: Psychophysiological perspectives]. Brussels: Pierre Mardaga.

Mathews, M. E., & Fozard, J. L. (1970). Age differences in judgments of recency for short sequences of pictures. *Developmental Psychology, 3*, 208-217.

Michon, J. A. (1967). *Timing in temporal tracking*. Assen, The Netherlands: Van Gorcum.

Michon, J. A. (1972). Processing of temporal information and the cognitive theory of time experience. In J. T. Fraser, F. C. Haber, & G. H. Müller (Eds.), *The study of time* (pp. 242-258). Heidelberg: Springer-Verlag.

Michon, J. A. (1978). The making of the present: A tutorial review. In J. Requin (Ed.), *Attention and performance* (Vol. VII, pp. 89-111). Hillsdale, NJ: Lawrence Erlbaum Associates.

Michon, J. A. (1985). The compleat time experiencer. In J. A. Michon & J. L. Jackson (Eds.), *Time, mind, and behavior* (pp. 20-52). Berlin: Springer-Verlag.

Michon, J. A. (1989). Timing your mind and minding your time. In J. T. Fraser (Ed.), *Time and mind: Interdisciplinary issues* (pp. 17-39). Madison, CT: International Universities Press.

Michon, J. A., & Jackson, J. L. (1984). Attentional effort and cognitive strategies in the processing of temporal information. In J. Gibbon & L. Allan (Eds.), *Timing and time perception* (pp. 298-321). New York: New York Academy of Sciences.

Michon, J. A., & Jackson, J. L. (1985). The psychology of time. In J. A. Michon & J. L. Jackson (Eds.), *Time, mind, and behavior* (pp. 2-17). Berlin: Springer-Verlag.

Morton, J. (1968). Repeated items and decay in memory. *Psychonomic Science, 10*, 219-220.

Murdock, B. B. (1974). *Human memory: Theory and data*. Hillsdale, NJ: Lawrence Erlbaum Associates.

Peterson, L. R. (1967). Search and judgment in memory. In B. Kleinmuntz (Ed.), *Concepts and the structure of memory* (pp. 153-180). New York: Wiley.

Pylyshyn, Z. W. (1980). Computation and cognition: Issues in the foundations of cognitive science. *The Behavioral and Brain Sciences, 3*, 111-169.

Robinson, J. A. (1986). Temporal reference systems and autobiographical memory. In D. C. Rubin (Ed.), *Autobiographical memory* (pp. 159-190). Cambridge: Cambridge University Press.

Rubin, D. C. (Ed.). (1986). *Autobiographical memory*. Cambridge: Cambridge University Press.

Shiffrin, R. M. (1968). *The temporal dimension in the memory search* (Rep. No. 69-80). Bloomington: Indiana University, Indiana Mathematical Psychology Program.

Shiffrin, R. M., & Cook, J. R. (1978). Short-term forgetting of item and order information. *Journal of Verbal Learning and Verbal Behavior, 17*, 189-218.

Shiffrin, R. M., & Schneider, W. (1977). Controlled and automatic human information processing: II. Perceptual learning, automatic attending, and a general theory. *Psychological Review, 84*, 127-190.

Shultz, R. W. (1955). Generalization of serial position in rote serial learning. *Journal of Experimental Psychology, 49*, 267-272.

Squire, L. R., Chase, P. M., & Slater, P. C. (1975). Assessment of memory for remote events. *Psychological Reports, 37*, 223-234.

Thomas, E. A. C., & Weaver, W. B. (1975). Cognitive processing and time perception. *Perception & Psychophysics, 17*, 363-367.

Toglia, M. P., & Kimble, G. A. (1976). Recall and use of serial position information. *Journal of Experimental Psychology: Human Learning and Memory, 4*, 431-445.

Tulving, E., & Madigan, S. A. (1970). Memory and verbal learning. *Annual Review of Psychology, 21*, 437-484.

Tzeng, O. J. L., Lee, A. T., & Wetzel, C. D. (1979). Temporal coding in verbal information processing. *Journal of Experimental Psychology: Human Learning and Memory, 5*, 52-64.

Tzeng, O. J. L., & Cotton, B. (1980). A study-phase retrieval model of temporal coding. *Journal of Experimental Psychology: Human Learning and Memory, 6*, 705-716.

Underwood, B. J. (1969). Attributes of memory. *Psychological Review, 76*, 559-573.

Underwood, B. J. (1977). *Temporal codes for memories: Issues and problems.* Hillsdale, NJ: Lawrence Erlbaum Associates.

Underwood, B. J., & Malmi, R. A. (1978). An evaluation of measures used in studying temporal codes for words within a list. *Journal of Verbal Learning and Verbal Behavior, 17*, 279-293.

Vierordt, K. (1868). *Der Zeitsinn nach Versuchen* [Empirical studies of time experience]. Doctoral dissertation, Universitat Tübingen, West Germany.

Wagenaar, W. A. (1986). My memory: A study of autobiographical memory over six years. *Cognitive Psychology, 18*, 225-252.

White, R. T. (1982). Memory for personal events. *Human Learning, 1*, 171-183.

Wickelgren, W. A. (1972). Trace-resistance and the decay of long-term memory. *Journal of Mathematical Psychology, 9*, 418-455.

Wickelgren, W. A. (1974). Single-trace fragility theory of memory dynamics. *Memory & Cognition, 2*, 775-780.

Yntema, D. B., & Trask, F. P. (1963). Recall as a search process. *Journal of Verbal Learning and Verbal Behavior, 2*, 65-74.

Zacks, R. T., Hasher, L., Alba, J. W., Sanft, H., & Rose, K. C. (1985). Is temporal order encoded automatically? *Memory & Cognition, 12*, 387-394.

Zimmerman, J., & Underwood, B. J. (1968). Ordinal position knowledge within and across lists as a function of instructions in free-recall learning. *Journal of General Psychology, 79*, 301-307.

Zola-Morgan, S., Cohen, N. J., & Squire, L. R. (1983). Recall of remote episodic memory in amnesia. *Neuropsychologia, 21*, 487-500.

8 Timing in Human Movement Sequences

Jeffery J. Summers
Bruce D. Burns
University of Melbourne

A characteristic of many motor skills is that they require the coordination of several movements into a smooth pattern. In such skills, each movement must occur in the correct order and at the appropriate moment in time in relation to the other movements making up the activity. The execution of one component too early or too late will disrupt the continuity of the skill. The ability to precisely time movements, therefore, is an important aspect of motor performance.

The question of how movements are timed has been the subject of considerable debate. In this chapter we review some of the mechanisms that have been proposed to underlie movement timing. Although a great deal has been written on the subject of timing, most of this work has been concerned with the subjective experience of time over relatively long intervals such as seconds, minutes, or hours. In most motor tasks (e.g., playing a musical instrument, executing a gymnastic routine), however, the time between actions is less than a second. This review, therefore, is restricted to the timing of fast motor actions.

A central issue in the movement-timing literature is whether time per se is directly specified in the control of movement production. On the one hand, information-processing theorists argue for the central control of timing in terms of temporal codes in stored motor programs or central time-keeping mechanisms. On the other, proponents of the ecological approach to perception and action argue that time is not directly controlled in movement. Rather, timing is seen as an emergent property of the dynamic behavior of the neuromotor system itself. The conclusion we wish to draw from this review of the motor-timing literature is that no single mechanism can account for timing behavior in the motor domain. It appears that the human has available a variety of sources of information and processes that can be used to precisely time movements. The particular level at which timing is controlled is determined by such factors as the nature of the task to be performed and the stage of learning.

This chapter focuses primarily on a discussion of the mechanisms of movement timing that have emerged from the information-processing and ecological approaches to motor behavior. In recent years, however, there has been a growing interest in activation (connectionist) models of cognition. Although this approach to cognition is still in its infancy, it may have important implications for theories of motor timing, and an overview of these models is presented.

THE INFORMATION-PROCESSING APPROACH

Historically, a major issue in the field of motor behavior has been the importance of central and peripheral mechanisms in the control of movement. An early theory of movement timing, for example, suggests that the timing of a response depends on proprioceptive feedback from a previous response, either directly, or by way of sensory trace decay in short-term memory (e.g., Adams, 1977; Adams & Creamer, 1962; Schmidt & Christina, 1969). However, growing evidence against a feedback-based account of timing (e.g., Kelso, 1978; Wing, 1977) and the emergence of the information-processing approach within the field of experimental psychology, has led motor theorists to propose central mechanisms in spatiotemporal motor control.

The Motor Program

Of particular importance in information-processing accounts of motor timing is the concept of a motor program (see Keele, 1981; Summers, 1981, 1989, for review). Early motor-program theory suggested that practice on a motor task results in the acquisition by the higher centers of the central nervous system, of a neuromotor program containing all the information necessary for movement sequencing and timing. Keele (1968), for example, defined a *motor program* "as a set of muscle commands that are structured before a movement begins, and that allows the entire sequence to be carried out uninfluenced by peripheral feedback" (p. 387). Motor-program theory does not deny that feedback plays an essential role in movement control, but suggests that feedback-response associations are not the mechanism through which sequences of movements are timed (Keele & Summers, 1976).

In recent years, the concept of motor programs, as applied to learned sequences of actions, has undergone considerable modification. A particular difficulty for the motor-program concept is to account for the tremendous flexibility and variety evident in human skill. For example, it is apparent that the motor system can produce a wide range of movements that subserve identical or closely related goals or outcomes, but through the action of different movements and different muscles. It would seem extremely inefficient and cumbersome for a separate motor program to be stored for every variation of an action that can be performed. Yet, despite the great flexibility evident in the movements people produce, an obvious feature of skilled performance is the consistency in the way an action is performed. A person's characteristic style of handwriting, for example, is evident for words written with the right and left hands, with a pen held in the mouth, and with a pen strapped to the foot (Raibert, 1977). The fact that certain properties of an action remain constant on different occasions suggests the existence of some underlying memorial representation of a movement pattern.

These features of skilled motor behavior have led motor-program theorists away from the notion of a single level of control specifying every detail in the response and toward the view of a multilevel or hierarchic system. The motor program is now seen as a hierarchic memory structure in which an abstract representation of action is elaborated into its more specific components as information descends the hierarchy (Keele, 1981, 1986; Summers, 1981, 1989). Evidence in support of the hierarchical representation of movement sequences has come from the analysis of sequencing errors in speech and typing, preparatory reaction-time studies and the grouping of responses during on-line production of motor sequences (see Keele, 1986, 1987; MacKay, 1987a; Rosenbaum, 1985, for a review). Recent models of rhythm perception (e.g., Povel, 1981; Povel & Essens, 1985) also propose that temporal patterns are encoded hierarchically (see Jones, 1985, chapter 9, this volume, for a review). A basic assumption of such models is that subjects detect underlying "beats" that occur at equal time intervals throughout a sequence. The beat interval is then used to organize other shorter intervals in the pattern into a limited number of within-beat structures. Beat intervals may be empty, filled with equal intervals, or filled with unequal intervals that relate as 1:2 or 1:3 (Essens & Povel, 1985).

Schmidt (1975), in an application of schema theory to motor learning, proposed the concept of a generalized motor program. The generalized motor program is an abstract memory structure that governs a class of movements possessing a common movement pattern. Variations in the movements within a movement class are produced by the specification of certain parameters necessary for the execution of the generalized motor program. Changing the parameter values produces changes to the "surface features" of the response without changing the basic pattern of action (Shapiro & Schmidt, 1982).

Much of the recent work from the motor-programming perspective has focused on identifying the features of a movement sequence that are represented in the generalized program and those features or parameters that can be varied to meet specific task demands. Two lines of evidence suggest that the specification of timing plays a special role in programming that is not shared by other components of a movement sequence, such as the spatial and muscular aspects.

The first is the search for invariances in motor behavior that indicate the features of movement that are coded in the abstract memory structure. A general finding that has emerged in a wide variety of movement behaviors is that the phasing (or relative timing) of movements seems to be an essential part of the motor program representation (see Schmidt, 1984). The temporal structure (i.e., the ratios of certain temporal events in the movement divided by the total movement time) of a movement series appears to remain approximately constant across changes in the speed and size of an action. Evidence for invariant temporal characteristics has been cited from studies of typing (Terzuolo & Viviani, 1979), handwriting (Viviani & Terzuolo, 1980), speech (Tuller, Kelso, & Harris, 1982), locomotion (Shapiro, Zernicke, Gregor, & Diestal, 1981), arm movements (Armstrong, 1970; Shapiro, 1977), and sequential finger-tapping (Summers, 1975).

The second line of evidence for the importance of time in the motor-programming process has come from choice reaction-time studies. A basic assumption of the motor-program concept is that the program is set up in advance of movement onset and that such organization takes measurable time. The reaction time to begin movement, therefore, reflects the time to construct the appropriate motor program. Of particular relevance to the present discussion is the finding that the organization of the timing aspect of a response is a critical determinant of initiation time (e.g., Heuer, 1984; Ivry, 1986; Klapp & Greim, 1979; Rosenbaum, Inhoff, & Gordon, 1984). For example, uncertainty about the temporal structure of sequences of finger movements increases initiation time to a far greater extent than uncertainty about which fingers to use (Rosenbaum et al., 1984). Rosenbaum (1985) concluded from a review of choice reaction-time studies that "the timing of movement sequences can be readied independently of the muscle commands needed to realize that timing" (p. 17).

Research into the contents of motor programs suggests that the features of a learned movement pattern that are represented in the abstract program are: (a) the relative timing inherent in the sequence, (b) the sequencing of actions, and (c) the relative force of muscle contractions (Schmidt, 1980, 1984). Variations in the basic motor pattern are produced by the addition of parameters specifying the overall duration and overall size of the movements. In recent years the "generalized motor program with a multiplicative rate parameter" (Gentner, 1987, p. 254) has been the dominant information-processing model of movement timing.

Independence of Sequencing and Timing Mechanisms

An issue that has generated much recent debate is whether the sequencing and timing of action are controlled by different mechanisms. Rosenbaum (1985), for example, proposed a scheduling view of motor programming in which the mechanism that controls movement timing also controls serial order:

> A motor program is a *schedule* of motor events or, more precisely, a list of associations between labels for motor commands and clock pulses. Motor programming, according to this hypothesis, is the process of determining which motor commands are to be employed and with which clock pulses they are to be associated. Executing a motor program is the process of allowing responses to be triggered when their associated clock pulses occur. (p. 16)

According to this view, the timing mechanism determines the sequencing of action directly by specifying the time each component action is to occur. Errors in the sequencing of movements arise through the incorrect assignment of clock pulses to motor instructions causing responses to occur at the wrong time. MacKay (1987a, 1987b), however, has argued that errors in speech production rarely involve the simple misordering of components in time. Rather, substituted components nearly always belong to the same sequential class (e.g., nouns interchange with nouns). Such sequential regularities in speech errors would not be predicted if the sequencing of behavior is determined by the timing mechanism (MacKay, 1987a, 1987b).

At the other extreme it has been proposed that a mechanism that controls the sequencing of movement also determines movement timing.

Rumelhart and Norman (1982), for example, simulated many aspects of skilled typing without recourse to a specific mechanism controlling movement timing. In their model, the timing of successive keystrokes is determined by the states of activation of motor commands present in the motor program for a typing sequence. The activation level reflects the sum of the excitation or inhibition received and such factors as decay and random fluctuations (noise) in the resting level of activation. The correct temporal ordering of keystrokes is achieved through inhibition of successive keypress commands by the one currently active. Following a keypress there is a release of inhibition and the next most highly activated keypress is produced. Errors in the sequencing of movements (e.g., transposition errors) occur when fluctuations in the background level of activation occasionally lead to the wrong keystroke being most highly activated and occurring out of order. Simulation of such transposition errors showed that the keystroke interval following an error is typically much shorter than in errorless sequences. However, examination of transposition errors made by skilled typists (Grudin, 1982) do not show the changes in keystroke intervals predicted by the model. Rather the timing profile is very similar to that observed when the sequence is typed correctly. Furthermore, Rumelhart and Norman's model cannot easily account for changes in speed and fluency of typing that occur with practice (Long, Nimmo-Smith, & Whitefield, 1983).

The inability of a single mechanism to satisfactorily account for both the sequencing and timing of motor behavior suggests that timing and sequencing are closely related but independent processes in the programming of movement (Keele, 1987; MacKay, 1985, 1987b; Schmidt, 1980). Support for the independence assumption comes from the fact that the same sequence of movements can be produced with different timing characteristics (e.g., the maintenance of constant relative timing across changes in tempo). Furthermore, errors in the sequencing of movements can occur without disrupting the timing of successive movements (e.g., transposition errors in typing, spoonerisms in speech). There is some evidence, however, in tasks requiring the precise timing of movements, that with practice timing may become an integral part of sequencing. Summers (1977), for example, using a sequential finger-tapping task, trained subjects to execute a sequence of eight keypresses containing an inherent temporal structure specifying the interval between one response and the next. Following training, subjects performed a series of test trials in which the sequence previously learned was occasionally disrupted by an event occurring out of its proper order and/or time. The results showed that the occurrence of an out-of-sequence event at the expected time caused a greater disruption in performance than a similar event occurring either early or late in time. Sequencing and timing, therefore, appear to involve independent but closely coupled mechanisms (MacKay, 1987b). Summers, Sargent, and Hawkins (1984) suggested that a strong coupling between sequencing and timing may be especially evident in skills involving rhythmic timing structures.

The Internal Clock

In addressing the question of how the abstract specifications of time contained in the generalized motor program are translated into patterned sequences of movements in real time, motor-program theorists have appealed to the notion of an internal clock or timekeeper. Rosenbaum (1985), for example, proposed that "motor commands are triggered when their associated clock pulses occur" (p. 19). Keele (1981) similarly argued that the timing of movements is under the control of an internal clock and that "a motor program specifies not only the order of movements but how they interface with the clock" (p. 1412).

The notion of an internal clock or timekeeper that emits pulses at regular intervals but with some variability has been a common feature of many cognitive models of movement timing and rhythm perception (see Povel & Essens, 1985). Wing and Kristofferson (1973), for example, proposed a two-process model of self-paced responding in which fluctuations from periodic timing may arise from imprecision in a hypothetical timekeeper and from temporal noise in the production of responses triggered by the clock (Figure 8.1). Assuming that the timekeeper intervals and response delays are independent random variables, each interresponse interval is viewed as the sum of the timekeeper's cycle time plus the difference in motor delays associated with the responses that initiate and terminate the period. The main prediction of the model is that successive interresponse intervals will be negatively correlated. That is, if one interresponse interval is by chance shorter than the average the next interval will be longer than average and vice versa. An important contribution of the Wing and Kristofferson model is that it allows for the separation of total timing variance into central and peripheral components.

Evidence in support of the model has come predominantly from studies using repetitive finger tapping tasks (e.g., Vorberg & Hambuch, 1978; Wing, 1977, 1980). These tasks typically involve an induction phase in which subjects attempt to synchronize their finger taps with a sequence of tones presented at regular intervals, followed by a continuation phase, in which the subject tries to reproduce the pattern previously

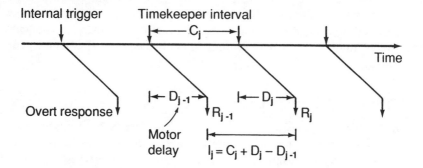

Figure 8.1. Wing and Kristofferson's (1973) two-process model of self-paced periodic responding. At time intervals, C, a timekeeper emits trigger pulses, each of which initiates a motor response. The motor system introduces a delay, D, between the trigger pulse and the occurrence of the overt response, R. Each interresponse interval is the sum of a timekeeper interval plus the difference in motor delays associated with the responses that initiate and terminate the period: $I_j = C_j + D_j - D_{j-1}$. (From Wing, Keele, & Margolin, 1984. Reprinted by permission.)

induced. Negative covariance between adjacent interresponse intervals is usually observed during the self-paced tapping (continuation) phase. Furthermore, increases in the duration of the intertap interval produces increases in clock variance while motor variance remains constant (Wing, 1980). This result provides support for the differentiation of timing variability into central and peripheral components. Negative covariance of adjacent intervals has been reported also in typewriting, but only when the text demands a strict alternation between the hands (Shaffer, 1978).

Vorberg and Hambuch (1984) have extended the two-process model of motor timing to the production of sequences composed of unequal intervals. The results suggested that timing in such patterns involves the use of several independent timekeepers arranged hierarchically but capable of running simultaneously.

Recently, Keele and his colleagues have had some success in using the Wing and Kristofferson method to identify the neural mechanisms involved in timing (Ivry & Keele, 1987; Ivry, Keele, & Diener, 1987; Keele & Ivry, 1987). Within-subject comparisons on a tapping task showed that increased variability when tapping with the impaired hand for peripheral neuropathy patients was solely attributed to the motor delay component. In contrast, Parkinson patients exhibited increased variability only in the clock process, whereas cerebellar patients showed increases in both clock and motor-delay estimates, when tapping with the affected hand. The research with neurological patients suggests that the timing system consists of a circuit "from cortex to cerebellum and basal ganglia and back to the cortex" (Keele, 1987, p. 479). This circuit is seen as constituting the motor program.

Common Timing Mechanisms for Perception and Action

It has been suggested that not only do different effectors share a common timekeeper but that the same timing mechanism also underlies the perception of time (Keele, 1987; MacKay, 1987a, 1987b). Support for this view has come from a significant correlation (.53) obtained between performance on a timed tapping task and performance on a perceptual task involving judgments concerning the durations of brief intervals between auditory events (Keele, Pokorny, Corcos, & Ivry, 1985). An interaction between perceptual and motor timing has also been demonstrated. Pokorny (cited in Keele, 1987) had subjects gener-ate a series of equal-interval finger taps. During some of the intertap intervals a pair of tones was presented and subjects were required either to make duration judgments, loudness judgments, or to ignore the tones. In all three conditions the intertap interval in which the tones occurred was lengthened. These results are consistent with a common timing mechanism governing both perceptual and motor timing. The apparent ease with which people can synchronize movement (e.g., key taps) with auditory patterns also indicates a close relationship between perception and action (Prinz, 1987).

Finally, recent work comparing the performance of Parkinson, cerebellar, cortical, and peripheral neuropathy patients on tapping and perception of time tasks has shown that only the cerebellar patients exhibit deficits on both tasks. This finding suggests that within the timing circuit (cortex-cerebellum-basal ganglia) the cerebellum functions like an internal clock, computing the timing requirements for the motor program (Ivry & Keele, 1987; Keele & Ivry, 1987).

Bimanual Coordination

A further source of evidence that has been cited in support of the notion of a central timing system has come from studies of interlimb coordina-tion. The general conclusion that emerges from these studies is that there are strong temporal constraints on the performance of simultane-ous motor actions. For example, Kelso, Southard, and Goodman (1979) examined the ability of subjects to make two-handed movements to separate targets that differed in size and in distance from the resting position. Under these conditions, the hands appeared to move in synchrony, so that they arrived at their respective targets at the same time. Thus, even though the spatial demands for the two limbs were quite different, the timing relations between the two limbs remained constant.

Studies using bimanual tapping tasks also show a similar disposition toward simple timing relations in the coordination of the two hands (Klapp, 1979; Peters, 1977). Subjects can easily produce two isochronous sequences in parallel, one with each hand, when the sequences have identical or harmonically related time intervals. However, great difficulty is experienced in the concurrent performance of nonharmonically related motor sequences, such as polyrhythms (Deutsch, 1983; Klapp, Hill, Tyler, Martin, Jagacinski, & Jones, 1985; Summers, 1987). Recent studies using the choice-reaction time paradigm indicate that the temporal incompatibility effects arise not only during the execution of movement but also at a central level during the programming of movement. Longer reaction times are produced when the choice is between movements with the left and right hand that differ in timing than when the movements have identical timing requirements (e.g., Heuer, 1984, 1986).

The temporal constraints evident in bimanual performance suggest the existence of a single timing mechanism controlling the right- and left-hand motor subsystems. It is assumed that the central mechanism is limited in the extent to which it can maintain different timing specifications for the two hands. Peters (1981, 1985) argued that when performing concurrent bimanual tasks the central controller assigns priorities, through the allocation of attention, so that one limb drives the other and the two hands become synchronized. It is further assumed that in the guidance of concurrent tasks there is a preferential allocation of attention to the preferred hand. Support for this view has come from studies showing performance asymmetries in bimanual tasks (e.g., Ibbotson & Morton, 1981; Peters, 1981, 1985). For example, when subjects are required to tap out a rhythm with one hand and a simultaneous regular beat with the other, performance is better when the preferred hand taps the rhythm and the nonpreferred hand the beat than vice versa (Ibbotson & Morton, 1981).

Problems With the Motor-Program Model of Movement Timing

The model of movement timing developed thus far has two basic components: a generalized motor program with a multiplicative rate parameter and one or more internal clocks that pace the production of motor responses in real time. Information in the abstract program specifies the interface between motor commands and clock pulses, whereas the rate parameter presumably controls the cycle time of the underlying clock mechanism(s). Perceptual and motor processes appear to share the same timing mechanisms.

Recently, a number of lines of evidence suggest that this model does not provide an accurate description of movement timing. Gentner (1987), for example, challenged the assumption that relative timing is determined by the program and duration by a parameter of the program. He completed a thorough reanalysis of the evidence cited to support the idea of an invariance in relative timing across changes in movement speed. Reanalysis of the data from a variety of laboratory tasks and highly practiced skills (e.g., locomotion, handwriting, speech, typewriting) failed to support the assumption of relative timing invariance. Rather, the data indicated "a composite model of motor control in which performance is determined by both central and peripheral mechanisms" (Gentner, 1987, p. 255).

Evidence against the view that relative timing is one of the invariant characteristics of a generalized motor program has come also from experiments examining transfer effects. According to motor-program theory perfect transfer would be expected between motor patterns with the same relative timing but different overall durations. Poor transfer, however, should occur when a shift is required to a motor pattern with a different relative timing and duration because a new motor program must be developed. Heuer and Schmidt (1988) tested these predictions in two experiments in which subjects practiced a particular spatio-temporal pattern of elbow flexion movements. Following practice subjects transferred either to a pattern with a new duration but identical relative timing or to a pattern involving both a new duration and relative timing. In both experiments there was no evidence that transfer is impaired if relative timing is changed. These results argue strongly against the view of a generalized motor program with mandatory invariant relative timing. Rather, the ability of subjects to quickly adopt a new relative timing suggests that the previously observed invariance may reflect "strategic factors having to do with patterns of timing that are in some way *preferred* as compared with others" (Heuer & Schmidt, 1988, p. 251). The strategic view suggests that a given generalized motor program may control movements with a range of natural temporal patterns, the range being determined by the spatial characteristics of the movements. Perfect transfer would be expected to a new relative timing when the new timing belongs to the range of natural patterns controlled by the motor program. The hypothesis that different timing patterns may differ with regard to their naturalness has also been proposed to explain the break down, in finger-tapping tasks, of some temporal patterns under speed instructions and when a secondary task is introduced (Summers, 1975; Summers et al., 1984). In such tasks, rhythmic timing structures may constitute the preferred relative timing (Summers et al., 1984).

Recent studies of handwriting also argue against the central control of timing (e.g., Teulings, 1988; Thomassen & Teulings, 1985; Wann, 1986). A detailed analysis of the factors determining the production of writing movements at the macro- (word), meso- (letter), and micro- (stroke) levels suggests that temporal information is not part of the abstract motor program of a handwriting pattern. Rather the "programs for letter shapes merely prescribe spatial relationships and general, ordered sequences of movements to achieve the corresponding spatial patterns, or to reach the successive goals within the pattern" (Thomassen & Teulings, 1985, p. 261). Timing in handwriting, therefore, appears to be primarily a reflection of the biomechanical constraints on the muscle systems involved, such as fingers, hand, and arm. Similarly, the timing observed in typewriting may be determined to a large extent by peripheral factors, such as the structure of the hands and keyboard (Rumelhart & Norman, 1982).

The concept of an internal clock or timekeeper underlying the timing of human movement has also been criticized by several authors. Kolers and Brewster (1985) have argued against the assumption that there is a central clock shared by motor and perceptual systems. They found that the variability of tapping performance was affected by the modality (visual, auditory, or tactile) used to present sequences to subjects. The authors suggest that performances were not based on a single timing mechanism, but, rather a different timing strategy was employed for the different modalities. As Kolers and Brewster (1985) pointed out:

> A logical problem with the notion of timers lies in the difficulty of specifying what is being timed and thus of setting a limit on their number and function. By extension, the notion of timer becomes indistinguishable from the temporal regularity of movement. (p. 165)

Shaffer (1982, 1985) criticized the idea that movements are triggered by pulses emitted by a central clock. He argued that it is more realistic to assume that movements are timed relative to the moment at which they produce their effects rather than from their moments of onset. Trigger theories of movement timing cannot easily explain anticipatory movement that is a common feature of many motor tasks, such as hitting or catching an approaching ball, or tapping in synchrony with a metronome. Co-articulatory movement in speech, typing, and piano playing also suggests that movements are constructed to anticipate temporal goals. Shaffer (1985) proposed that "there are procedures in the motor system, containing a wealth of background knowledge about movement, which can compute muscle actions that will achieve goals designated by a motor program" (p. 227). Thus, the motor system itself can act as a timekeeper by translating a given time interval into a movement trajectory having that duration (Shaffer, 1982). Shaffer suggested, however, that in certain motor tasks, such as playing music, the motor system may make use of a superordinate clock or timekeeper, not directly involved in movement production, which can, on instruction from the motor program, "generate a time scale to control the time course of performance" (Shaffer, Clarke, & Todd, 1985, p. 64). That is, the superordinate clock does not trigger movement directly but provides temporal reference points for movements produced by the motor system and enables the coordination of movements in independent motor systems. Examination of the timing evident in a variety of motor skills suggests that timing may be either a secondary consequence of movement logistics or it may be constructed by the motor system (Shaffer, 1982, 1985). In constructing movements having a given time span or temporal goal the motor system can make reference to an underlying clock to pace the motor output.

THE ECOLOGICAL APPROACH

The ecological or action system approach to the study of motor behavior rejects the view that timing in movement results from an a priori prescription in terms of temporal codes stored in a motor program, central clocks, or timers. Rather, time per se is not directly controlled; it is a consequence of the dynamic behavior of the neuromotor system (Kelso, 1981). The key concept in the ecological approach is the coordinative structure (Easton, 1972). A coordinative structure is a group of muscles often spanning several joints that is constrained to act as a single functional unit. These units of action are not "hard wired" but are flexibly assembled to perform a specific act. Once assembled, a coordinative structure operates relatively autonomously achieving its goal with minimal voluntary intervention (Saltzman & Kelso, 1987).

Proponents of the ecological approach have focused on the periodicities evident in cyclic repetitive movements, such as locomotion and bimanual movements. They suggest that the timing of such movements is a consequence of underlying oscillatory processes. Coordinative structures, therefore, function as nonlinear, limit-cycle oscillators (see Kelso, Holt, Rubin, & Kugler, 1981). Nonlinear oscillatory systems possess a number of properties that form the basis for their model of motor timing. In particular, limit-cycle oscillators always exhibit interaction or entrainment. One form of interaction is mutual entrainment that occurs when coupled oscillators with slightly different frequencies become synchronized at an intermediate frequency. Another form is subharmonic entrainment that results when one oscillator adopts a frequency that is an integer multiple of another to which it is coupled (as when two limbs are moved at different rates).

Evidence for entrainment-like phenomena in voluntary human actions has come from studies of cyclic finger or hand movements. Kelso et al. (1981), for example, asked subjects to move the index fingers of one or both hands in a cyclical (flexion-extension) manner. The preferred frequency of each limb in isolation was first determined and then possible interactions between the limbs when they performed together were examined. When the two hands moved together mutual entrainment effects were observed. In right-handed subjects the left hand was "attracted" to the right hand. Subharmonic entrainment was also observed when subjects were asked to move one finger at a preferred frequency and to move the other finger at a different frequency. In nearly all cases, subjects employed low integer subharmonics such as 2 to 1 and 3 to 1. Yamanishi, Kawato, and Suzuki (1980) have also obtained results consistent with the view that bimanual coordination in finger tapping is controlled through coupled oscillatory neural networks, one for each finger. They required subjects to maintain various phase differences between the two hands. For both musically trained and untrained subjects accurate and stable performance was obtained when the two hands tapped in synchrony (in-phase) or alternated (180 degrees out of phase). Furthermore, intermediate phase differences between the two hands produced unstable performance and a tendency to entrain to the nearest stable phase (synchrony or alternation). The authors conclude that in-phase motion and antiphase motion are stable modes of coupling the hands. Recent work, however, suggests that the in-phase relation is more stable. When subjects using an antiphase motion of the hands are asked to increase the cycling rate an abrupt shift to an in-phase relation is observed at a critical driving frequency (Kelso, 1981, 1984). Such behavior has been successfully modeled using the mathematics of nonlinear oscillator theory (see Haken, Kelso, & Bunz, 1985; Kelso & Scholz, 1985).

The ecological approach, therefore, argues that task-specific ensembles of coordinative structures are the units of control and coordination of action. Such a scheme does not require an explicit representation of time; rather, it is an emergent property of the dynamical structure of the motor system. Flexibility in behavior is attained by adjusting control parameters over the entire unit (Kelso & Scholz, 1985). It is further assumed that the setting of parameters is specified directly via perception. In particular, action-system theorists have developed Gibson's (1966, 1979) notion of the optical flow field. Lee (1976), for example, has argued that optic flow information can be used for the regulation of action. In tasks in which the timing of actions is determined by how the organism is moving relative to the environment (e.g., locomotion), or how an object is moving relative to the organism (e.g., hitting or catching a ball), the flow of optical texture in the visual field provides time-to-contact information. For example, the time-to-contact (called the *tau-margin*) of a ball on a collision course with an organism's eye is the inverse of the rate of dilation of the image of the ball on the retina (Lee & Young, 1986). Lee and others have successfully applied the notion of the tau-margin to a variety of sports skills (e.g., ski jumping, long jumping) and everyday activities (e.g., driving, crossing the road, stair climbing) (see Lee & Young, 1986, for a review). The importance of the concept to the ecological approach is that time-to-contact is a directly available, nonderived property of the visual input itself (Kelso & Kay, 1987).

The ecological approach to the study of movement timing, therefore, contrasts dramatically with the information-processing approach outlined previously. Time is not seen as an independent variable in the control of movement. The spatiotemporal behavior of individual components in a movement sequence emerges from the inherent dynamics of the particular task-specific assemblage of neuromuscular elements. In its purest form, action-system theory rejects the notion of high-level controllers supposing a direct link between sensory input and motor output. Craske and Craske (1986), however, have criticized this view:

> We cannot see how dynamical considerations alone can model a goal directed system; it seems that in such systems order to a specific end must be absent, however much emergent organization there may be. (p. 122)

Craske and Craske proposed the existence of a motor controller that is responsive to sensory input and "can translate intention into action by starting stopping, and modifying parameters of oscillator mechanisms to which it has access" (p. 122).

ACTIVATION MODELS OF MOVEMENT TIMING

Recent years have witnessed the emergence of activation or connection-ist models of cognition. These models typically have either not directly addressed the issue of movement timing, or have assumed that timing is derived from the order of events (e.g., Anderson, 1983; Rumelhart & Norman, 1982). MacKay (1982, 1985), however, has developed an activation theory of action in which timing and sequencing are seen as closely related but independent processes. The basic components for organizing actions in the theory are networks of simple processing units (nodes). Nodes have a number of dynamic properties (see MacKay, 1985, 1987b, for a detailed discussion), the two most important being priming and activation. Activation of nodes occurs in an all-or-none fashion and continues for a specifiable period of time before being terminated through a process of self-inhibition. *Priming* refers to the simultaneous subthreshold activation of all nodes directly connected to an activated node, and is a necessary prerequisite for activation.

The theory proposes that nodes are organized into two general systems that can operate independently: a mental system that contains cognitive units representing the components of an action sequence and the relationship between them, and a muscle movement system which specifies muscle-specific patterns of movement. These general systems are seen as comprising of a number of hierarchically organized sub-systems. In speech production, for example, the mental system contains two subsystems: a sentential system and a phonological system (see Figure 8.2).

Each system in MacKay's model has three types of nodes: "*content nodes* represent the form or content components of an action or percep-tion; *sequence nodes* represent the order in which content nodes become activated; and *timing nodes* determine when to activate the sequence nodes, which in turn activate the content nodes" (MacKay, 1987b, p. 16). Timing nodes, therefore, provide the mechanism for the temporal organization of the output. They determine both when the sequence nodes become activated and determine the overall rate of behavior. Timing nodes for different systems have different periodicities or average rates of activation, with the higher level systems (e.g., sentential system) exhibiting a slower periodicity than lower level systems (e.g., muscle movement system). Different timing nodes, however, can be coupled so that if a high-level timing node is speeded up, the timing nodes at lower levels will speed up proportionally.

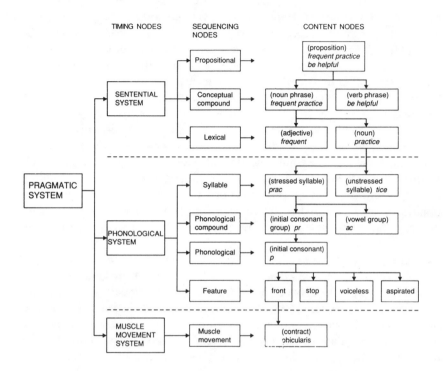

Figure. 8.2. An overview of MacKay's node structure theory. The hypothetical structure underlying the production of the sentence "Frequent practice is helpful" is shown. (From MacKay, 1982. Reprinted by permission.)

The coupling of different effectors to the same timing node produce the temporal constraints on interlimb coordination described previously. However, the ability of skilled performers, such as pianists, to generate two differently timed motor sequences in parallel is due to the development, with prolonged practice, of independent timing nodes for the two hands. Alternatively, a single timing node and a counter could be used for controlling temporally incompatible activities (MacKay, 1987b). The counter determines which pulses emitted by the timing node trigger the movement (i.e., activate the most primed nodes) for one hand, and which pulses trigger the movement for the other.

To engage and disengage timing nodes a high-level decision is required. MacKay (1985) proposed that such decisions are made within a higher level cognitive control system; the pragmatic system. The pragmatic system also sets the rate or tempo of action by determining how fast the coupled timing nodes for all other systems become activated.   Furthermore, by directly controlling timing nodes the pragmatic system is able to determine the mode of output. For example, by engaging high-level timing nodes but not those for the muscle movement system imagined action can occur. A general overview of the basic theoretical constructs of node structure theory is provided in Figure 8.2.

MacKay's model of timing differs from those previously discussed in that timing is seen as a distributed characteristic.   Timing neither emerges nor is it imposed at any particular level, it is present at all levels through the activation of different timing nodes at each level. "Rhythm, rate, and timing permeate the entire process of producing well-practiced behaviors, and cannot be tacked on as an independent stage at some point in the theoretical specification of the output" (MacKay, 1987b, p. 91).

There are, however, some aspects of the node-structure theory of timing that need further elaboration. First, it is not explained how the pragmatic system selectively activates the timing nodes.   Second, the organization of the timing nodes is unclear. Different organizations are proposed to explain various phenomena.   Such flexibility makes it difficult to formulate definite predictions from the model. This must be done or the model is in danger of being seen as just a metaphor for the all-pervasiveness of periodic movement.

An advantage of dynamic models such as MacKay's is that they have the potential for mapping psychological constructs onto the functional organization of the nervous system (see MacKay, 1985).   Furthermore, by attempting to explain hierarchical concepts in cognition in terms of the parallel nature of the neuron, they may help to refocus or resolve the current debate between motor programming and ecological theories of movement timing. It remains to be seen, however, whether the node structure approach can provide a complete account of the complexities of timing evident in motor performance.

THE TIMING OF MOVEMENT SEQUENCES

In this chapter we have examined the question of how sequences of movements are timed from three perspectives: the information process-ing, ecological, and node-structure approaches to motor behavior. Information-processing models stress the central control of movement via generalized motor programs stored in long-term memory and internal clocks or timekeepers. Ecological approaches to action, in contrast, deny that time per se is directly controlled in any movement activity, preferring to argue that order and regulation in movement are a consequence of the motor system's dynamic structure and parameterization. Finally, the node-structure approach emphasizes the distributed nature of timing with separate timing mechanisms operating throughout a hierarchically organized system of production units. The general conclusion that emerges from this review is that in some motor activities time need not be independently specified in the control of movement. This seems to be the case in skills like typing, handwriting, and speech, where the maintenance of precise timing between movements is not an explicit part of the activity. In such activities timing may be a natural consequence of well tuned, smoothly operating output systems (Thomassen & Teulings, 1985).

This does not mean, however, that central control is not or cannot be exerted in the performance of such tasks. As MacKay (1987b) pointed out, people, especially the highly skilled, can and often do generate perfect or near perfect periodicity in skills that do not demand rhythmic timing (e.g., typing, speech, handwriting). Gentner (1987), for example, showed that skilled typists can vary their overall typing rate at will. When typing at their slowest rate, typing seems to be paced by a central timekeeper, with peripheral constraints becoming more important as speed is increased. In activities, such as typing, higher level periodicity may often be masked by lower level constraints, such as the structure of the hands and keyboard (MacKay, 1987b). Furthermore, timing periodicities are most frequently observed in highly skilled performers suggesting that higher level control of timing emerges with practice. In MacKay's node-structure theory, this is due to the fact that timing nodes only become connected during the final stages of skill acquisition, when the skill has become largely automatic.

There is also evidence that motor interactions (i.e., entrainment) commonly observed between the two hands are not a necessary consequence of bimanual performance. Summers, Bell, and Burns (1989) compared the ability of subjects to tap out simple temporal patterns using two hands or one hand (where motor interactions are not involved). The results showed almost identical performance under the two response conditions. The authors conclude that the perceived temporal structure was the main determinant of performance in both response modes. Klapp et al. (1985) have similarly argued that the difficulty in responding to incompatible rhythms (i.e., polyrhythms) may be primarily due to perceptual factors rather than interference between the two hands. Even in studies where motor interactions between the two hands have been observed, there is evidence that the interaction may be weakened by learning. Yamanashi et al. (1980) noted that the entrainment between the hands in bimanual tapping was much stronger for unskilled than skilled (musically trained) subjects. These results suggest that in tasks requiring the precise phasing of the two hands central control can be exerted over low-level oscillatory mechanisms. There is increasing evidence that most motor skills are cognitively penetrable. Many actions that have been previously considered as low-level automatisms, such as the maintenance of upright posture, locomotion, and reflexive responses to unexpected perturbations of movement, can be influenced by specific cognitive states such as expectations, goals or knowledge (Hughes & Stelmach, 1986).

There is also strong evidence to suggest that sensory information can be used to control the timing of movements, particularly in tasks requiring extrinsic timing (Lee & Young, 1986). In these activities, time-to-contact information derived from visual input may directly control movement timing.

In tasks where the maintenance of a particular temporal structure is essential to successful performance (e.g., playing music), timing may form part of the high-level representation of action. Shaffer (1984), for example, has shown that the free use of rubato and tempo variation by a skilled pianist are highly reproducible in repeat performances of a piece played a year apart. This suggests that "the timing information in a motor program contains a formal schedule, obtained from the written music, together with its expressive modulations" (p. 422). It is not surprising, therefore, that the strongest evidence for the central control of movement timing has come from laboratory studies in which the subject's task is to reproduce precisely the temporal relations between successive events in a presented pattern (e.g., Povel, 1981; Vorberg & Hambuch, 1984; Wing, 1980). Michon (1985) has suggested that when temporal information is processed it is "largely a deliberate cognitive activity, requiring a great deal of attention and strategic flexibility on the part of the individual" (p. 35).

Some support for this view has come from studies examining the effects on performance of changes in the nature of a task. Summers, Hawkins, and Mayers (1986), for example, compared performance in tasks involving either the reproduction or spontaneous production of simple temporal patterns. The results suggested that different timing strategies were employed by subjects in the two tasks. The reproduction data were consistent with the notion that an internal clock was used as a basis to specify the temporal structure of a pattern (Povel & Essens, 1985). In the production task, however, subjects appeared to adopt a more primitive timing strategy based on the organizing principles of distinction and assimilation (Fraisse, 1978). Whether or not an internal clock is generated has also been shown to depend on the structural characteristics of a temporal pattern (Essens & Povel, 1985). Differences in performance obtained across different pattern structures, tasks, or modalities (Kolers & Brewster, 1985) provide support for the view that different strategies may be employed in the performance of timing tasks.

CONCLUDING REMARKS

It appears, therefore, that there are number of mechanisms that can be used to control the spatiotemporal patterning of individual components in a movement sequence. The particular timing option adopted will be determined by the task demands, sources of information available (e.g., optic flow) and stage of learning. Gentner (1987) has similarly concluded that "control of timing is determined at several levels in the perceptual-cognitive-motor system, and the nature and relative importance of these control levels can shift with skill acquisition and in response to the task environment" (p. 275).

Future work in the area must provide a more rigorous account of the timing mechanisms involved in motor performance and the particular conditions that determine their use. Understanding the interface between cognitive processes and low-level neurological mechanisms is clearly an important issue for research in the timing of movement sequences.

ACKNOWLEDGMENT

Preparation of this chapter was supported by the Australian Research Grants Scheme, Project No. A28115899.

REFERENCES

Adams, J. A. (1977). Feedback theory of how joint receptors regulate the timing and positioning of a limb. *Psychological Review, 84,* 504-523.

Adams, J. A., & Creamer, L. R. (1962). Proprioception variables as determiners of anticipatory timing behavior. *Human Factors, 4,* 217-222.

Anderson, J. R. (1983). *The architecture of cognition.* Cambridge, MA: Harvard University Press.

Armstrong, T. R. (1970). *Training for the production of memorized movement patterns* (Tech. Rep. No. 26). Ann Arbor: University of Michigan, Human Performance Center.

Craske, B., & Craske J. D. (1986). Oscillator mechanisms in the human motor system: Investigating their properties using the aftercontraction effect. *Journal of Motor Behavior, 18,* 117-145.

Deutsch, D. (1983). The generation of two isochronous sequences in parallel. *Perception & Psychophysics, 34,* 331-337.

Easton, T. A. (1972). On the normal use of reflexes. *American Scientist, 60,* 591-599.

Essens, P. J., & Povel, D.-J. (1985). Metrical and nonmetrical representations of temporal patterns. *Perception & Psychophysics, 37,* 1-7.

Fraisse, P. (1978). Time and rhythm perception. In E. C. Carterette & M. P. Friedman (Eds.), *Handbook of perception* (Vol. 8, pp. 203-254). New York: Academic Press.

Gentner, D. R. (1987). Timing of skilled motor performance: Tests of the proportional duration model. *Psychological Review, 94,* 255-276.

Gibson, J. J. (1966). *The senses considered as perceptual systems.* Boston: Houghton-Mifflin.

Gibson, J. J. (1979). *The ecological approach to visual perception.* Boston: Houghton-Mifflin.

Grudin, J. T. (1982). *Central control of timing in skilled typing* (Tech. Rep. No. 8202). San Diego: University of California, Center for Human Information Processing.

Haken, H., Kelso, J. A. S., & Bunz, H. (1985). A theoretical model of phase transitions in human movements. *Biological Cybernetics, 51,* 347-356.

Heuer, H. (1984). Binary choice reaction time as a function of the relationship between durations and forms of response. *Journal of Motor Behavior, 16,* 392-404.

Heuer, H. (1986). Intermanual interactions during programming of aimed movements: Converging evidence on common and specific parameters of control. *Psychological Research, 48,* 37-46.

Heuer, H., & Schmidt, R. A. (1988). Transfer of learning among motor patterns with different relative timing. *Journal of Experimental Psychology: Human Perception and Performance, 14,* 241-252.

Hughes, B. G., & Stelmach, G. E. (1986). On Bernstein as a contributor to cognitive theories of motor behavior. *Human Movement Science, 5,* 35-45.

Ibbotson, N. R., & Morton, J. (1981). Rhythm and dominance. *Cognition, 9,* 125-138.

Ivry, R. B. (1986). Force and timing components of the motor program. *Journal of Motor Behavior, 18,* 449-474.

Ivry, R. B., & Keele, S. W. (1987). *Timing functions of the cerebellum* (Tech. Rep. No. 87-2). Eugene: University of Oregon, Cognitive Psychology Program.

Ivry, R. B., Keele, S. W., & Diener, H. C. (1987). *Dissociation of the lateral and medial cerebellum in movement timing and movement execution* (Tech. Rep. No. 87-3). Eugene: University of Oregon, Cognitive Psychology Program.

Jones, M. R. (1985). Structural organization of events in time. In J. A. Michon & J. L. Jackson (Eds.), *Time, mind, and behavior* (pp. 192-214). Berlin: Springer-Verlag.

Keele, S. W. (1968). Movement control in skilled motor performance. *Psychological Bulletin, 70,* 387-403.

Keele, S. W. (1981). Behavioral analysis of movement. In V. Brooks (Ed.) *Handbook of physiology: Motor control* (pp. 1391-1413). Washington, DC: American Physiological Society.

Keele, S. W. (1986). Motor control. In J. K. Boff, L. Kaufman, & J. P. Thomas (Eds.), *Handbook of perception and human performance: Vol. II. Cognitive processes and performance* (pp. 1-60). New York: Wiley.

Keele, S. W. (1987). Sequencing and timing in skilled perception and action: An overview. In A. Allport, D. MacKay, W. Prinz, & E. Scheerer (Eds.), *Language perception and production* (pp. 463-487). New York: Academic Press.

Keele, S. W., & Ivry, R. B. (1987). Modular analysis of timing in motor skill. In G. Bower (Ed.), *The psychology of learning and motivation* (Vol. 21, pp. 183-228). New York: Academic Press.

Keele, S. W., Pokorny, R. A., Corcos, D. M., & Ivry, R. (1985). Do perception and motor production share common timing mechanisms? A correlational analysis. *Acta Psychologica, 60*, 173-191.

Keele, S. W., & Summers, J. J. (1976). The structure of motor programs. In G. E. Stelmach (Ed.), *Motor control: Issues and trends* (pp. 109-142). New York: Academic Press.

Kelso, J. A. S. (1978). Joint receptors do not provide a satisfactory basis for motor timing and positioning. *Psychological Review, 85*, 474-481.

Kelso, J. A. S. (1981). Contrasting perspectives on order and regulation in movement. In J. Long & A. Baddeley (Eds.), *Attention and performance* (Vol. IX, pp. 437-457). Hillsdale, NJ: Lawrence Erlbaum Associates.

Kelso, J. A. S. (1984). Phase transitions and critical behavior in human bimanual coordination. *American Journal of Physiology: Regulatory, Integrative and Comparative, 246*, R1000-R1004.

Kelso, J. A. S., Holt, K. G., Rubin, P., & Kugler, P. N. (1981). Patterns of human interlimb coordination emerge from the properties of non-linear, limit-cycle oscillatory processes: Theory and data. *Journal of Motor Behavior, 13*, 226-261.

Kelso, J. A. S., & Kay, B. A. (1987). Information and control: A macroscopic analysis of perception-action coupling. In H. Heuer & A. F. Sanders (Eds.), *Perspectives on perception and action* (pp. 3-32). Hillsdale, NJ: Lawrence Erlbaum Associates.

Kelso, J. A. S., & Scholz, J. P. (1985). Cooperative phenomena in biological motion. In H. Haken (Ed.), *Complex systems: Operational approaches in neurobiology, physics, and computers* (pp. 124-149). New York: Springer-Verlag.

Kelso, J. A. S., Southard, D. L., & Goodman, D. (1979). On the coordination of two-handed movements. *Journal of Experimental Psychology: Human Perception and Performance, 5*, 229-238.

Klapp, S. T. (1979). Doing two things at once: The role of temporal compatibility. *Memory & Cognition, 7*, 375-381.

Klapp, S. T., & Greim, D. M. (1979). Programmed control of aimed movements revisited: The role of target visibility and symmetry. *Journal of Experimental Psychology: Human Perception and Performance, 5*, 509-521.

Klapp, S. T., Hill, M. D., Tyler, J. G., Martin, Z. E., Jagacinski, R. J., & Jones, M. R. (1985). On marching to two different drummers: Perceptual aspects of the difficulties. *Journal of Experimental Psychology: Human Perception and Performance, 11*, 814-827

Kolers, P. A., & Brewster, J. M. (1985). Rhythms and responses. *Journal of Experimental Psychology: Human Perception and Performance, 11*, 150-167.

Lee, D. N. (1976). A theory of visual control of braking based on information about time-to-collision. *Perception, 5*, 437-459.

Lee, D. N., & Young, D. S. (1986). Visual timing of interceptive action. In D. Ingle, M. Jeannerod, & D. N. Lee (Eds.), *Brain mechanisms and spatial vision* (pp. 1-30). Dordrecht, The Netherlands: Nijhoff.

Long, J., Nimmo-Smith, I., & Whitefield, A. (1983). Skilled typing: A characterization based on distribution of times between responses. In W. E. Cooper (Ed.), *Cognitive aspects of skilled typewriting* (pp. 145-195). New York: Springer-Verlag.

MacKay, D. G. (1982). The problems of flexibility, fluency and speed-accuracy trade-off in skilled behavior. *Psychological Review, 89,* 483-506.

MacKay, D. G. (1985). A theory of the representation, organization and timing of action with implications for sequencing disorders. In E. A. Roy (Ed.), *Neurological studies of apraxia and related disorders* (pp. 267-308). Amsterdam: North-Holland.

MacKay, D. G. (1987a). Theories of sequencing and timing. In A. Allport, D. MacKay, W. Prinz, & E. Scheerer (Eds.), *Language perception and production* (pp. 407-430). New York: Academic Press.

MacKay, D. G. (1987b). *The organization of perception and action.* New York: Springer-Verlag.

Michon, J. A. (1985). The compleat time experiencer. In J. A. Michon & J. L. Jackson (Eds.), *Time, mind, and behavior* (pp. 20-52). Berlin: Springer-Verlag.

Peters, M. (1977). Simultaneous performance of two motor activities: The factor of timing. *Neuropsychologia, 15,* 461-465.

Peters, M. (1981). Attentional asymmetries during concurrent bimanual performance. *Quarterly Journal of Experimental Psychology, 33A,* 95-103.

Peters, M. (1985). Constraints in the performance of bimanual tasks and their expression in unskilled and skilled subjects. *Quarterly Journal of Experimental Psychology, 37A,* 171-196.

Povel, D.-J. (1981). Internal representation of simple temporal patterns. *Journal of Experimental Psychology: Human Perception and Performance, 7,* 3-18.

Povel, D.-J., & Essens, P. (1985). Perception of temporal patterns. *Music Perception, 2,* 411-440.

Prinz, W. (1987). Ideo-motor action. In H. Heuer & A. F. Sanders (Eds.), *Perspectives on perception and action* (pp. 47-76). Hillsdale, NJ: Lawrence Erlbaum Associates.

Raibert, M. H. (1977). *Motor control and learning by the state space model* (Tech. Rep.). Cambridge, MA: Massachusetts Institute of Technology, Artificial Intelligence Laboratory.

Rosenbaum, D. A. (1985). Motor programming: A review and scheduling theory. In H. Heuer, U. Kleinbeck, & K. H. Schmidt (Eds.), *Motor behavior: Programming, control, and acquisition* (pp. 1-33). Berlin: Springer-Verlag.

Rosenbaum, D. A., Inhoff, A. W., & Gordon, A. M. (1984). Choosing between movement sequences: A hierarchical editor model. *Journal of Experimental Psychology: General, 113,* 372-393.

Rumelhart, D. E., & Norman, D. A. (1982). Simulating a skilled typist: A study of skilled cognitive-motor performance. *Cognitive Science, 6,* 1-36.

Saltzman, E., & Kelso, J. A. S. (1987). Skilled actions: A task-dynamic approach. *Psychological Review, 94,* 84-106.

Schmidt, R. A. (1975). A schema theory of discrete motor skill learning. *Psychological Review, 82,* 225-260.

Schmidt, R. A. (1980). On the theoretical status of time in motor program representations. In G. E. Stelmach & J. Requin (Eds.), *Tutorials in motor behavior* (pp. 145-165). Amsterdam: North-Holland.

Schmidt, R. A. (1984). The search for invariance in skilled movement behavior. *Research Quarterly for Exercise and Sport, 56,* 188-200.

Schmidt, R. A., & Christina, R. W. (1969). Proprioception as a mediator in the timing of motor responses. *Journal of Experimental Psychology, 81,* 303-307.

Shaffer, L. H. (1978). Timing in the motor programming of typing. *Quarterly Journal of Experimental Psychology, 30,* 333-345.

Shaffer, L. H. (1982). Rhythm and timing in skill. *Psychological Review, 89,* 109-122.

Shaffer, L. H. (1984). Timing in musical performance. In J. Gibbon & L. Allan (Eds.), *Timing and time perception* (pp. 420-428). New York: New York Academy of Sciences.

Shaffer, L. H. (1985). Timing in action. In J. A. Michon & J. L. Jackson (Eds.), *Time, mind, and behavior* (pp. 226-241). Berlin: Springer-Verlag.

Shaffer, L. H., Clarke, E. F., & Todd, N. P. (1985). Metre and rhythm in piano playing. *Cognition, 20,* 61-77.

Shapiro, D. C. (1977). A preliminary attempt to determine the duration of a motor program. In D. M. Landers & R. W. Christina (Eds.), *Psychology of motor behavior and sport* (Vol. 1, pp. 17-24). Champaign, IL: Human Kinetics.

Shapiro, D. C., & Schmidt, R. A. (1982). The schema theory: Recent evidence and developmental implications. In J. A. S. Kelso & J. E. Clark (Eds.), *The development of movement control and co-ordination* (pp. 113-150). New York: Wiley.

Shapiro, D. C., Zernicke, R. F., Gregor, R. J., & Diestal, J. D. (1981). Evidence for generalized motor programs using gait analysis. *Journal of Motor Behavior, 13,* 33-47.

Summers, J. J. (1975). The role of timing in motor program representation. *Journal of Motor Behavior, 7,* 229-241.

Summers, J. J. (1977). The relationship between the sequencing and timing components of a skill. *Journal of Motor Behavior, 9,* 49-59.

Summers, J. J. (1981). Motor programs. In D. H. Holding (Ed.), *Human skills* (pp. 41-61). Chichester: Wiley.

Summers, J. J. (1989). Motor programs. In D. H. Holding (Ed.), *Human skills* (2nd ed., pp. 48-69). Chichester: Wiley.

Summers, J. J. (1987, September). *The production of polyrhythms.* Paper presented at the Second Workshop on Rhythm Perception and Production, Marburg, Germany.

Summers, J. J., Bell, R., & Burns, B. D. (1989). Perceptual and motor factors in the imitation of simple temporal patterns. *Psychological Research, 51,* 23-27.

Summers, J. J., Hawkins, S. R., & Mayers, H. (1986). Imitation and production of interval ratios. *Perception & Psychophysics, 39,* 437-444.

Summers, J. J., Sargent, G. I., & Hawkins, S. R. (1984). Rhythm and the timing of movement sequences. *Psychological Research, 46,* 107-119.

Terzuolo, C. A., & Viviani, P. (1979). The central representation of learned motor programs. In R. E. Talbort & D. R. Humphrey (Eds.), *Posture and movement* (pp. 113-121). New York: Raven Press.

Teulings, H.-L. (1988). *Handwriting movement control.* Nijmegen, The Netherlands: NICI.

Thomassen, A. J. W. M., & Teulings, H.-L. (1985). Time, size and shape in handwriting: Exploring spatio-temporal relationships at different levels. In J. A. Michon & J. L. Jackson (Eds.), *Time, mind and behavior* (pp. 253-263). Berlin: Springer-Verlag.

Tuller, B., Kelso, J. A. S., & Harris, K. S. (1982). Interarticulator phasing as an index of temporal regularity in speech. *Journal of Experimental Psychology: Human Perception and Performance, 8*, 460-472.

Viviani, P., & Terzuolo, C. (1980). Space-time invariance in learned motor skills. In G. E. Stelmach & J. Requin (Eds.), *Tutorials in motor behavior* (pp. 525-533). Amsterdam: North-Holland.

Vorberg, D., & Hambuch, R. (1978). On the temporal control of rhythmic performance. In J. Requin (Ed.), *Attention and performance* (Vol. VII, pp. 535-555). Hillsdale, NJ: Lawrence Erlbaum Associates.

Vorberg, D., & Hambuch, R. (1984). Timing of two-handed rhythmic performance. In J. Gibbon & L. Allan (Eds.), *Timing and time perception* (pp. 390-406). New York: New York Academy of Sciences.

Wann, J. P. (1986). Handwriting disturbances: Developmental trends. In H. T. A. Whiting & M. G. Wade (Eds.), *Themes in motor development* (pp. 207-223). Dordrecht: Nijhoff.

Wing, A. M. (1977). Perturbation of auditory feedback delay and the timing of movement. *Journal of Experimental Psychology: Human Perception and Performance, 3*, 175-186.

Wing, A. M. (1980). The long and short of timing in response sequences. In G. E. Stelmach & J. Requin (Eds.), *Tutorials in motor behavior* (pp. 469-486). Amsterdam: North-Holland.

Wing, A. M., Keele, S. W., & Margolin, D. I. (1984). Motor disorder and the timing of repetitive movements. In J. Gibbon & L. Allan (Eds.), *Timing and time perception* (pp. 183-192). New York: New York Academy of Sciences.

Wing, A. M., & Kristofferson, A. B. (1973). Response delays and timing of discrete motor responses. *Perception & Psychophysics, 14*, 5-12.

Yamanishi, J., Kawato, M., & Suzuki, R. (1980). Two coupled oscillators as a model for the coordinated finger tapping by both hands. *Biological Cybernetics, 37*, 219-225.

9 Musical Events and Models of Musical Time

Mari Riess Jones
The Ohio State University

When we consider "models of time," one question that immediately arises concerns that of time as an abstract dimension apart from other dimensions that define the world of real events. It seems difficult to meaningfully abstract "time" from activities such as conversations, speeches, dances, sports, and so on. To be sure, each of these things takes a certain amount of total time, and each has various embedded intervals of time. But on closer examination of such events, two things seem evident.

First, it is clear that the total duration of an intact event is framed by a stylistic beginning and ending that seem intrinsic to the event itself. Such markers may consist of certain gestures, as when a tennis player arches to serve, or specific pitch/amplitude changes, as when a speaker or singer begins or closes a phrase. Furthermore, these events contain subparts that themselves are characteristically marked and so yield nested time spans. A whole melody, for instance, contains briefer phrases that are outlined by distinctive pitch and time changes. In short, beginnings and endings of whole events and of their subparts have several aspects. They are part of the entire relational structure of the event, and at the same time they are markers, in time, of durations that belong to the event. Finally, this means that the abstraction of one time interval rather than another crucially depends on our talents for identifying their beginnings and endings. Often, we resort to conventions for these identifications. Unfortunately, sometimes these conventions are tacit ones, especially at the theoretical level.

A second observation that emerges in grappling with models of time involves the word *time* itself. This seemingly innocuous word tends to conjure up in most of us either a void or a "line" (or both). Along a time line we find "instants" arbitrarily marking out abstract intervals. Such constructs help in formalizations because points in time and abstract time intervals facilitate summations and other operations. Yet instants, which in reality may mark either beginnings or endings, convey little functional distinctiveness. These concepts suggest that characteristically different events with similar time spans can be conceived as interchangeable voids; the information that fills them is irrelevant. But interchangeability has risks, and such constructs are mathematically useful only after we know how to apply them.

I refer to the latter conception of time as *high church time*. High church time relies on arbitrary markers and an abstract time line to define, respectively, points in time ("instants") and arbitrary time periods. It is not clear how this concept advances our understanding of the complex time relations that are found in many world events. It reflects an awesome abstraction of time that too often bequeaths to us a version of psychological time that ignores event structure itself. Psychological models of time that spring from this faith therefore also focus on abstract time intervals and arbitrary time limits, ones that often bear little relationship to the intact structure of the event. Psychological time becomes abstract, with perhaps arbitrarily defined "psychological moments." Sadly, there is usually little agreement on a single value for some psychological moment (e.g., Michon, 1978; Stroud, 1955). In fact, given the range and diversity of unsuccessful theories and conflicting data that arise from this conception, I am not sure that it has granted us much in the way of general explanatory power.

Perhaps we need to start more simply. These sorts of observations suggest that a more fruitful approach is one that takes its cue from the way in which time actually functions in everyday events rather than the way it functions, disembodied, in our imagination. Consider that subtly marked time periods of various sorts are insinuated into most of our interactions with the world. Time is part of events. This is *garden variety time*. Time periods play an intrinsic role in the relational structure of everyday events. Not only do we find characteristic markers that identify commonplace events, but these markers often outline characteristic time periods, ones of constrained lengths, that also go along with these events. That is, conversations, turntaking times, symphonies, and so on cannot take on any value; there are limits to the tempi found in action patterns, in speech, and in music and there are natural limits to whole event durations as well.

DYNAMIC EVENT STRUCTURE AND RELATIVE TIME

Garden variety time is the time of everyday events. It is found in the dynamically changing structure of the environment that surrounds and engulfs us. It is the time of patterns of speech, music, body gestures, and so on. I have suggested that time within such events forms an integral aspect of their whole structure (Jones, 1976). This means that, rather than abstracting arbitrary time intervals from such events, we should look more closely at ways in which distinctive time relationships work within intact events. In dynamic contexts, it is time relationships that exhibit and express constraints on particular time values, and it is these relational properties of events that we typically confront.

Temporal relationships refer to relative time: time relative to something else. In this chapter I consider two kinds of relative time, and I try to show how various models of time capture these relationships. One kind of relative time involves time change relative to space or spacelike change. This is the time of velocity, flow fields, and generally *motional properties* of events. The second kind of relative time involves one time change relative to another. This is the essence of relative timing and generally *rhythmic properties* of events.

In this chapter, the models of psychological time that I consider place different emphases on motional and rhythmic properties of events. On the one hand, clock models primarily address rhythmic event properties, and they do so by formalizing relations among time intervals. On the other hand, dynamic event structure models address both motional and rhythmic properties, and they do so by formalizing each in terms of higher-order event relationships. Both kinds of models strive for generality by abstracting temporal properties from the event structure, but both have claims to addressing garden variety time in that they attempt to tie their abstractions to structure of intact everyday events.

Time Relative to Spacelike Change:
Motional Properties of Events

An elementary way in which time enters into event structure is through its function in defining rates of change. Velocity and flow rate are based on this function of time, and much recent research shows that these motional properties are important to understanding the ways in which people and other organisms "use" relative time (e.g., Gibson, 1979; Lee, 1980). Similarly, characteristic motion patterns conveyed by body gestures supply critical information for observers who can recognize in these patterns a friend's walk or a distinctive folk dance (Cutting & Kozlowski, 1977; Johansson, 1973). Other gestures also transcribe characteristic velocity profiles (e.g., a speaker's jaw motions or a tennis player's swing). Many musical gestures, too, create velocity patterns because hands and fingers move over space along some instrument to produce sound sequences.

To an observer, the dynamics of time relative to space is a motion pattern. It is directly evident to one who sees an action. With purely auditory events, such as musical ones, a listener hears but does not necessarily view some musical performer; nevertheless information for something we can call an *auditory motion* is in the sound pattern. In part, this information comes across in the speed of certain sound changes: the rate of change of amplitude or of frequency. In fact, I refer to changes in loudness and pitch as *spacelike* changes; when they occur over a given time span an auditory motion occurs. And just as a spatial layout provides the basis for optic flow pattern, so the temporal layout can provide a basis for acoustic flow patterns that are velocity profiles (Hahn & Jones, 1981; Jones, 1976; Shepard, 1984).

To summarize, velocity patterns contribute to aspects of relative time in dynamic events. This is a traditional sort of relative time, one that figures prominently in classical physics and is often conceived in Western philosophies as linear rather than cyclic time. Because these philosophical distinctions tempt us into abstractions characteristic of high church time, I refer to this sort of relative time as motional. In later sections, when it is formalized in dynamic event structure models, motional time is also referred to as *horizontal* event time. It turns out that these kinds of models are more congenial for formalizing motional relative time than are clock models.

Time Relative to Time:
Rhythmic Properties of Events

Temporal relationships involve things like the patterning of time periods within a larger context. Whenever a recurrent sequence of durations (e.g., long-short-long) or some variation of this occurs, it is relationships among both successive durations and some overarching (higher-order) period that embody time-relative-to-time. Simply put, this information concerns rhythmic constraints that appear in many complex events including speech, music, and body movements. Here, I interpret the term *rhythmic* broadly to include both constraints involving the relation between successive durations (truly rhythmic patterns) and that between lower- and higher-order time periods (metric patterns; see section on music terminology).

Purely rhythmic constraints operate in naturally created events, quite apart from motional constraints. This is clear from a study by Kelso, Southard, and Goodman (1979). They found that people timed their two hands to arrive *simultaneously* at two different targets in spite of the fact that one hand had to move with greater velocity to reach its goal. This finding suggests the importance of synchronicity and more generally of time-relative-to-time.

The *synchronicity principle* underlies a full understanding of relative time in natural events. Briefly, it states that "the interaction of the perceiver with moving world patterns is described by the principle of synchronization" (Jones, 1976, p. 328). It suggests that whenever overlapping time intervals are involved there is a tendency to equate their durations so that they begin and end synchronously. This implies that a favored time ratio obtains between co-occurring time intervals (e.g., 1.00 in Kelso et al., 1979); it also implies that other favored integer time ratios exist among (recurrent) nested time periods because these too maximize simultaneities (i.e., periods related by multiples of 2, 3, 4, etc.). For similar reasons, favored phasing relationships should exist between events that do not start simultaneously (Boltz & Jones, 1986; Hahn & Jones, 1981; Jones & Boltz, 1989). In summary, the synchronicity principle suggests the kind of mathematical relationships that should reflect psychologically meaningful rhythmic constraints among observed periodicities.

Rhythmic constraints enter in whenever temporal coordination of activities is critical. This seems like a fairly broad mandate. But, consider simply the temporal play of gestures of one person, where substantial self-synchrony appears. A speaker's hands and head move together in lawful ways: Co-occurring gestures are phase locked or they are predictably timed relative to one another (Kelso et al., 1979; Klapp 1979, 1981). Even among different individuals there is synchronicity. Of course one might expect this if several people are engaged in a dance or a performance where a premium exists on coordination. But curiously, lawful relative timings also occur spontaneously in everyday interactions. One person nods precisely when another begins to wave (see, e.g., Kendon, 1977; Newtson, Hairfield, Bloomingdale, & Cutino, 1987). Underlying all of this is the general principle of synchrony: the use of relative time between an attender and a to-be-attended event (Jones, 1976; Jones, Kidd, & Wetzel, 1981). If attending itself is taken to be an activity with extension in time then for attending to be optimal there must be synchronicity between attender and producer as well.

Rhythmic time is the sort of relative time suggested in Eastern philosophies of time because it incorporates "return" or cyclicity. In this, it differs from the linear time suggested by analyses of motions and their velocity profiles. But, I refrain from abstractions implied by cyclicity per se and refer instead to event rhythmicities. Both clock models and dynamic event structure models address event rhythmicities, but in different ways. Clock models typically focus on abstracting a recurrent and fixed interval time from an event. Rhythmic properties then fall out as operations of one or more clock timers that determine both a person's production and perception of various other time intervals. In contrast, dynamic event structure models appeal directly to higher-order time relationships among time intervals within the event (temporal invariants). Here, rhythmic properties depend on abstraction and use of rhythmic generators to explain productions and perception of temporal events. Both approaches have some potential for realizing mathematical constraints suggested by a synchronicity principle.

Summary

In order to understand psychological time and the way we respond to temporalities in our world we need to understand the sculpting in and over time that is the essence of garden variety time. We do not begin with time that is abstracted from everyday events, namely high church time. Instead, we should stick more closely to the dynamics of event structure itself. This means we must begin to find ways to identify reliable markers of time periods that characterize everyday events and to formalize any characteristic dependencies among marked time intervals and other aspects of event structure.

Finally, all psychological modeling must abstract at some point to generalize. The models I consider do this in different ways. Clock models propose operations based on abstractions of recurrent time intervals, whereas dynamic event structure models propose ones based on abstractions of various higher-order relationships among time intervals. Yet, most can rightly claim to address garden variety time, the time of everyday events. In this chapter, I limit my consideration to models that concern a special class of everyday events, namely musical ones. They encourage a refreshing look at some old psychological problems. In this context, issues raised by clock models, on the one hand, and dynamic event structure models, on the other, have meaning beyond the scope of musical events.

MUSICAL TIME

Musical events are created (composed and performed) by humans in order to communicate to other humans. Time enters into both the *production* and *perception* of musical events. Indeed, musical time models considered in this chapter address both production and perception. And in this sense they also speak to traditional psychological issues that are concerned with the production and perception of "time."

Therefore, before we turn to these models, it is worth considering musical production and perception in light of two preliminary topics. The first concerns the problem of "time" production versus perception as conceived within traditional psychological approaches to time estimation. The second concerns the same distinction as viewed from a traditional musical theoretic perspective. In brief, I suggest that simple interpretations from either tradition are challenged by emerging research on production and perception of musical events.

Time Estimation and Production Versus Perception of Time

A typical time-estimation task requires a subject to judge or reproduce a fixed interval of time, either filled or empty. Given the history of research on time estimation (Allan, 1979; Fraisse, 1984), we know that methodological issues are intimately involved in understanding findings from such studies. For instance, different stimulus presentations and estimation methods (reproduction, judgment) do not consistently yield comparable estimates of the same time period (Allan, 1979; Woodrow, 1951). Indeed, perhaps the hallmark of time-estimation research is variability in reported findings (see Block, 1989; Jones & Boltz, 1989).

But problems surrounding time estimation take on a new dimension when the times involved cover musical events. Indeed, the issue of estimating the "pure time" of high church time arises immediately because time in music is difficult to tease apart from the structure of the event itself. Musical events include both filled and empty time spans, but all are part of a larger whole. In this context, the production and perception of time intervals can no longer center on use of abstracted and isolated time intervals but rather they must deal with estimates of whole sequences of meaningfully marked periods. Furthermore, musical time intervals serve functions that are intimately connected with musical communication and these functions are typically not those found in laboratory time estimations. Time intervals are produced and responded to as a byproduct of the communication from performer to listener. And neither participant in this tacit interaction typically stops to abstract and estimate the length of a given time interval, as such, from the ongoing musical event.

In short, temporal production and estimation have special meanings in musical contexts. Perhaps this is significant in itself for what it may due to stretch tacit boundaries established by traditional psychological approaches to time estimation. It is possible that the notorious variability in findings in time-estimation research can be explained by taking account of the structure and function of events to be judged in various tasks (Jones & Boltz, 1989). With the study of production and perception of natural events such as music there is the potential to discover the extent to which task and event structure determine people's responses to time and temporal relationships, namely to garden variety time.

Musical Terminology and Some Psychological Implications

If we opt to study natural events such as musical patterns, there is the temptation to eschew laboratory constraints and solely rely on musical terminology to explain their perception and production. However, as we begin to explore the complexities of traditional musical definitions as well as the distinctions between scored and played music, it becomes clear that strict interpretations of musical terms also do not tell the whole story about production and perceptions of musical timing. Somewhere between conventions established in the two disciplines of psychology and music is a middle ground that may permit new conceptions of psychological time as it figures in music. Conventional musical terms such as *tempo, meter, musical rhythm,* and *phrasing* need to be taken seriously and explored in the context of experiments on perception and production of temporal events.

Tempo. Loosely speaking, the musical term *tempo* refers to the pace of a musical piece. Often it is equivalent to the frequency of a given note duration such as the *beat period*. The beat period is specified in the time signature. Thus, in 3/4 time the beat period is equivalent to a quarter note, (from the lower number, 4). But this tells us little about the real value of tempo as interpreted and produced by a musical artist nor of how listeners hear tempi.

In modern times, characteristic values of the beat period are summarized roughly by metronomic guidelines (e.g., $\downarrow$ = M.M. 100), as well as by suggestions from the composer using scored terms such as *adagio* (relatively slow) or *allegro* (relatively fast). But, finally, determination of tempo is up for grabs in the sense that it is an important variable at the disposal of a creative performer who selects and changes tempo according to his or her interpretation of its role in the musical event as a whole. Rarely does a performer abide by a fixed tempo; instead accelerations and decelerations are the rule. In fact, modulations in tempo with a given piece can be quite consistent with a given performer (see e.g., Clynes & Walker, 1986; Gabrielsson, 1986).

On the other hand, listeners are not especially good at detecting tempo changes (Wapnik, 1980). Much remains to be determined about the perception of tempo and tempo change. A number of factors, quite apart from the stipulated beat period, may contribute to perceived tempo. These include the average local duration of note-to-note time changes, the frequency distribution of different note durations, the style of playing (e.g., connected, termed *legato*; or disconnected, termed *staccato*). Even melodic transitions and the shape of melody as conveyed by its pitch pattern, namely its motional properties, may have potential for determining how quickly a sequence of notes within a musical piece "seems" to unfold in time to a listener (e.g., Dowling, 1978; Jones, Maser, & Kidd, 1978; Kronman & Sundberg, 1987).

In terms of the psychological models considered shortly, both clock models and dynamic event structure models must confront issues of surrounding production and perception of some unit time period. For clock models, the issue is a straightforward one, the beat period or a multiple of it realizes the clock itself. For dynamic structure models, the relevant tempo unit enters into a motional component (i.e., becomes part of horizontal time), and so is a function of melodic context.

Meter. *Meter* refers to temporal grouping. In contrast to tempo where motional properties are at issue, meter signifies time change relative to time, namely rhythmic constraints. Temporal grouping implies that smaller time periods are embedded within larger overlapping ones. This embedding appears in all music but in Western music it capitalizes on time ratios. Time ratios are explicit in the definition of meter and are specified in a score. This naturally raises the question of the psychological validity of time ratios and meter as strictly defined.

In Western music, meter is notated by a time signature that communicates to the performer two things: the unit time per group, and the number of unit time periods per group (Apel, 1972). For instance, in 3/4 time the unit time is a quarter note and there are three quarter notes per group. Thus, *temporal embedding* is given as a ratio (i.e., 3:1 in the case of 3/4 meter). This determines, at the least, a two-level time hierarchy where small time values (e.g., ♩) are nested (i.e., embedded) within larger durations (e.g., within ♩, where ♩ = ♩ + ♩). Often, more than two

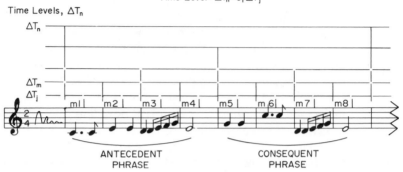

A DUPLE METER TIME HIERARCHY

Time Ratio : $C_t = \Delta T_m / \Delta T_j = 2$

Time Level : $\Delta T_n = C_t \Delta T_j^{n-j}$

Figure 9.1. Antecedent-consequent phrases of a melody in the key of C (first note). The meter is 2/4 with eight measures (M1 - M8) shown by bar lines. The metric time hierarchy corresponding to these measures is indicated above: ΔT_j refers to the beat period, ΔT_m to the measure level, and so on; and C_t refers to the time ratio of 2 (for duple meter) which obtains between any two adjacent time levels. (From Jones, 1987. Reprinted by permission.)

time levels are involved. Therefore, meter embodies a metric time hierarchy. Figure 9.1 shows a metric hierarchy for a 2/4 meter that suggests a 2:1 time ratio.

In Western music, notated meters express time change relative to time change. In Figure 9.1, we see two properties typical of metrical meters: (a) recursiveness, in that the period covering ♩ + ♩ contains or embeds smaller time periods; and (b) ratio relationships, in that grouping properties realize some invariant time ratio (Jones, 1981a). Although metric ratios differ depending on composer guidelines, three common kinds are: (a) *duple meters* that are based on ratios of 2:1 (2/4, 2/8, etc.); (b) *triple meters* that incorporate ratios of 3:1 (3/4, 3/8, etc.); and (c) *compound meters* that incorporate complex ratios (6/4, 9/8, etc.) and can be considered combinations of duple and triple meters (Apel, 1972).

Just as with scored and produced tempo, no neat equation relates scored meter to produced (or perceived) meter. For a precise realization of duple or triple meter in a produced sound pattern we would need to find correspondingly precise evidence for time ratios of 2 and 3 in these sequences. Although some evidence exists for such temporal proportionality, it is misleading to say that precise time ratios are produced. Discrepancies between scored and produced metric relationships abound even in performances of the best musicians (e.g., Gabrielsson, 1987; Shaffer, 1982; Vos & Handel, 1987). Many causes for these discrepancies have been proposed. Some cite the influence of structural complexity (i.e., *unintentional* time errors), whereas others focus on interpretive license (i.e., *intentional* time changes) (Jones, 1987a; Palmer, 1989; Shaffer, 1981). The most significant factors are probably the following:

1. *Ratio bias*: Performers appear to unconsciously favor some time ratios over others (Essens, 1986; Fraisse, 1982; Klapp, 1981; Povel, 1981).
2. *Tempo shifts*: Performers rarely abide by a fixed tempo (Gabrielsson, Bengtsson, & Gabrielsson, 1983; Shaffer, 1981, 1982).
3. *Symmetry violations*: As artists, performers will consciously violate the symmetry associated with time ratios to achieve certain interpretive effects (Gabrielsson, 1986; Jones, 1981b; Palmer, 1988, 1989; Todd, 1985).
4. *Variable markings*: Performers do not uniformly and consistently mark relevant beginnings and endings of metric time periods and so validation of meaningful time intervals is problematic (Sloboda, 1983; Vos & Handel, 1987).

As we see, all of this presents problems for certain versions of clock and dynamic event structure models. That is, in their simpler forms both kinds of models turn out to predict that precise time ratios should appear in produced musical sound patterns.

Finally, what of a listener's perception of meter? While there is evidence that duple and triple meter distinctions are important to listeners (Monahan & Carterette, 1985), meter perception remains one of the unsolved problems in research on music time. Various solutions have been proposed (e.g., Lerdahl & Jackendoff, 1983; Longuet-Higgins & Lee, 1984; Povel & Essens, 1985). Lerdahl and Jackendoff, for example, suggest guidelines for meter perception based on well-formedness and preference rules applied to musical scores that are heavily imbued with Gestalt principles. Recent research with simple melodies suggests the psychological validity of at least some of their guidelines that involve temporal and melodic accenting (Deliege, 1987).

Nevertheless, significant problems remain. One involves the fact that perceived meter does not always reflect scored meter. In part, this is related to the fact that produced meter does not always reflect scored meter (as previously indicated). That is, performers deviate from scored norms and different performers may do this in characteristically different ways (i.e., via temporal, stress accents, or chord asynchronies; Palmer, 1988, 1989; Sloboda, 1983, 1985). The best performers avoid heavy-handed stressing of every measure, but may introduce hardly noticeable chord asynchronies at measure onsets, for example (Palmer, 1988). Other factors such as melodic structure and background pace complicate assessment of perceived meter (Handel, 1984; Steedman, 1977; Vos, Leeuwenberg, & Collard, 1978). In short, many unknown factors intervene between scored meter and perceived meter.

In summary, the mystery deepens. How do listeners ever perceive the metric groupings suggested by the composer? I return to this problem later in considering other solutions posited by various models of musical time. For the present, it is sufficient to observe that the most promising approaches to this problem are ones that emphasize that the psychology of performing and listening is not found in strict interpretations of musical scores, but rather in understanding how activities change over time. That is, listening may be initially sensitive to certain temporal invariants, which when are detected later guide expectancies about temporal groupings. Such an expectancy driven interpretation means that the presence of markings that directly contradict a given metric expectation may cause more problems for a listener than absences of markers that directly confirm a metric expectation (see Povel, 1985; Povel & Essens, 1985). From the perspective of a performer, tacit knowledge of this fact means that clever instantiation of metric relationships early in a piece renders unnecessary the heavy handed marking of every metric level in a metric time hierarchy.

Musical Rhythm. The term *rhythm* has many meanings ranging from simple periodic recurrences of some event to special patterning of durations. By *musical rhythm* I mean a special patterning of durations. In Western metrical music, patternings are special by virtue of their metrical constraints. Like meter, musical rhythm manifests relative time constraints built on time proportionalities. Finally, however, the essence of musical rhythm is invariance and transformation of temporal relationships. Ultimately this is realized in rhythmic themes and their variations.

Rhythms are developed within metrical constraints. On paper (the score) they capture durational configurations based on time ratios (subdivisions/multiples of a standard duration). For example, in the rhythmic figure ♪♪$_o$ the note durations of whole note (o) to sixteenth note ($♪$) bear the following binary time relations to one another: $_o = 2↓$ $= 4↓ = 8♪ = 16♪$. Scores also suggest stylistic variations of such ratio norms (e.g., *legato*, *staccato*), and performers are consistent in their use of these styles (Palmer, 1989). In addition, they add interpretive changes in tempo that further modulate the resulting sound pattern.

Nevertheless, there is a basic rhythmic theme implied by the notation, one that is often designed to accompany the recurrence of a given pitch sequence within a larger piece. Variations of the theme are time transformations that speed it up or slow it down while still preserving important aspects of its temporal proportions. Some variations may actually permute parts of the rhythmic figure, convert it to an entirely new meter, or both.

Various theorists have proposed relational distinctions that apply to the theme itself. Cooper and Meyer (1959), for example, emphasized patterning terminologies based on types of prosodic feet such as iamb (ua), dactyl (auu), and so on. Yeston (1976), on the other hand, stressed the role of the time ratios themselves as they enter into the rhythmic texture of a piece, distinguishing between consonant rhythmic forms (i.e., based on integer time ratios) and dissonant forms (noninteger time ratios). This dichotomy reinforces the synchronicity principle, which relies on similar distinctions between ratio time invariants (Jones, 1976). Such analyses are useful in summarizing important relational properties within scored rhythms because they can focus on thematic coherence and transformational novelty. Nevertheless, they are incomplete to the degree that they are tied to analyses of scored rhythms only.

By now it should not surprise the reader to learn that produced musical rhythms do not usually conform to their notated versions. For example, a pattern such as ♩♩ (in 3/4 meter) with a notational ratio of 2:1 is often not realized as such in actual performances where observed average ratios can differ noticeably depending on the performer and the musical genre (see Gabrielsson, 1986, for an excellent review). Nevertheless, recent studies suggest that there is a relational logic to preserved rhythmic patterns (Hutchinson & Knopoff, 1987). Finally, the facts of rhythmic theme and transformation in music present challenges to production and perception models based on either clock or dynamic structure. As we see here, the latter offers a more parsimonious approach to the problem.

Phrase-Based Time Periods. Perhaps the most captivating way in which lawful temporal relationships emerge in music is found in the way musical phrases relate to one another. This is most simply illustrated in terms of monophonic (one voice) melodies such as that shown in Figure 9.1. A musical phrase forms an intact subpart of a larger melody, much like speech phrases form subparts of an utterance. Musical phrases define time periods, ones that do not always coincide with those outlined by measures. This fact sets the stage for interesting analyses of musical time relationships that concern temporal phasing of metric and melodic time periods.

Melodic phrases are structurally and functionally distinct from metrical partitionings of a tune. Unlike metric time periods, which are marked by stressed beats, melodic time periods are marked by tonally significant beginning and ending pitches. In Figure 9.1, for example, the phrase opens with a tonal accent critical to the melodic theme (the tonic, or anchor pitch, C), and it ends on a tonally related pitch (E). Functionally, melodic phrases supply an auditory motion pattern or pitch velocity profile that is "shaped" within the phrase by the succession of pitch (spacelike) changes relative to the tempo base (Dowling, 1978; Jones, 1981b, 1982; Jones, Summerell, & Marshburn, 1987; Rosner & Meyer, 1986). Accelerations and decelerations of melodic and harmonic motions contribute to a phrase's distinctive beginning, middle, and end (Friberg, Sundberg, & Fryden, 1987; Jones, Maser, & Kidd, 1978; Kramer, 1982).

Although melodic phrases differ from measure spans in contributing to a motional component, they do share with metric time hierarchies a rhythmic component. Durations of successively outlined phrases are lawful. Often they form groups with regular higher-order time spans; in addition, subdivisions of the phrases within these groups are also lawful suggesting that temporal embeddings, based on phrase durations, are coherent over several nested time levels (Cone, 1968; Jones & Boltz, 1989; Kramer, 1982; Lerdahl & Jackendoff, 1983).

In effect then, when we consider the rhythmic implications of melodic phrasing, it is clear that the phrase structure of music offers melodic time hierarchies. These hierarchies can either compete or coordinate with metric time hierarchies. Both kinds of hierarchies illustrate the importance of time-relative-to-time found in rhythmical constraints. Metrical time hierarchies refer to time periods of measures, whereas melodic time hierarchies refer to those of melodic phrases. Because time periods of both can co-occur in music, the principle of synchronicity applies to suggest which kinds of temporal phasing relationships among the two hierarchies might be psychologically simpler (Boltz & Jones, 1986). The complexities of temporal phase relations in musical time presents challenges to both clock models and those based on analysis of dynamic event structure.

Summary

The terms *tempo, meter,* and *musical rhythm* have certain conventional meanings that apply to scored music and its time properties.   In this section, I made two points: (a) Neither conventional psychological approaches to time estimation nor standard music terminology and its scored instantiations offer sufficient bases for explaining production and perception of musical time; (b) The phenomena of tempo, meter, musical rhythm, and melodic phrasing all embody some aspects relative time, either in the form of motional time (e.g., tempo, melodic phrasing) or as rhythmic time (e.g., meter, musical rhythm, etc.).

MODELS OF TIME PRODUCTION IN MUSICAL EVENTS

Musical productions that are created from a visual score typically require an expert musician to generate the actual sound pattern that is ultimately heard by a listener. Some of the models outlined in this section propose how such musicians do this.   Others focus on productions of musicians with different degrees of expertise, requiring them to produce or reproduce sound patterns from presented examples.   In all theories, a recurrent issue involves the nature of temporal relationships that guide productions: Are these relationships fundamentally interval or ratio in nature?   Clock models emphasize the psychological primacy of interval time relationships, whereas dynamic event structure models focus on ratio-time relationships.

A related issue concerns performers and their skills at creating various kinds of time relationships within musical sound patterns. On the face of it, a musical production task offers a rare opportunity to study the production method of time estimation in a natural environment and so to discover whether the most successful productions favor interval or ratio descriptions of time. After all, performers/producers are experts that can be "instructed" to create durations in complex contexts. Yet, as Sloboda (1983) pointed out, musical expertise is different from that found in other contexts (chess, programming, etc.) because criteria for success are less clear cut. Musical experts are artists and their skill resides in inter- pretation of musical scores in ways that are difficult to assess. For exam- ple, the best musicians often violate the ratio-timed norms suggested in scored note durations. Does this mean that finally they cannot produce proportional times, as some suggest (e.g., Sternberg, Knoll, & Zukofsky, 1978)? Or is something else going on? Although the answers are not simple, it appears that something else is going on. Musical experts often achieve successful communication of musical ideas by intentionally violating certain ratio-based time norms. To the extent this is so, it suggests that time proportionalities have an intriguing function in musical communication. As such, they cannot be considered irrelevant.

Both clock models and dynamic event structure models are confounded by the experts on this matter. We see here that, if taken in their simplest forms, both kinds of models predict precise production timings either of fixed time intervals (clocks) or of specified time ratios (dynamic event structure models). Thus, it is interesting to consider those production models that emerged to address this problem. Specifically, to accommodate timing variations, some clock models introduce stretchable clock intervals, whereas certain dynamic structure models posit tradeoffs between the way experts use an event's motional and rhythmic relationships to produce a sound pattern. But let us begin at the beginning with the work of Paul Fraisse, whose ideas had a powerful orienting influence.

The Work of Paul Fraisse

Fraisse (1956, 1982, 1984) studied production and reproduction of time intervals using tapping responses. His stimuli and task were not explicitly musical, but his results have had implications for subsequent research on musical time. He found that when people tapped out sequences of durations, they tended to temporally group taps using two kinds of time intervals: a short duration (150-300 ms) separated within group taps while a longer one (500-900 ms) separated groups themselves. One of Fraisse's most influential discoveries was his finding that the ratio of long-to-short times tended toward 2:1. Furthermore, in reproducing certain timed sequences, biases for this ratio could enter in to distort the actual intervals produced.

Note that Fraisse does not refer to *embedded* time ratios (i.e., hierarchical time relations). Instead, his use of short and long time periods seems to be rather abstract. The time-ratio property really applies to the relationship between two broad categories of time intervals that can segment a sequence. In other respects, Fraisse's approach appeals to Gestalt principles of good form in time patterns as well as to notions of assimilation and contrast (see Jones, 1978).

In extending these ideas to musical analyses, Fraisse has claimed that most Western music exhibits this dichotomous approach to the use of time intervals (e.g., Fraisse, 1982). In fact, he concluded that each of a variety of surveyed musical pieces capitalizes largely upon two distinct categories of time intervals such as ♩ versus ♪ or ♩ versus ♪, which bear the 2:1 time ratio. Needless to say, many composers and musicians would object to such an oversimplification, as Gabrielsson (1986) rightly pointed out. Nevertheless, Fraisse's ideas served as a beginning from which others focused on either interval time relationships (clock models) or ratio time relationships (dynamic structure models).

Clock Models and Interval Time Relations

Clocks are interval timers. They build on abstractions of certain recurrent time intervals, intervals evident in music as beat periods or measures. To the extent some unit interval is fixed, clocks can render predictions about temporal patterns that contain time periods that are integer multiples of this unit period. In this way clock models realize certain constraints suggested by the synchronicity principle. Current models are built on assumptions about the operations of a single clock or about those of multiple clocks.

Single Clocks. Povel (1981) tested Fraisse's claims about simple time ratios. He presented people with various serial combinations of time intervals such as 250-250-250-750, where a 3:1 ratio between long- and short-interval components obtains, and examined their tapping reproduction times. A decisive factor in timing accuracy turned out to be the embedding property of the context, a factor not considered by Fraisse. Sequences with ratios of 3:1 or 4:1 were accurately reproduced provided that the lower-order series of intervals combined to create equal higher-order periods that in turn evenly divided the total duration of the sequence (i.e., 1,500 = 750 + 750 in this example). Although biases for 2:1 serial time ratios were evident, especially in difficult sequences, there was also evidence for preferred embedding ratios of 2:1 or 3:1 (see also Essens, 1986; Essens & Povel, 1985; Monahan, Kendall, & Carterette, 1987).

A single clock model was later developed from Povel's beat-based model. Povel and Essens (1985) proposed that timed serial productions depend on the operation of one "best clock" that is induced during perception. This notion implies that a cognitive array of potential interval timers exists and is surveyed; finally the mental clock that best fits a given sequence is selected by the performer. Povel and Essens used to-be-produced patterns where brief pulses (accented and unaccented) defined different serial arrangements of time periods. They showed that the way accented pulses divided up the sequences was critical in determining the clock involved. That is, the best clock for a sequence was that which generated fewest mismatches of its strict interval markers with various accented periods.   Povel and Essens outlined degrees of sequence simplicity in terms of the amount and kind of discrepancy between a pattern's accent structure and the best clock engaged for it. Experimentally, they found that both timing accuracy of pattern productions and complexity judgments about the sequences varied as a function of predicted simplicity.

Although not developed in an explicitly musical task, Povel's work has implications for understanding meter production.   His metrical versus nonmetrical distinction can be framed in terms of simplicity criteria. Thus, a given meter is most clearly instantiated by sequences that provide fewest deviations from their best clock (see also Boltz & Jones, 1986).

Multiple Clocks.   Others have taken a different approach to musiclike productions, one that relies on the concept of joint operation of several clocks. Some clocks control produced times over longer (higher-order) time intervals, whereas others control shorter (embedded) time intervals.

Vorberg and Hambuch (1978, 1984) relied on earlier work by Wing and Kristofferson (1973) to analyze higher-order timing dependencies (covariances) among interresponse intervals created by serial tapping. They deduced support for hierarchical time constraints among different clocks that were assumed to jointly guide rhythmic productions (Vorberg & Hambuch, 1984). Following up on this, Jagacinski, Marshburn, Klapp, and Jones (1988) found that two-handed tapping to a polyrhythmic sequence revealed the influence of embedded time ratios.   In addition, they also found that other aspects of event structure affected the precision with which the ratio-based hierarchy was revealed in productions. For example, whenever the presented polyrhythm was realized by interleaving tones of two very different frequencies rather than two similar ones, tapping performance declined. This finding underscores the intimate linkage between perception and production.

The hierarchical clock model has been used extensively by Shaffer to explain rhythmical time constraints evident in musical productions of expert pianists who play scores of Chopin, Bach, and Bartok (Shaffer, 1982; Shaffer, Clarke, & Todd, 1985). Shaffer's clocks reflect abstractions of interval-time properties of motor events themselves, and his support comes from covariance analyses of production times.   These remarkable studies follow earlier pioneering work of Povel (1977). It is the striking dependencies among production time intervals, suggesting the operation of a recurrent beat period as well as various higher-order time periods, that imply the existence of nested clocks.   Interactions among clocks are used to indirectly explain various higher-order rhythmic constraints observed in production timing, such as the fact that time periods of measures may be more regular than those of nested beat periods. Although clock interactions can successfully explain metric influences on produced times, it remains unclear how these models explain the production of rhythmic themes and variations.

Simple hierarchical clock models, although more powerful than nonhierarchical clock models, face other problems as well. A generic problem for clock models, whether they apply to production or perception of time intervals, involves phenomena that suggest that the nature of information that fills the time intervals can distort the observed psychological time. In the case of production models, this takes the form of melodic phrasing influences on produced times. Performers bring artistic interpretation and expressive intention to melodic phrases that fill to-be-produced intervals; they may play "off beat" (early or late) and change the tempo locally (rubato). These systematic departures from notated timings regularly appear in produced sound patterns and cannot be accounted for by any simple clock model.

Shaffer's hierarchical clock model is the only one that attempts to confront this issue directly. He proposed that clocks that govern musical productions are responsive not only to musical (melodic) syntax but also to expressive markers that can change a clock's rate and deform its time intervals (i.e., stretch or shrink the unit time). Others working along the same lines find additional support for this view (for reviews, see Gabrielsson, 1986; Jones, 1987a).

In summary, models based on single or multiple clocks can express some of the constraints found in musical event timing. Once set in motion, a clock's interval timer runs its course. Depending on the kind and number of clocks, these timers can explain simple to tap sequences as well as observed higher-order embedding constraints arising from metrical properties. Nevertheless, because clocks reflect strict interval time abstractions, they can be inflexible. To add flexibility and to capture observed violations of musical metricality, "stretchable" clock units have been proposed. Finally, however even the modified clock models leave unanswered certain questions. They do not succinctly explain productions of rhythmic themes and variations. Nor are the ways that "stretching" and "shrinking" unit-time intervals occur always clear.

Dynamic Structure and Relative Time

There are subtle differences between models that emphasize the operation of interval-timing clocks and those that posit a more direct approach to time proportionalities. In clock models, embedding time ratios fall out indirectly as a function of the hierarchical operation of clocks, whereas in dynamic structure models, temporal relationships are primary.

Event Structure and Systematic Variations. Gabrielsson's views on dynamic event structure are not explicitly formalized in a relative time model (Gabrielsson, 1974, 1985, 1986; Gabrielsson, et al., 1983). However, he has argued for important distinctions among three production components—structural, motional, and emotional—and he identified relationships within musical sequences that corresponds to each. For Gabrielsson, the structural component refers to metric and rhythmic time properties that appear in a score; it involves metric/rhythmic coherences. Motional factors involve tempo and rate properties, whereas emotional aspects refer to special relationships that contribute to temporal deviations from a score. Emotional factors especially make artistically performed music an act of expressive communication and it is these that explain deviations from scored timing. Gabrielsson's work and his ideas are convincing in their illustrations that in serving its communicative function real music systematically departs from mechanical timing norms.

Along these lines, Clynes' (1977, 1986) work on the dynamic shape of expression suggests that both amplitude and pitch changes over time to create special motional patterns. In this view, each composer communicates, via his music, a characteristic pulse that shapes amplitude over time at various metric levels and thus distinctively modulates periods such as beat and measure times. Clynes also proposed that different emotional shapes (joy, grief, etc.) in time are reflected in the dynamics of melodic contours.

The Temporal Perspective Model: A Two-Component Production Model. Recently, I proposed a production model, the temporal perspective model, which incorporates direct sensitivities to dynamic event relationships that a performer uses to influence the way listeners attend in time (Jones, 1987a). It builds on the basic assumption that these sensitivities derive from fundamental rhythmicities of people (and other living things).

The model is a two-factor model in which a musician is portrayed as a refined user of relative time relationships in music. One factor reflects the artist's use of relative time hierarchies (the vertical time component). This factor captures invariances in temporal embeddings of various time hierarchies (metric, melodic, etc.). By using vertical time, a performer attempts to encourage different temporal views (perspectives) associated with different musical time levels (i.e., beat period, measure, etc.). The second component, reflects sensitivity to motional information (the horizontal time component). This factor captures the shape and pacing of a melodic line, the velocity profiles of melodic phrases. The horizontal component communicates various things, among these momentum and expressive feeling. By using horizontal time, the performer "shapes" melodic phrases to create motional objects that can be heard then from different temporal perspectives. (The terms *vertical* and *horizontal* here refer to relative time relationships; they are not synonymous with the popular usage of these terms to reflect pitch structure: harmonic vs. melodic.)

Vertical and horizontal production components are associated with different communication goals. The vertical component is associated with a goal of proportional ("correct") timing, whereas the horizontal component is associated with expressive violations of this timing. Effectively, artistic expertise resides in achieving a compromise between these potentially conflicting goals. The successful artist (in Western music) conveys both coherent time proportionalities while also achieving an acceptable degree of violation from ratio norms to permit play in the motional properties.

The vertical production component summarizes a performer's use of rhythmic embedding constraints to convey multiple time levels. The performer here literally *creates* time hierarchies with a *rhythm generator*. A rhythm generator is not a clock. It is an abstracted ratio reflecting the performer's knowledge (e.g., of meter) and use of rhythmical constraints (Jones, 1976, 1981a). The idea is that the performer initially aligns some produced time span with a time level (e.g., beat period or measure span) that is suggested by a score, and this periodicity becomes a predominant temporal perspective that the performer shares with the audience. During a performance, other durations are created from this referent time period by multiplying and subdividing it, within limits (Jones, 1987a). Finally, however, if this dynamic event structure model rested only on abstractions of temporal embeddings ratios, it could not handle production phenomena which show that people violate such ratios.

This simple version of a ratio generator model meets the same fate as simple hierarchical clock models. Temporal productions that deviate from strict interval constraints also violate strict time ratio constraints. The temporal perspective model meets this challenge via incorporating operations of the horizontal component. This production component captures the impact of tempo variations, among other things. The rate of change of a melodic line and its trajectory are created through operations of a motion generator (e.g., velocity vectors). Tempo is quickened or slowed to create a meaningful "velocity profile" (Jones, 1976, 1981b,

1982). In contrast to the vertical component, the horizontal component is essentially motional.

Whereas clock models meet the challenge posed by violations of "precision" timing via hypothesizing "stretchable" clock units, the temporal perspective model resolves this issue by assuming that vertical and horizontal production components often raise conflicting goals. The nature and degree of ratio time deviations depend on the way a performer resolves this conflict. That is, the performer who is dominated by motional relationships (horizontal goal) may whip through a score with little regard for preserving its rhythmic coincidences or the synchronicity of both hands (a vertical goal) thus achieving a poor compromise of horizontal and vertical components. Conversely, the pianist who is dominated by rhythmic relationships may play the score precisely as notated but with no feeling or directionality, an equally unhappy compromise of the two production forces.

The juxtaposition of these two different production components is illustrated in Figure 9.2. The vertical time component is reflected by the rhythm generator, denoted as C_t. For this musical passage C_t is 2, reflecting duple meter. The metric time hierarchy is then created by multiplying (magnifying) and dividing (minifying) a referent time span. The referent span is shown as ΔT_j, a beat period level of the hierarchy. Use of C_t^n then yields hierarchic levels, n, greater $(n > j)$ and less $(n < j)$ than the beat period in value. The rhythm generator can also yield durations of rhythmic figures (rhythmic themes and variations on a metric base). Against all of these ratio-generated durations plays the horizontal component. Because this component creates auditory motions based on tempo, horizontal goals can yield changes in the value of the beat period. Time changes, subservient to the shape of a phrase, add or subtract from the time base. Ultimately, such temporal variations change the ratio character of durations in both the metric hierarchy and rhythmic figures.

Two combinations of vertical and horizontal components appear in Figure 9.2 in order to illustrate ways these two components can play off against one another. The version shown in Figure 9.2a reflects a mechanical or deadpan performance where the motional component is based on a fixed referent beat period (tempo constant). (In Figure 9.2a, pitch values of the notes are not shown; they correspond to the first phrase of Figure 9.1.) A more expressive performance is shown in Figure 9.2b. Here melodic phrasing is "shaped" in time as the tempo base changes from slow to fast to slow again. The important point here is that the time value of the referent period changes in response to the performer's goals in shaping the velocity profile of the entire melodic phrase with the consequence that observed durations change.

In summary, in contrast to clock models, this view portrays the performer as an artistic *interpreter* of musical events. To this end, a performer "uses," in a generative fashion, both rhythmic and motional relative time information that are suggested by the composer. But because this information can raise conflicting timing goals, the successful artist is one who resolves the conflict in creative ways.

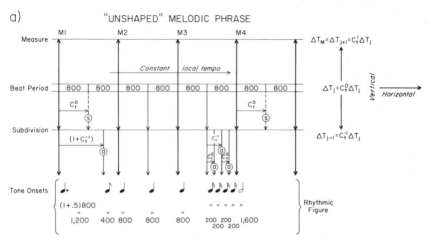

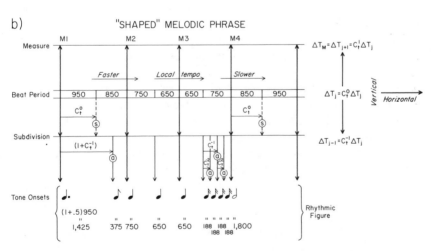

Figure 9.2. Rhythmic patterns underlying the antecedent melodic phrase of Figure 9.1 can be mechanically produced (Figure 9.1a) or expressively produced (Figure 9.1b). In the former the horizontal component is based on a constant tempo unit (ΔT_j), whereas in the latter it reflects a modulated one. (From Jones, 1987. Reproduced by permission.)

Summary

Hypotheses about musical productions derive from clock models and dynamic event structure formulations. In sophisticated versions of each, there is an attempt to reflect the joint influence of rhythmical time (the synchronicity principle) and of tempo and phrasing variations that violate this principle. Clock models achieve this through abstractions of interval time relations in the form of clocks and nestings of clocks to which are added assumptions concerning variations in the timer itself. Dynamic event structure models achieve this via abstractions of ratio time relationships of two sorts: time-relative to spacelike change (motional) and time-relative-to-time (rhythmic) which may raise conflicting goals and tradeoffs between two different production components.

PERCEPTION AND MUSICAL TIME

When we consider perception and musical time, the old issue of "perceiving time" re-enters the picture. Some have proposed that people perceive time as such (e.g., Massaro & Idson, 1976; see Michon, 1985, for a review), whereas others have taken the position that one can either attend "to" time or "to" something else (e.g., Thomas & Brown, 1975; see also Michon, 1985, p. 36). Both perspectives rest on the assumption that time is separable from other dimensions. They deal with high church time. Whereas this assumption often makes for simple models, I have doubts about its long-run tenability.

Others are more bold. Ornstein (1969) maintained that one neither perceives nor represents time as such. Longer and/or more complex events only "seem" longer because their nontemporal information produces more elaborate nontemporal mental codes. At the other extreme, Gibson (1975) has also argued against pure time perception, but not at the cost of denying the reality of time. For Gibson, time is part of the flow structure of events themselves. Although very different, these approaches agree in suggesting that the question of perceiving "pure time" is a moot one.

I agree with Gibson's perspective that time is inseparable from event structure. This is garden variety time. But I suspect the role of garden variety time is more complicated than he originally envisioned. Further, there are pitfalls in interpreting Gibson's statement as license to ignore meaningful and ecologically valid questions about time estimation. People, rightly or wrongly, routinely make judgments about elapsed time intervals. How is this accomplished if people do not abstract out "pure" time intervals? The issues here are complicated and beyond the scope of this chapter (see chapters 1 & 3, this volume). However, it is fair to say that although people do judge intervals of time in our society, they do so with a good deal of assistance (external clocks) and with varying success.

In this section, I focus on a subset of issues related to time estimation with musical events and their implications for the two kinds of models already considered, namely, clock models and dynamic event structure models. On the face of it, clock models might seem to have an advantage over dynamic event structure models when it comes to time estimation. They can readily explain time interval judgments in terms of reference to some mental "clock." However, even for clock models, problems quickly become complicated because musical events are effectively sequences of time intervals. There is far more to time perception in music than merely judgments about isolated intervals. How do listeners gauge a musical meter or recognize a rhythm pattern under changes of tempo? In the latter cases, parsimony favors models that assume that people respond directly to higher-order temporal relationships (dynamic event structure).

Clock Models and Coded Time Intervals

Povel's coding approach follows in the tradition established by Fraisse that finds perception and production inseparable. Production turns out to be one good way of measuring perception, in this case the perception of a sequence of time intervals. According to Povel and Essens (1985), metrical time patterns, namely those with regular accentings, are perceived more accurately than nonmetrical ones. This is confirmed with evidence from both pattern reproductions and complexity judgments. Metricality here depends on the best clock induced. Consequently, Povel suggested that distinctly different perceptual/memory strategies underlie coding of time intervals in metrical and nonmetrical events. Metrical time sequences are perceived through the clock induction activities, whereas nonmetrical patterns are coded via grouping and counting of the unevenly distributed accents.

One characteristic of many coding models that is shared by Povel's temporal encoding model is their neglect of attending *as a temporal event unfolds*. In Povel's clock model, for example, a best clock is selected only after the whole sequence is matched with all possible clocks that can be induced. Effectively, influences of earlier parts of a rhythmical sequence on perceiving later parts can only be indirectly incorporated into a final event code. Other approaches maintain that initial expectancies about future outcomes within a patterned sequence are critical to understanding its perceived difficulty or temporal complexity (Garner, 1974; Jones, 1976; see Jones, 1978, 1985, for reviews). In fact, Povel himself recently moved toward this position. He showed that temporal expectancies for upcoming beats in a sequence determined people's judgments about its temporal coherence (Povel, 1985).

More generally, clock models have been criticized for certain inflexibilities in their approach to time perception (Jones & Boltz, 1989; Ornstein, 1969). We see an example of this in reproduction experiments where clock constructs work best when musical-like sequences are metrical. Perhaps, more complex clock models that envision various hierarchical linkages and distortable time units can surmount such problems. However, those theories in which such constructs figure (e.g., Shaffer, 1982) make no claims about musical time perception.

Event Structure and Event-Related Expectancies

Whether perception involves judgments about meter or event durations, the same event relationships which govern production may also influence attending to and perceiving musical sound patterns (Jones, 1976, 1987a). Two important differences exist when we focus on the attender who experiences a created event and must make judgments about it rather than the skilled performer who produces it.

The first difference involves familiarity. The listener who experiences a novel event does not "know" its rhythmic invariances so well as the skilled performer who creates it. Instead, I suggest that the listener resorts to abstracting initial and prominently marked embedding relationships in an unfolding event. These relations are then provisionally "used" to anticipate "when" the next time interval will begin. Such anticipations are termed *temporal expectancies*, and they guide attending.

This view assumes that expectancies depend on temporal invariants that are initially abstracted from unfolding events. In contrast to clock models, higher-order time relationships thus come to serve as rhythm generators that can, in turn, bias attending in certain ways. The principle of synchronicity is fundamental in determining a listener's initial bias toward the pick-up and use of simpler rhythmic generators. More consonant embedding time ratios (e.g., $C_t = 1, 2, 3$) correspond to simpler time patterns, and these are initially preferred. Musical events that initially play to these biases encourage quick detection of temporal invariants.

The second difference between attender and performer is related to the first. It involves *expectancy violations*. The basis for expectancy violations can be created by either the composer or the performer (i.e., we have seen that performers intentionally introduce violations of ratio norms in production). From a listener's perspective, any deviation of observed from expected timing is an expectancy violation that brings potential "surprise." Such deviations are termed *temporal contrast.*

Expectancies and temporal contrasts play important roles in meter perception and time interval estimation. In the perceiver, these two aspects of attending parallel ones found in the more skilled performer, namely vertical and horizontal production components. The vertical component, which is based on ratio time generators, provides the temporal invariants for temporal expectancies in the listener; whereas the horizontal component, which is based on motion generators, contributes to systematic violations of these expectancies in the form of temporal contrasts.

Meter Perception. Opening embedding time ratios are abstracted from prominently marked intervals to create metric expectancies in a listener according to this account. This means that melodic accents as well as metric ones can sometimes determine perceived meter. But any such expectancies are provisional for a listener. Expectancy violations (temporal contrasts) provide additional information about viability of an initial (provisional) time ratio. For example, if an initial time interval (call it ΔT_0) is followed by another that determines the overlapping period (or ΔT_1), these two together can provisionally determine a triple meter expectancy (i.e., $C_t = \Delta T_1 / \Delta T_0 = 3$) (Jones, 1976). As the pattern continues these expectancies can be violated. The idea of expectancy violations as correctives during listening suggest that the means by which a listener come to a metric judgment (i.e., a final C_t value) involves reacting to contrasting time relations, namely time markers that occur "early" or "late."

The problem of meter perception is also addressed by Longuet-Higgins and Lee (1982, 1984) in a framework that shares some similarities with that previously described. They address the central question of how one arrives at a particular metric interpretation, given that the whole sequence can be interpreted in many different ways. They, too, focus on biasing influences associated with opening embedding time ratios (i.e., determined by onsets of the first three markers). Over various modifications of this model they elaborate on the nature of this activity. Recently, Lee (1985) has suggested that people initially expect that successive durations will be equal and that notes with durations longer than expected are most likely to be perceived as marking onsets of higher order time periods (measures). This approach gives weight to metric markings by temporal accents and to an initial bias for equal time intervals (i.e., a preference for $C_t = 2$ in Jones' model).

Finally, determinations of perceived meter are tricky. Perceived metric stress and "naturalness" are not always easily deduced from analyses of sound pattern structure (e.g., Vos & Handel, 1987). Furthermore, meter perception depends, in complex ways, on other structural relationships including melodic structure and repetitions, as well as rhythmic figure-background properties and tempo (Handel, 1984; Handel & Oshinsky, 1981; Steedman, 1977). All of this indicates that problems concerning both psychologically salient markers and initial temporal expectancies are at the center of the mystery of meter perception.

Time Estimation. A major problem for a theory of relative timing involves time interval estimation. We return to nagging questions about duration judgment. How do people judge event durations, if as rhythmical attenders, they respond primarily to time ratios? The discussion thus far suggests listeners do somehow judge musical durations. Clock models might lead us to believe that they do so by abstracting pure time intervals. Do people judge "pure time" or is relative time somehow involved?

A case can be made for involvement of relative time in estimations of time intervals. Meaningful duration judgments always occur in some temporal context in which they can be conceived as relative time judgments (Jones & Boltz, 1989; Ornstein, 1969). In laboratory settings people are usually asked to estimate one time span relative to another. In other settings, including those involving musical events, the context also sets the stage for relative time judgments. The influence of prior context is typically not incorporated into clock models. They assume instead that time intervals as such are directly perceived and abstracted. Among other things, this makes clock models rather inflexible.

Other time estimation models add flexibility and/or attempt to address context effects (e.g., Ornstein, 1969; Underwood & Swain, 1973). A central issue for these models involves the role of nontemporal information that fills a to-be-judged time period (e.g., Allan, 1979). Many propose that time intervals filled with more information (Ornstein, 1969) or attentional effort (Underwood & Swain, 1973) should be judged proportionately longer. Some data support these hypotheses leading to the notion of a "filled-interval effect." However, although such findings are difficult for simple clock models, data are by no means unequivocal in their support of the contention that time intervals filled with more information always seem longer (see Block, 1989; Jones & Boltz, 1989).

One overlooked factor that may contribute to conflicting reports surrounding the filled-interval effect involves the relative time structure outlined by information that fills these time spans (Jones & Boltz, 1989). That is, the issue is not "how much" information fills an interval, but rather "how" it fills the interval. In particular, information may be temporally patterned in ways that can evoke temporal expectancies for "when" an interval "should" end. Duration judgments then are a function of the way these expectancies are confirmed or violated (Jones & Boltz, 1989).

The hypothesis that information filling time intervals has the potential to evoke temporal expectancies that influence judgments about the entire duration is one that explains how an inherently rhythmical attender can wind up making judgments that seem interval in nature. This hypothesis found support from duration judgments of musical events, namely simple folk tunes. We held total information per tune constant, while manipulating expectancies about "when" they should end by varying relative durations of embedded melodic phases. Expectancies were also sometimes violated by altering final melodic phrasings so that some tunes "seemed" to end early and others to end late relative to the provisionally expected ending time. Actually, all pairs of tunes were identical in total time. We predicted that people would generate temporal expectancies about the total durations of these events based on relative durations of opening phrases, and that durations judgments would be biased by temporal contrast associated with tune endings. Events that ended unexpectedly "late" were predicted to be judged "long" (relative to a standard duration), whereas those ending unexpectedly "early" were predicted to be judged "short." The idea is that temporal contrast, which accompanies an expectancy violation, systematically affects judgments about the duration of the whole melody (Jones & Boltz, 1989).

We found support for this interpretation. Furthermore, alternative predictions based on models such as Ornstein's (1969) or Underwood and Swain's (1973) received only limited support largely because they ignore the role of relative timing in generating temporal expectancies. And even though clock models emphasize coding of time intervals, they too have problems with these data because they fail to explain how context-specific expectancies and their violations systematically bias time judgments.

In summary, temporal relations in music affect the way people perceive meter and may be involved in their perception and identification of recurrent rhythmic forms. Invariant time relations, summarized as time ratios, that underlie meter and rhythm are abstracted and used to generate temporal expectancies. But finally, even these do not tell the whole story, because people may initially abstract the "wrong" relationship and so generate inappropriate metric expectancies. Both expectancies and expectancy violations must play a role in meter perception. It turns out that they also figure in time estimation: One's sense of how long a musical event lasts is influenced by expectancies about its duration and by the way these expectancies are violated.

SUMMARY

Classically, the study of time in psychology has conceived of time as a domain apart from other aspects of stimulation. Indeed the field of time perception is a distinct area of study with methods such as estimation, production, or reproduction all contributing to ways of understanding how people respond to "pure" time. However, when we conceive of time as it figures in the events psychologists have begun to study, namely, time in gait production/perception, time in speech production/perception, time in motion production/perception, and finally time in music production/perception it becomes clear that temporal relationships play an intimate role in producing and perceiving everyday events. This garden variety time is relational time, tied tightly to the structure of the events involved. In music, relevant time relationships can be conceived in terms of motional and rhythmic event properties. In this chapter, I considered the ways in which two general categories of psychological models, clock models and dynamic event structure models, have depicted garden variety time in musical events. Both have the potential for generating predictions about complex serial timings within musical productions, and both in principle can be applied to the perception of musical timing.

ACKNOWLEDGMENTS

The author is indebted to several colleagues who read and commented on earlier versions of this chapter. Among these are Richard Block, Marilyn Boltz, Sue Holleran, Caroline Palmer, Dirk-Jan Povel, and Jackie Ralston. This research was sponsored in part by Grant BNS-8204811 from the National Science Foundation.

REFERENCES

Allan, L. G. (1979). The perception of time. *Perception & Psychophysics, 26,* 340-354.
Apel, W. (1972). *Harvard dictionary of music* (2nd ed.). Cambridge, MA: Belknap Press of Harvard University Press.

Block, R. A. (1989). Experiencing and remembering time: Affordances, context, and cognition. In I. Levin & D. Zakay (Eds.), *Time and human cognition: A life-span perspective* (pp. 333-363). Amsterdam: North-Holland.

Boltz, M., & Jones, M. R. (1986). Does rule recursion make melodies easier to reproduce? If not, what does? *Cognitive Psychology, 18,* 389-431.

Clynes, M. (1977). *Sentics, the touch of emotion.* New York: Doubleday.

Clynes, M. (1986). When time is music. In J. R. Evans & M. Clynes (Eds.), *Rhythm in psychological, linguistic, and musical processes* (pp. 169-224). Springfield, IL: Charles C. Thomas.

Clynes, M., & Walker, J. (1986). Music as time's measure. *Music Perception, 4,* 85-119.

Cone, E. (1968). *Musical form and musical performance.* New York: W. Norton & Company.

Cooper, G. W., & Meyer, L. B. (1959). *The rhythmic structure of music.* Chicago: The University of Chicago.

Cutting, J. E., & Kozlowski, L. T. (1977). Recognizing friends by their walk: Gait perception without familiarity cues. *Bulletin of the Psychonomic Society, 9,* 353-356.

Deliege, I. (1987). Grouping conditions in listening to music: An approach to Lerdahl & Jackendoff's grouping preference rules. *Music Perception, 14,* 325-359.

Dowling, W. J. (1978). Scale and contour: Two components of a theory of memory for melodies. *Psychological Review, 85,* 341-354.

Essens, P. J. (1986). Hierarchical organization of temporal patterns. *Perception & Psychophysics, 40,* 69-73.

Essens, P. J., & Povel, D.-J. (1985). Metrical and nonmetrical representations of temporal patterns. *Perception & Psychophysics, 37,* 1-7.

Fraisse, P. (1956). *Les structures rythmiques* [Rhythmic structures]. Louvain: Editions Universitaires.

Fraisse, P. (1982). Rhythm and tempo. In D. Deutsch (Ed.), *The psychology of music* (pp. 149-180). New York: Academic Press.

Fraisse, P. (1984). Perception and estimation of time. *Annual Review of Psychology, 35,* 1-36.

Friberg, A., Sundberg, J., & Fryden, L. (1987). How to terminate a phrase: An analysis-by-synthesis experiment on a perceptual aspect of music performance. In A. Gabrielsson (Ed.), *Action and perception in rhythm and music* (pp. 49-55). Stockholm: Royal Swedish Academy of Music.

Gabrielsson, A. (1974). Performance of rhythm patterns. *Scandinavian Journal of Psychology, 15,* 63-72.

Gabrielsson, A. (1985). Interplay between analysis and synthesis in studies of performance and experience of music. *Music Perception, 3,* 59-86.

Gabrielsson, A. (1986). Rhythm in music. In J. R. Evans & M. Clynes (Eds.), *Rhythm in psychological, linguistic, and musical processes* (pp. 131-167). Springfield, IL: Charles C. Thomas.

Gabrielsson, A. (1987). Once again: The theme from Mozart's piano sonata in A major (K. 331): A comparison of five performances. In A. Gabrielsson (Ed.), *Action and perception in rhythm and music* (pp. 81-103). Stockholm: Royal Swedish Academy of Music.

Gabrielsson, A., Bengtsson, I., & Gabrielsson, B. (1983). Performance of musical rhythm in 3/4 and 6/8 meter. *Scandinavian Journal of Psychology, 24,* 193-213.

Garner, W. R. (1974). *The processing of information and structure.* Hillsdale, NJ: Lawrence Erlbaum Associates.

Gibson, J. J. (1975). Events are perceivable but time is not. In. J. T. Fraser & N. Lawrence (Eds.), *The study of time II* (pp. 295-301). New York: Springer-Verlag.

Gibson, J. J. (1979). *The ecological approach to visual perception.* Boston: Houghton-Mifflin.

Hahn, J., & Jones, M. R. (1981) Invariants in auditory frequency relations. *Scandinavian Journal of Psychology, 22,* 129-144.

Handel, S. (1984). Using polyrhythms to study rhythm. *Music Perception, 1,* 465-484.

Handel, S., & Oshinsky, J. S. (1981). The meter of syncopated auditory polyrhythms. *Perception & Psychophysics, 30,* 1-9.

Hutchinson, W., & Knopoff, L. (1987). The clustering of temporal elements in melody. *Music Perception, 4,* 281-303.

Jagacinski, R. J., Marshburn, E., Klapp, S. T., & Jones, M. R. (1988). Tests of parallel versus integrated structure in polyrhythmic tapping. *Journal of Motor Behavior, 20,* 416-442.

Johansson, G. (1973). Visual perception of biological motion and a model for its analysis. *Perception & Psychophysics, 14,* 201-211.

Jones, M. R. (1976). Time, our lost dimension: Toward a new theory of perception, attention, and memory. *Psychological Review, 83,* 323-335.

Jones, M. R. (1978). Auditory patterns: Studies in the perception of structure. In E. C. Carterette & M. P. Friedman (Eds.), *Handbook of perception: Vol. 8. Space and object perception* (pp. 255-288). New York: Academic Press.

Jones, M. R. (1981a). Only time can tell: On the topology of mental space and time. *Critical Inquiry, 7,* 557-576.

Jones, M. R. (1981b). Music as a stimulus for psychological motion: Part I. Some determinants of expectancies. *Psychomusicology, 1,* 34-51.

Jones, M. R. (1982). Music as a stimulus for psychological motion: Part II. An expectancy model. *Psychomusicology, 2,* 1-13.

Jones, M. R. (1985). Structural organization of events in time. In J. A. Michon & J. L. Jackson (Eds.), *Time, mind, and behavior* (pp. 192-214). Berlin: Springer-Verlag.

Jones, M. R. (1986). Attentional rhythmicity in human perception. In J. R. Evans & M. Clynes (Eds.), *Rhythm in psychological, linguistic, and music processes* (pp. 13-40). Springfield, IL: Charles C. Thomas.

Jones, M. R. (1987a). Perspectives on musical time. In A. Gabrielsson (Ed.), *Action and perception in rhythm and music* (pp. 153-175). Stockholm: The Royal Swedish Academy of Music Publications.

Jones, M. R. (1987b). Some thoughts on the relevance of Bergson to contemporary psychology. In A. C. Papanicolacu & P. A. Y. Gunter (Eds.), *The legacy of Henri Bergson: Towards a unification of the sciences* (pp. 250-270). New York: Gordon & Breach Science Publishers.

Jones, M. R., & Boltz, M. (1989). Dynamic attending and responses to time. *Psychological Review, 96,* 459-491.

Jones, M. R., Kidd, G., & Wetzel, R. (1981). Evidence for rhythmic attention. *Journal of Experimental Psychology: Human Perception and Performance, 7,* 1059-1073.

Jones, M. R., Maser, D. J., & Kidd, G. R., (1978). Rate and structure in memory for auditory patterns. *Memory & Cognition, 6,* 246-258.

Jones, M. R., Summerell, L., & Marshburn, E. (1987). Recognizing melodies: A dynamic interpretation. *Quarterly Journal of Experimental Psychology, 39,* 89-121.

Kelso, J. A., Southard, D. L., & Goodman, D. (1979). On the nature of human interlimb coordination. *Science, 203*, 1029-1031.

Kendon, A. (1977). Movement coordination in social interaction: Some examples described. In *Studies in semiotics: Vol. 6. Studies in the behavior of social interaction* (pp. 53-77). Bloomington: Indiana University Press.

Klapp, S. T. (1979). Doing two things at once: The role of temporal compatibility. *Memory & Cognition, 7*, 375-381.

Klapp, S. T. (1981). Temporal compatibility in dual motor tasks: II. Simultaneous articulation and hand movement. *Memory & Cognition, 9*, 398-401.

Kramer, J. (1982). Beginnings and endings in Western art music. *Canadian University Music Review, 3*, 1-14.

Kronman, U., & Sundberg, J. (1987). Is the musical ritard an allusion to physical motion? In A. Gabrielsson (Ed.), *Action perception in rhythm and music* (pp. 57-68). Stockholm: Royal Swedish Academy of Music.

Lee, C. S. (1985). The rhythmic interpretation of simple musical sequences: Towards a perceptual model. In P. Howell, I. Cross, & R. West (Eds.), *Musical structure and cognition* (pp. 53-69). London: Academic Press.

Lee, D. N. (1980). The optic flow field: The foundation of vision. *Philosophical Transactions of the Royal Society of London, 290*, 169-179.

Lerdahl, F., & Jackendoff, R. (1983). *A generative theory of tonal music.* Cambridge, MA: MIT Press.

Longuet-Higgins, H. C., & Lee, C. S. (1982). The perception of musical rhythms. *Perception, 11*, 115-128.

Longuet-Higgins, H. C., & Lee, C. S. (1984). The rhythmic interpretation of monophonic music. *Music Perception, 1*, 424-442.

Massaro, D. W., & Idson, W. L. (1976). Temporal course of perceived auditory duration. *Perception & Psychophysics, 20*, 331-352.

Michon, J. A. (1978). The making of the present: A tutorial review. In J. Requin (Ed.), *Attention and performance* (Vol. VII, pp. 89-111). Hillsdale, NJ: Lawrence Erlbaum Associates.

Michon, J. A. (1985). The compleat time experiencer. In J. A. Michon & J. L. Jackson (Eds.), *Time, mind, and behavior* (pp. 20-52). Berlin: Springer-Verlag.

Monahan, C. B., & Carterette, E. C. (1985). Pitch and duration as determinants of musical space. *Music Perception, 3*, 1-32.

Monahan, C. B., Kendall, R., & Carterette, E. C. (1987). The effect of melodic and temporal contour on recognition memory for pitch change *Perception & Psychophysics, 41*, 576-600.

Newtson, D., Hairfield, J., Bloomingdale, J., & Cutino, S. (1987). The structure of action and interaction. *Social Cognition, 5*, 191-237.

Ornstein, R. E. (1969). *On the experience of time.* Harmondsworth, England: Penguin.

Palmer, C. (1988). *Timing in skilled music performance.* Unpublished doctoral dissertation, Cornell University, Ithaca, NY.

Palmer, C. (1989). Mapping musical thought to musical performance. *Journal of Experimental Psychology: Human Perception and Performance, 15*, 331-346.

Povel, D.-J. (1977). Temporal structure of performed music: Some preliminary observations. *Acta Psychologica, 41*, 309-320.

Povel, D.-J. (1981). Internal representation of simple temporal patterns. *Journal of Experimental Psychology: Human Perception and Performance, 7*, 3-18.

Povel, D.-J. (1985). Time, rhythms, and tension: In search of the determinants of rhythmicity. In J. A. Michon & J. L. Jackson (Eds.), *Time, Mind, and Behavior* (pp. 215-225). Berlin: Springer-Verlag.

Povel, D.-J., & Essens, P. (1985). Perception of temporal patterns. *Music Perception, 2,* 411-440.

Rosner, B., & Meyer, L. (1986). The perceptual roles of melodic process, contour and form. *Music Perception, 4,* 1-39.

Shaffer, L. H. (1981). Performances of Chopin, Bach & Bartok: Studies in motor programming. *Cognitive Psychology, 13,* 326-376.

Shaffer, L. H. (1982). Rhythm and timing in skill. *Psychological Review, 89,* 109-122.

Shaffer, L. H., Clarke, E. F., & Todd, N. P. (1985). Meter and rhythm in piano playing. *Cognition, 20,* 61-77.

Shepard, R. N. (1984). Ecological constraints on internal representation: Resonant kinematics of perceiving, imagining, thinking, and dreaming. *Psychological Review, 91,* 417-447.

Sloboda, J. A. (1983). The communication of musical meter in piano performance. *Quarterly Journal of Experimental Psychology, 35,* 377-390.

Sloboda, J. A. (1985). *The musical mind.* Fair Lawn, NJ: Oxford University Press.

Steedman, M. J. (1977). The perception of musical rhythm and metre. *Perception, 6,* 555-569.

Sternberg, S., Knoll, R., & Zukofsky, P. (1978). Timing by skilled musicians. In D. Deutsch, *The psychology of music* (pp. 181-239). New York: Academic Press.

Stroud, J. M. (1955). The fine structure of psychological time. In H. Quastler (Ed.), *Information theory in psychology: Problems and methods* (pp. 174-205). Glencoe, IL: The Free Press.

Thomas, E. A. C., & Brown, I. (1975). Time perception and the filled duration illusion. *Perception & Psychophysics, 16,* 363-367.

Todd, N. (1985). A model of expressive timing in tonal music. *Music Perception, 3,* 33-58.

Underwood, G., & Swain, R. A. (1973). Selectivity of attention and the perception of duration. *Perception, 2,* 101-105.

Vorberg, D., & Hambuch, R. (1978). On the temporal control of rhythmic performance. In J. Requin (Ed.), *Attention and performance* (Vol. VII, pp. 535-555). Hillsdale, NJ: Lawrence Erlbaum Associates.

Vorberg, D., & Hambuch, R. (1984). Timing of two-handed rhythmic performance. In J. Gibbon & L. Allan (Eds.), *Timing and time perception* (pp. 390-406). New York: New York Academy of Sciences.

Vos, P. G., & Handel, S. (1987). Playing triplets; facts and preferences. In A. Gabrielsson (Ed.), *Action and perception in rhythm and music* (pp. 35-47). Stockholm: The Royal Swedish Academy of Music Publications.

Vos, P. G., Leeuwenberg, E. L., & Collard, R. F. (1978). *What melody tells about meter in music* (Rep. No. 78 FU 03). Nijmegen, The Netherlands: University of Nijmegen.

Wapnik, J. (1980). The perception of musical and metronomic tempo changes in musicians. *Psychology of Music, 8,* 3-12.

Wing, A. M., & Kristofferson, A. B. (1973). Response delays and timing of discrete motor responses. *Perception & Psychophysics, 14,* 5-12.

Woodrow, H. (1951). Time perception. In S. S. Stevens (Ed.), *Handbook of experimental psychology* (pp. 1224-1236). New York: Wiley.

Yeston, M. (1976). *The stratification of musical rhythm.* New Haven: Yale University Press.

10 Time Reversal in Human Cognition: Search for a Temporal Theory of Insanity

Suchoon S. Mo
University of Southern Colorado

TIME AND INSANITY

My aim is not so much to derive a cognitive theory of time as to arrive at a temporal theory of cognition. Consider the following limerick, as quoted by Narlikar (1978):

> There was a young girl named Miss Bright
> Whose speed was far faster than light.
> She departed one day in a relative way
> And came back the previous night.

Human mental activities, including human cognition, depend on temporal direction. As Denbigh (1981) stated, it is difficult to conceptualize *un*knowing or *un*observing in conjunction with knowing or observing. Miss Bright is confined to science fiction, to theoretical physics, or to the realm of insanity. In short, if one is neither a novelist nor a theoretical physicist, one risks the chance of being regarded as insane by addressing the issue of time reversal in cognition. However, it is also possible that time reversal may, in fact, be a fundamental process underlying phenomena that appear to be illogical, irrational, delusionary, or insane. For example, if one claims to have a power of precognition to receive a message before it is sent, such a claim is often regarded as delusionary, and tends to be condemned to the normative realm of abnormality or paranormality. However, the end-means relationship is

241

as pertinent to animal evolution as the cause-effect relationship. Human cognition, as a part of evolutionary process, is capable of anticipating, expecting, and axiomatizing before receiving information. In short, cognition is capable of incorporating some kind of time reversal. At least, if cognition is to be understood, the issue of insanity must be studied without resorting to normative criteria.

TIME AND LOGIC

One way of relating time to logic is to talk about the distinction between two different kinds of time: A-series and B-series. *A-series* refers to time with tense, that is, time in terms of future, present, and past. *B-series* refers to time with succession defined by the "before than" or "after than" relation. This distinction was originally made by McTaggart (1908, 1927). How one kind of time is related to the other is a very controversial question (see Gale, 1968a, 1968b). Logical asymmetry arises with respect to the A-series, because the past is closed, whereas the future is open. What is past can be true or false; what is not yet may be neither true nor false. Logic of the future, such as modal or three-value logic, is characteristically different from logic of the past.

Instead of discussing future and past, I focus on intension and its extension. A logical term, idea, or concept has its intension and extension. Seventeenth-century Port Royal Logic made a distinction between intension (comprehension) and extension. Intension of a general term is the set of attributes that it implies. Extension is the set of things to which such attributes apply (Kneale & Kneale, 1962). Intension is a kind of abstraction. Because more attributes apply to a lesser number of things, the relation between intension and extension can be regarded as an inverse relation. For example, a square has more attributes than a rectangle; therefore, there are more rectangles than squares.

Our desire to cast human cognition in the light of exact science leads to reduction of the logic of intension to that of extension. The *Thesis of Extensionality* proposes that all logic, and all language, is extensional, and that intensional phenomena are surface phenomena (Kneale & Kneale, 1962). Linguistically, the deep structure of language is extensional; surface phenomena of language are intensional (Bealer, 1982). Because truth values are extensional, and because truth values favor the past over the future, the Thesis of Extensionality exudes an attitude that is resistant and hostile to the temporality of human cognition. To reduce human cognition to the deep structure of language is to reject the temporality inherent in human cognition. An alternative approach, in accordance with Brentano's notion (see Bealer, 1982), is to regard intension as being *about* something and extension as being *from* something. In terms of information, we may say that information about something is intensional; information from something is extensional. Because there is no way of obtaining information from the future, information about the future is intensional. By the same reasoning, we can say that information from the past is extensional. If one knows more about something, there is less need to obtain information from it. The inverse relation between future and past information still holds. Reichenbach (1956), by borrowing Brentano's notion of intension and extension, regarded negentropy and entropy as intensional and extensional information, respectively. Although discussion of the nature of relation between negentropy and information is beyond my aim, it should be noted that the relationship between negentropy and entropy is inverse as between intension and extension.

Study of the psychological relationship between time and logic has, in the past, been largely left to phenomenological speculation. One typical example is that of Dufrenne (1966), who reduced the notion of logical a priori to immediacy of consciousness. Such phenomenological reduction of a priori is similar to perceptual Gestalt. The difficulty is that, as with James' (1890) "specious present," the temporality of immediacy is not specified. Is the immediacy in terms of succession, duration or tense? The answer is not clear. As Gale (1968a) pointed out, two different tones in close temporal proximity may constitute the specious present. Yet they do not constitute a chord.

In order to understand the relation between time and cognition at an elementary level, consider the case of the temporal experience of pure duration. A signal begins at a particular moment and ends at a particular later moment. At the beginning, one has little information as to how long the signal is going to last, if the information is extensional. As time passes, more time information is gained from the duration. Time information from the duration is an increasing function of passage of time, or what is known stochastically as "aging," in the duration. Such time information may be called *posterior time information*. On the other hand, one may have, at the beginning of the duration, prior information as to how long the duration is going to last. Such time information may decay over time, and is a decreasing function of passage of time in duration. Such time information may be called *prior time information*. The relation between prior and posterior time information is, as with intensional and extension, an inverse relation. At the beginning of the foreperiod, no time information can be obtained from the foreperiod. Prior time information is intensional. As time passes in the foreperiod, time information can be obtained from time duration that has passed. Posterior time information is extensional. Temporality of logical asymmetry is specified by such reciprocal relationship between prior and posterior time information.

SCHIZOPHRENIA AND TIME INFORMATION

Consider the case of a typical simple reaction time experiment. A warning signal is followed by an imperative stimulus to which one must respond promptly, usually by depressing a key. The duration between the onset of the warning signal and the onset of the imperative stimulus, usually called the *foreperiod*, affects reaction time in a systematic way. For example, if the foreperiod is variable from trial to trial, reaction time tends to be shorter for a longer foreperiod. Such an effect is regarded as being due to the decreasing time uncertainty associated with a longer foreperiod duration (Drazin, 1961; Karlin, 1959; Klemmer, 1956; Zahn & Rosenthal, 1966). However, the foreperiod effect is not always due to time uncertainty. Subjective probability as to the occurrence of the signal to respond confounds the foreperiod effect. For example, if the probability that the signal to respond will follow the warning signal is varied, then the reaction time is a decreasing function of such probability, even if the foreperiod is constant at a duration as short as 1 s (Näätänen & Koskinen, 1975).

There are two kinds of time information at any given moment during the foreperiod duration: prior time and posterior time information. Information at the beginning of the foreperiod duration consists entirely of prior time information. Time information near the end of the duration consists predominantly of posterior time information. Because prior time information and posterior time information are, respectively, intensional and extensional, the relation between them is an inverse one. Prior time (intensional) information decreases, and posterior time (extensional) information increases, progressively, as time progresses during the foreperiod duration. This inverse relation between two kinds of time information points to an aspect of temporality common to both logic and cognition.

Consider schizophrenia, which is generally regarded as a disorder of cognition (see Bleuler, 1911; Spitzer, Endicott, & Robins, 1978). Formal thought disorder, thought broadcasting, illogical thinking, delusions, and other forms of disorder of cognition characterize schizophrenia. Studies of the use of time information in schizophrenics may lead to a better understanding of the nature of the temporality associated with insanity.

If the foreperiod duration is variable, the reaction time of schizo-phrenics is a decreasing function of foreperiod. When the foreperiod duration is constant, their reaction time is an increasing function of foreperiod. Such a "cross-over phenomenon," although not unique to schizophrenics, is quite exaggerated among them (see Cromwell, 1975). Shakow (1962) theorized that schizophrenics segmentalize the fore-period because of future-past reversal in terms of motivation. In a situa-tion calling for future orientation, such as in reaction time experiments, schizophrenics are motivated by the needs of the past. However, the way in which such a past orientation would result in a cross-over phenomenon is not clear.

Assume that an auditory warning signal is followed by a single dark dot, and that the task is to judge the duration of the dot. The duration estimation of the dot is an increasing function of the foreperiod duration (that is, the duration of the warning signal) if the foreperiod duration is variable from trial to trial. The reason is that expectancy of arrival time of the dot is stronger for a longer foreperiod, resulting in earlier onset of the duration estimation process and the subsequent longer temporal experience of the duration of the dot (Mo & George, 1977). In terms of uncertainty, all durations are alike at their beginning. A longer duration is merely a shorter duration that is prolonged. Consequently, time uncertainty decreases as duration is increased. In short, the effect of foreperiod duration originates from the passage of time associated with the foreperiod. Such a foreperiod effect is due to posterior time infor-mation, and is extensional. On the other hand, if the pitch of the warning signal is correlated with the foreperiod duration, then the pitch would function as prior time information, at the beginning of the fore-period, as to how long the foreperiod is going to last. The effect of the foreperiod, being due to prior time information, is intensional. Thus, the effect of foreperiod on duration estimation of the dot should be the inverse of the effect of foreperiod lacking prior time information. That is, the duration estimation should decrease as a function of foreperiod duration. Experimental results show that there is no difference between schizophrenics and nonschizophrenics in terms of the posterior time information effect, that is, the effect of foreperiod for which the pitch of the warning signal is uncorrelated with foreperiod duration. However, schizophrenics are greatly affected by prior time information, whereas nonschizophrenics are unaffected. Specifically, if the pitch of the warning signal is correlated with foreperiod duration so that the pitch functions as prior time information concerning how long the foreperiod is going to be, the increasing effect of foreperiod is either eliminated or attenuated (Mo & Kersey, 1977; Mo, Kersey, & Lowe, 1977). In short, schizophrenia cannot be distinguished on the basis of extensionality alone. In a way, to say that some aspect of cognition is "irrational" may be an admission that the Thesis of Extensionality, and the notion of rationality, is inadequate to account for human cognition.

Generally, schizophrenics are intensionally oriented. This is another way of saying that a delusionary system is a highly intensional system. Delusion resists reality. One reason is that intension is prior in time to extension, and no information can be obtained from that which is not yet in existence. Whether or not extension is the deep structure of cognition is irrelevant. The issue is not one of how deep; it is one of *when*.

TIME REVERSAL AND LATERAL REVERSAL

An experimental study (Mo, LeFevre, & Kersey, 1984) was conducted to explore brain hemisphere locus of the inverse relation between prior and posterior time information. As with previous experiments (e.g., Mo & Kersey, 1977), an auditory warning signal of variable duration was followed by a single dark dot, and the task was to judge the duration of the dot. In the uncorrelated condition, the pitch of the warning signal was uncorrelated with foreperiod. The foreperiod effect on the duration estimation would be due to posterior time information from the foreperiod itself. In the correlated condition, the pitch of the warning signal was correlated with foreperiod duration. In this condition, the foreperiod effect is due to prior time information. The dot to be estimated in terms of its duration was presented to either the left, the center, or the right visual field. That is, a duration estimate was made on the basis of visual information to either the right or the left hemisphere, or to both hemispheres.

For nonschizophrenic controls (reformed alcoholics) in the uncorrelated condition, duration estimates increased as a function of foreperiod duration. This increasing effect of foreperiod was stronger for the right visual field (left hemisphere). In the correlated condition, the foreperiod effect was stronger for the left visual field than for the right. It is apparent that the relation between prior and posterior time information is an inverse relation with respect to laterality of brain hemisphere. Temporal asymmetry is apparently spatialized in terms of lateral asymmetry. Among schizophrenics, brain hemisphere laterality itself is laterally reversed. In the uncorrelated condition, the foreperiod effect is stronger for the left hemisphere. That is, in schizophrenics the inverse relation between prior and posterior time information is reversed in terms of brain hemisphere laterality. In short, brain hemisphere laterality associated with time information in schizophrenics is a mirror image, a spatialized enantiomorph, of that in nonschizophrenics.

What such findings imply is that the cognition that characterizes schizophrenia involves some kind of time reversal, specifically, reversal between "before" and "after," and that such time reversal is spatialized in terms of reversed brain hemisphere laterality. Time reversal manifests itself in spatialized laterality. "Before" and "after" are spatialized in terms of "left" and "right," and temporal reversal is spatialized in terms of lateral reversal. In terms of logical asymmetry, such a reversal is associated with the reversal between intension and extension. Suppose that a situation calls for gaining information from an event, but one believes that he or she already knows all about that event. In such a situation, the person is not so much ignorant as delusionary. If delusion is an aspect of insanity, then temporal reversal of logical asymmetry is not an issue of intelligence, but rather of insanity. Conversely, suppose that a situation calls for knowing about an event, but one attempts to gain information from the event. This reversal is likely to involve a process of segmentalization such as Shakow (1962) discussed, and it is similar to the popular notion of inability to see a forest because one is too obsessed with the trees.

The literature on brain hemisphere laterality is vast, and the precise role of brain hemisphere laterality in schizophrenia is not a clearly decided issue (see Merrin, 1981). However, it has been shown that some schizophrenics show brain hemisphere lateral reversal even anatomically (Luchins, Weinberger, & Wyatt, 1979, 1982). Reversal in schizophrenics of brain hemispheres associated with time information is a phenomenon that should be taken into consideration when studying their cognitive processes.

It must be noted that human cognition tends to spatialize time. For example, the question "what time is it now?" is a question about the location of a point on a clock. The nonspatialized question "when time is it now?" is almost incomprehensible. Space is isotropic, so that directionality of space is arbitrary. However, if the process of spatialization of time is possible in nature, then, as so advocated by Kozyrev (1971), spatialization of time reversal would result in reversal of spatial asymmetry. In short, time reversal would result in some kind of enantiomorph. At least, such spatialized reversal may be the case in reversal of brain hemisphere laterality associated with reversal of time information.

SELF: SUBJECT-OBJECT REVERSAL

When one looks into a mirror, the reflected image is reversed laterally but not longitudinally. Although an exhaustive investigation of this "mirror-image paradox" is lacking, one plausible explanation advanced by Navon (1987) is that this apparent lateral reversal originates from a "front-to-front" encounter between two animals. In such an encounter, the animal being observed is laterally reversed with respect to the animal that observes it. We can carry this explanation much further. Evolution dictates that an object is a lateral reversal of a subject, and that, when the object moves to the left, the subject must move to the right in order for the subject to be in the proximity of the object. The mirror image of self is no exception. Self as being observed, conceptualized, and known is an object; self that observes, conceptualizes, and knows is a subject. We may speculate that self as an object, or, what may be called *objective self*, is an enantiomorph of subjective self, and is based on time reversal.

Chapman and his colleagues (Chapman, Chapman, & Raulin, 1976, 1978; Chapman, Edell, & Chapman, 1980) specified three dimensions that are pertinent to vulnerability to schizophrenia: perceptual aberration, physical anhedonia, and social anhedonia. These three dimensions, measured by questionnaire-type scales, refer to gross perceptual distortion of one's body image, lack of physical pleasure, and lack of pleasure in interpersonal relationships, respectively. Schizophrenics tend to score high on these three scales. However, among nonpsychotics these scales show very little correlation, pointing to a possibility that perceptual aberration may be unrelated to anhedonia (Simons, McMillan, & Ireland, 1982), and that perceptual aberration is more or less independent of other factors of vulnerability toward schizophrenia. One can infer that perceptual aberration is an extreme case of objectification of self. For example, when one feels strange toward one's body, feels that one's arms or legs are not his or hers, self is predominantly objective, and therefore, should constitute a laterally reversed enantiomorph. We can predict that prior and posterior time information would be reversed for those who score high on the scale of perceptual aberration, and that such temporal reversal manifests itself in terms of lateral reversal of locus of brain hemispheres associated with these two kinds of time information. An experimental study (Mo & Chavez, 1986) was conducted to test this prediction.

Eighteen college students participated in an experiment. Prior to experimentation, the perceptual aberration scale (PAB), physical anhedonia scale (PHA) and social anhedonia scale (SOA) were administered. In each experimental session, an auditory warning signal of 5-s duration was followed immediately by a single dark dot of either .08-s or .10-s duration. The task was to judge the duration of the dot and report the judgment by saying either "short" or "long." The duration of the warning signal constituted the foreperiod. The dot was presented either to the left visual field or to the right visual field in random order. The warning signal was presented to the left or the right ear, using a counter-balanced block design.

The rank-order correlation between the difference of duration estimation between the left and right ear, and PAB scale was significant (.69). The duration estimation of the dot tends to be longer for the right ear than the left for those who score high on the PAB scale. As to rank-order correlation coefficients among these three scales, they were: -.13 between PAB scale and PHA scale, .37 between PAB scale and SOA scale, and .35 between PHA scale and SOA scale. There was a complete reversal of ear dominance associated with time information between those who score high and those who score low on the PAB scale. Specifically, the left ear, and therefore, the right hemisphere, is dominant for those who score low on the PAB scale and the opposite is the case for those who score high on the PAB scale. Because the foreperiod remained constant at 5 s, time information associated with the foreperiod can be regarded as prior time information. Objectification of self is accompanied by spatial reversal as demonstrated in terms of lateral reversal of brain hemisphere locus of prior time information. Together with the finding of the previous study (Mo et al., 1984) that the inverse relation between prior and posterior time information is laterally reversed among schizophrenics, and because PAB is a characteristic of schizophrenia, it is reasonable to assume that time reversal can manifest itself in terms of lateral reversal, and that subject-object reversal is a case of such lateral reversal.

The tradition of natural science is to minimize the subject in a subject-object relation. The pursuit of objectivity of observation is often identified with control, minimization, or even elimination of subject variables, through experimental manipulation or by means of statistical operation. In psychology, which has the task of studying subject-object relations, obsession with objectivity is such that subject is objectified to the extreme extent that objects of experimental observation are often called *subjects*. Such a contradiction results from reversal of the subject-object relation (see Riegel, 1979). The notion of subject-object reversal, as well as of a Hegelian dialectic, is consistent with the experimental finding that perceptual aberration is accompanied by brain hemisphere lateral reversal of time information. The self that observes or knows is distinct from the self that is observed or known. One is an enantiomorph of the other. Is subject-object reversal also an issue of insanity rather than one of intelligence? The answer is affirmative.

IRRATIONALITY, DELUSION, AND THOUGHT DISORDER

If the nature of human cognition is to be regarded as rational, then irrationality must be regarded as an indication of insanity. Because it is no longer fashionable to talk about evil spirits, insanity is now commonly associated with mental illness. As Szasz (1970, 1977) asserted, the notion of insanity has transformed itself from a theological notion to a medical notion. The notion that irrationality originates from thought disorder is a convenient means to uphold the view that the nature of cognition is fundamentally rational. Consequently, if it can be shown that schizophrenics use rules of logic different from those of nonschizophrenics, as advocated by Arieti (1955), then we can regard irrationality as some kind of thought disorder, and therefore, we would be free from the burden of accepting irrationality as a fundamental dimension of cognition.

More recent research does not support the view that thought disorder is unique to schizophrenia. Watson and World (1981) compared schizophrenics and people suffering from brain damage, on measures of over-inclusiveness and syllogism error. The group differences disappeared when the factors of education, intelligence, and sampling were taken into consideration. Thought disorder is not unique to schizophrenia; it can even be detected among those suffering from affective disorders such as mania (Andreasen, 1979; Hoffman, Stopeck, & Andreasen, 1986; Simpson & Davis, 1985). In clinical situations, as in daily life, cognition is inferred from communication. However, speech or language disorder is not necessarily thought disorder. Among schizophrenics, phonology and syntax are more or less self-contained, so that the interaction between language and reality is determined mostly by semantics (Chaika, 1982). Inference of thought disorder from bizarre verbalization is not warranted, because bizarre verbalization is due to intermingling of present and past experience, and is related to personal life. Consequently, disordered logic is not a major factor in accounting for the bizarre language behavior of schizophrenics (Harrow & Prosen, 1978). Speech disorder is not necessarily an indication of thought disorder.

Delusion is a system of rigid ideas and beliefs. As such, it is prior to experience, and is highly intensional. Such intensionality of delusion is often regarded as an indication of irrationality, as would be the case of various types of delusion characterizing schizophrenia. To illustrate intensionality of delusion, I cite some studies done in the context of the theory of rational-emotive therapy (Ellis, 1962). According to this theory, "intensionally" oriented people are those whose cognition and affect are influenced by the word they use. "Extensionally" oriented people are more influenced by empirical observations (see Korzybski, 1933). Although such operational definition of intensionality and extensionality may not agree with their logical definition, it may be assumed that people who are influenced more by semantics than empirical observation are highly intensionally oriented. It has been shown that intensionally oriented people are more prone to form irrational beliefs, that is, delusion, than extensional people (Milford & Tobacyk, 1988). Furthermore, the degree of irrationality is inversely related to the level of performance in the tasks of reading and comprehension, but not in the tasks of writing and mathematics (Prola, 1985, 1988). Why? The tasks of reading and comprehension demand extraction of information *from* reading materials. In accordance with Brentano's distinction between intension and extension, we can say that such information is extensional. Consequently, intensionally oriented people perform poorly in the task. On the other hand, writing involves information *about* what to write, and, therefore, what has not been written yet. The task is intensional. Consequently, intensionally oriented people are not hampered in their performance. Mathematics is highly intensional in that is relies on abstract symbols. Again, intensionally oriented people can perform the task with little conflict.

High degree of intensionality alone does not lead to delusion. A highly abstract belief is not necessarily delusionary. Only the intensionality that is prior in time to extensionality can be delusionary. Stated in another way, delusion persists because it is prior in time to experience. It may be that intensionally oriented people tend to form irrational beliefs only because they are influenced more by the effect of prior time information than by the effect of posterior time information. In this way, the issue of irrationality may be reduced to the issue of temporality of cognitive processes.

The rationality-irrationality dimension makes sense only if the work is assumed to be totally extensional. Such a dimension is not in itself adequate as a means to understand cognition. Does evolution favor rational beliefs? It remains to be seen whether natural selection would favor those who believe that natural selection would favor true and rational strategies.

SUMMARY AND CONCLUSION

The dimension of insanity, as independent of the dimension of intelligence, is based on reversal of time information involved in cognition. There are two kinds of time information associated with duration. They are prior time information, which is *about* duration, and posterior time information, which is *from* duration. The relation between prior time information and posterior time information is an inverse relation. This inverse relation is little different from the inverse relation between logical intension and extension. Temporal reversal of these two kinds of time information in schizophrenics is associated with corresponding lateral reversal of brain hemisphere loci associated with such time information. Time reversal is spatialized in terms of the brain hemisphere lateral reversal. What are usually regarded as the abnormality and irrationality of cognition characterizing schizophrenia involve brain hemisphere lateral reversal of these loci. Extreme self-awareness, which is based on subject-object reversal of self, is also accompanied by brain hemisphere lateral reversal of such loci. Certainly, those who suffer from gross distortion of perception of their own bodies do manifest such hemispheric reversal. A conclusion is that the dimension of insanity is based on such time reversal.

REFERENCES

Andreasen, N. C. (1979). Thought, language and communication: II. Diagnostic significance. *Archives of General Psychiatry, 36*, 1325-1330.

Arieti, S. (1955). *Interpretation of schizophrenia*. New York: Basic Books.

Bealer, G. (1982). *Quality and concept*. Oxford: Clarendon Press.

Bleuler, E. (1911). *Dementia praecox or the group of schizophrenias*. New York: International Universities Press.

Chaika, E. (1982). Thought disorder or speech disorder in schizophrenia? *Schizophrenia Bulletin, 8*, 587-591.

Chapman, L. J., Chapman, J. P., & Raulin, M. L. (1976). Scales for physical and social anhedonia. *Journal of Abnormal Psychology, 85*, 374-382.

Chapman, L. J., Chapman, J. P., & Raulin, M. L. (1978) Body-image aberration in schizophrenia. *Journal of Abnormal Psychology, 87*, 399-407.

Chapman, L. J., Edell, W. S., & Chapman, J. P. (1980). Physical anhedonia, perceptual aberration, and psychosis proneness. *Schizophrenia Bulletin, 6*, 639-653.

Cromwell, R. L. (1975). Assessment of schizophrenia. *Annual Review of Psychology, 26*, 593-619.

Denbigh, K. G. (1981). *Three concepts of time*. Berlin: Springer-Verlag.

Drazin, D. H. (1961). Effects of foreperiod, foreperiod variability, and probability of stimulus occurrence on simple reaction time. *Journal of Experimental Psychology, 62*, 43-50.

Dufrenne, M. (1966). *The notion of the a priori*. Evanston, IL: Northwestern University Press.

Ellis, A. (1962). *Reason and emotion in psychotherapy*. New York: Lyle Stuart.

Gale, R. M. (1968a). *The philosophy of time*. London: McMillan.

Gale, R. M. (1968b). *The language of time*. London: Routledge & Kegan Paul.

Harrow, M., & Prosen, M. (1978). Intermingling and disordered logic as influences on schizophrenic "thought" disorders. *Archives of General Psychiatry, 35*, 1213-1218.

Hoffman, R. E., Stopeck, S., & Andreasen, M. C. (1986). A comparative study of manic vs. schizophrenic speech disorganization. *Archives of General Psychiatry, 43*, 831-838.

James, W. (1890). *Principles of psychology* (Vol. 1). New York: Henry Holt.

Karlin, L. (1959). Reaction time as a function of foreperiod duration and variability. *Journal of Experimental Psychology, 58*, 185-191.

Klemmer, E. T. (1956). Simple reaction time as a function of time uncertainty. *Journal of Experimental Psychology, 54*, 179-184.

Kneale, W., & Kneale, M. (1962). *The development of logic*. Oxford: Clarendon Press.

Korzybski, A. (1933). *Science and minds*. Lancaster, PA: Lancaster Press.

Kozyrev, N. A. (1971). On the possibility of experimental investigation of the properties of time. In J. Zeman (Ed.), *Time in science and philosophy* (pp. 111-132). Prague: Academia.

Luchins, D. J., Weinberger, D. R., & Wyatt, R. J. (1979). Schizophrenia: Evidence of a subgroup with reversed cerebral asymmetry. *Archives of General Psychiatry, 36*, 1309-1311.

Luchins, D. J., Weinberger, D. R., & Wyatt, R. J. (1982). Schizophrenia and lateral asymmetry detected by computed tomography. *American Journal of Psychiatry, 139*, 753-757.

McTaggart, J. M. E. (1908). The unreality of time. *Mind, 17*, 457-474.

McTaggart, J. M. E. (1927). *The nature of existence* (Vol. 2). Cambridge: Cambridge University Press.

Merrin, E. L. (1981). Schizophrenia and brain asymmetry: An evaluation of evidence for dominant lobe dysfunction. *Journal of Nervous and Mental Disease, 169*, 405-416.

Milford, G., & Tobacyk, J. (1988). Intensionality and irrational beliefs. *Psychological Reports, 56*, 236-238.

Mo, S. S., & Chavez, M. R. (1986). Perceptual aberration and brain hemisphere reversal of foreperiod effect on time estimation. *Journal of Clinical Psychology, 42*, 787-792.

Mo, S. S., & George, E. J. (1977). Foreperiod effect on time estimation and simple reaction time. *Acta Psychologica, 41*, 47-59.

Mo, S. S., & Kersey, R. (1977). Prior time uncertainty reduction of foreperiod duration in schizophrenia and old age. *Journal of Clinical Psychology, 33*, 53-58.

Mo, S. S., Kersey, R., & Lowe, W. C. (1977). Prior time uncertainty reduction of foreperiod duration under two different levels of event uncertainty in schizophrenia. *Journal of Clinical Psychology, 33*, 381-385.

Mo, S. S., LeFevre, P. A., & Kersey, R. (1984). Binocular locus of brain hemisphere reversal of time information in schizophrenia. *Journal of Clinical Psychology, 40*, 230-236.

Näätänen, R., & Koskinen, R. (1975). Simple reaction time with very small imperative-stimulus probabilities. *Acta Psychologica, 39*, 43-50.

Narlikar, J. U. (1978). Cosmic tachyons: An astrophysical approach. *American Scientist, 66*, 587-593.

Navon, D. (1987). Why do we blame the mirror for reversing left and right? *Cognition, 27,* 275-283.

Prola, M. (1985). Irrational beliefs and intellectual performance. *Psychological Reports, 57,* 431-434.

Prola, M. (1988). Intensionality in the irrational belief - intellectual performance relationship. *Journal of Clinical Psychology, 44,* 57-60.

Reichenbach, H. (1956). *The direction of time.* Berkeley: The University of California Press.

Riegel, K. F. (1979). *Foundations of dialectical psychology.* New York: Academic Press.

Shakow, D. (1962). Segmental set: A theory of the formal psychological deficit in schizophrenia. *Archives of General Psychiatry, 6,* 1-17.

Simons, R. F., McMillan, R. W., & Ireland, R. B. (1982). Reaction-time cross over in preselected schizotypic subjects. *Journal of Abnormal Psychology, 91,* 414-419.

Simpson, D. M., & Davis, G. C. (1985). Measuring thought disorder with clinical rating scales in schizophrenic and nonschizophrenic patients. *Psychiatry Research, 15,* 313-318.

Spitzer, R. L., Endicott, J., & Robins, E. (1978) *Research Diagnostic Criteria (RDC) for selected groups of functional disorders.* New York: New York State Psychiatric Institute.

Szasz, T. S. (1970). *The myth of mental illness.* New York: Harper & Row.

Szasz, T. S. (1977). *The theology of medicine.* Baton Rouge: Louisiana State University Press.

Watson, C. G., & World, J. (1981). Logical reasoning deficits in schizophrenia and brain damage. *Journal of Clinical Psychology, 37,* 466-471.

Zahn, T. P., & Rosenthal, D. (1966). Simple reaction time as a function of the relative frequency of the preparatory interval. *Journal of Experimental Psychology, 72,* 15-19.

11 Identity and Temporal Perspective

Frederick T. Melges[1]
Duke University Medical Center

Is the sense of identity related to how a person construes and experiences temporal perspective? This is the central question of this chapter. The question arose from clinical observations of acutely ill psychiatric patients. It appeared that when these patients' temporal perspective became chaotic they also lost their sense of self.[2] This spurred more systematic studies and explorations that I summarize in this chapter.

DEFINITIONS

Identity and temporal perspective are fundamental integrative cognitions of human experience. This integrative quality often gets lost if one attempts to define these terms precisely by breaking them down into their component parts. For example, identity is composed of the body image, attitudes toward the self and others, the person's emotional proclivities, dispositions toward passivity or action, social and occupational commitments, gender comfort, and reflections from significant others; but none of these represents the integration suggested by the term *identity*. In order to reflect the overall integrative quality of the

---

[1] The author is now deceased. The volume editor has done some minor editing of the chapter.

[2] For supporting data, background, and journal references for many of the assertions of this chapter, please refer to Melges (1982).

255

term *identity*, I stay close to its customary general meaning. In similar fashion, I deal with the broad meaning of *temporal perspective*.

According to Webster's dictionary, *identity* means "sameness of essential or generic character in different instances" and "unity and persistence of personality." This meaning is essentially the same as Erikson's (1956) definition of identity as "both a persistent sameness within oneself and a persistent sharing of some kind of essential character with others" (p. 102). This persistent sameness over time is the key to the feeling of identity. It is of great importance for mental health because it serves as a person's center of awareness or anchoring point in a variety of circumstances. In psychiatric illness, regardless of the specific diagnosis, some degree of impairment of identity is present.

Temporal perspective refers to how a person construes and experiences the past, present, and future. It refers to the span of awareness into the past and future as well as the relative attention given to the past, present, or future. For a person to make adequate distinctions between these divisions of "time's arrow," he or she has to have intact sequential thinking in which the present is differentiated from the past and future. Immediate memory, by enabling an ongoing grasp on the now, is important for this differentiation (Melges, 1988a). The distinction between the past (after-now) and the future (before-now) becomes progressively elaborated into spans of awareness that reflect constructions from long-term memory, particularly episodic memory, and anticipatory frames for testing predictions (Block, 1985; Kelly, 1955; Michon & Jackson, 1985; Tulving, 1984).

The relationship between identity and time has been the subject of intensive philosophical debate (Brockelman, 1985; Shalom, 1985). The crux of the issue is, how is the sense of permanence (identity) related to the sense of change (time)? However interesting such philosophical discussions are, I take a more empirical approach. In this chapter, I explore selected psychiatric and medical conditions in which the sense of time and of identity are impaired, and examine common themes in these pathological conditions.

CENTRAL THESIS

The essential proposal is as follows: The sense of identity is related to the continuity of temporal perspective, especially future time perspective.

The rationale for this thesis is threefold: (a) Because a person becomes familiar with his or her self over time, the disruption of the continuity of temporal perspective impairs this sense of familiarity, thereby giving rise to lack of self-sameness over time. This makes the self feel unfamiliar, and thus the self feels strange. (b) Of the various components of human time sense, such as sequence, rate, rhythm, and temporal perspective, the latter is the most permanent. Within the framework of temporal perspective, momentary changes of sequence, rate, and rhythm are evaluated. Thus, discontinuities in temporal perspective are more likely to disrupt that which is stable and relatively permanent about time. When this framework becomes blurred, the integration of the self (identity) also becomes compromised. (c) Because human beings are basically goal-correcting organisms, a firm grip on the personal future, such as having extended anticipations aimed at personal values, provides a key anchoring point for the continuity of temporal perspective. Future time perspective, as a means-to-ends process, gives order and direction to temporal perspective. When the personal future becomes clouded so does the direction of temporal perspective, thereby impairing the sense of identity.

This rationale for the central thesis becomes clearer as I deal with some of the pathological conditions in which temporal perspective and identity become diffused. For now, I elaborate on the importance of the future. The present may be understood in terms of the past from the standpoint of causality and determinism, but the meaning of present and past experiences comes into clearer focus when they become related to our constructions of the anticipated future (Kelly, 1955). Although the future is "empty" of perceptual content, it is rich in cognitive content such as anticipations, expectations, and goals. Projections into the future, which I term *futuring*, are highly important for foresight and the delay of gratification (Jacques, 1956; Melges, 1982).

DEPERSONALIZATION
AND TEMPORAL DISINTEGRATION

Depersonalization refers to the experience of the self as strange and unreal. It is the opposite of a firm sense of identity. Although depersonalization can occur in normal or neurotic individuals when they are faced with an impasse or need to block the reality of an event or emotion, its most extreme forms occur in acute psychosis, particularly when temporal disorganization is present (Melges, 1982). In acute schizophrenia, for example, it is common for the patient to state that the self feels "unreal" and is "going to pieces" when the patient has difficulty in keeping track of sequences over time.

In a series of studies, a research group at Stanford University investigated the relationship between depersonalization and temporal disintegration (see Melges, 1982, for a review). Depersonalization was measured by a 12-statement inventory of feelings of self-estrangement. Examples of such statements are: "I feel like a stranger to myself," "my body seems detached, as if my body and self are separate," "there is little distinction between 'me' and 'not-me'," and "I have the feeling that I am two people: One is 'going through the motions' while the other 'me' is observing me."

Temporal disintegration refers to the loss of sequential thinking and impaired goal-directedness. Cognitively, temporal disintegration was measured by a goal-directed serial-alternation (GDSA) task that requires subjects to make serial adjustments of addition and subtraction as they plan to reach a numerical goal. An example of the GDSA instructions to the subject is as follows: "Starting at 104, subtract 7, then add 1, 2, or 3, and keep alternating the subtraction of 7 with adding 1, 2, or 3, adjusting as you go down to prepare to reach the exact number of 51." Changes in performance on this cognitive measure were found to be highly correlated ($r = .74$) with changes in a 14-statement inventory of temporal integration. Examples of the latter, reworded to reflect temporal disintegration, are as follows: "My past, present, and future seem quite disintegrated with each other," "my past, present, and future seem all muddled up and mixed together," "my past and future seem to have collapsed into the present, and it is difficult for me to tell them apart," "my past, present, and future seem like separate islands of experience with little relation to each other," "my short-term goals do not seem to fit my long-term goals," and "I am not confident that my plans will accomplish my goals."

From these inventory items, it can be seen that temporal disintegration, particularly the indistinction of past, present, and future, is perhaps the most severe form of disruption of temporal perspective. Thus, temporal disintegration can be thought of as disrupting the timeline from past to present to future so that it seems discontinuous. In fact, temporal disintegration was substantially correlated with reports of this timeline as being "discontinuous" and also with measures that indicated foreshortening of future time perspective.

We tested the hypothesized relationship between depersonalization and temporal disintegration from several vantage points, using the same or similar measures each time, but employing different research designs. When psychiatric patients were tested only once shortly after admission to the hospital, the single-time correlation between depersonalization and temporal disintegration was .66 (Freeman & Melges, 1977). When another sample of acute psychiatric patients were tested at admission and then shortly before discharge from the hospital, the pre-post correlation of changes between depersonalization and temporal disintegration was .52 (Freeman & Melges, 1978).

These correlations, consistent with our hypothesis, suggested a relationship, but we did not know whether depersonalization and temporal disintegration were dynamically related as processes over time. Thus, we studied six psychiatric patients longitudinally over a 3-year period as an independent observer reported either a definite improvement or worsening of depersonalization. For these within-patient changes over time, the mean correlation between changes in depersonalization and temporal disintegration was .83. This suggested a dynamic interrelationship between the processes but we did not know whether the relationship was limited to psychiatric illness.

We thus asked, if we induce temporal disintegration in normal subjects, will they become depersonalized? To answer this question, we used tetrahydrocannabinol (THC), the active ingredient of marijuana and hashish, as a way to induce temporal disintegration. It is well known that THC is a potent drug for inducing changes in time sense; at higher doses in the range of hashish it produces marked temporal disintegration, perhaps by disrupting immediate memory as well as anticipatory processes (Hicks, Mayo, Gualtieri, & Perez-Reyes, 1984). For these manipulation experiments, we carefully selected normal individuals with no history of previous depersonalization experiences and tested them at various doses (including placebo and comparably intoxicating doses of alcohol, which produces much less time distortion) in an intensive crossover design that used each subject as his or her own control. Subjects were tested by research assistants who did not know the hypothesis.

In the first experiment (Melges, Tinklenberg, Hollister, & Gillespie, 1970), which employed orally ingested THC, we found a highly substantial covariance of within-subject changes between temporal disintegration and depersonalization (mean $r = .87$). A second experiment (Melges, Tinklenberg, Deardorff, Davies, Anderson, & Owens, 1974), which used smoked THC, replicated these findings (mean $r = .92$). From these findings, we felt we could make the strong inference that the induction of temporal disintegration in normal subjects also produces depersonalization that waxes and wanes in time and intensity with the degree of temporal disintegration.

Although concomitant changes over time within subjects that covary in intensity suggest a causal interaction, the findings did not definitely indicate which factor was primary. To explore this, we examined the time course of changes. We found that temporal disintegration appeared to slightly precede the onset of depersonalization. Thus, at least at the psychological level of inquiry, it appeared that temporal disintegration was fundamentally involved in the precipitation of depersonalization.

Of course, some other variable, perhaps at the biological level, may have accounted for the covarying changes. It should be noted, however, that changes in calculative ability or disorientation to clock time, as in a delirium, did not account for these changes. Whatever might be the underlying cause or causes, at the psychological level, we believe that once a time distortion takes place, it alters the form of consciousness. In these studies, it appeared that a breakdown of the timeline going from past to present to future altered the temporal form of consciousness through which these individuals had become familiar with their selves over time. With the sense of self unhinged from its customary timeline, they became depersonalized.

Although we feel a strong case can be made for temporal disintegration as an inducer of depersonalization, the converse is perhaps not true. From clinical experience, there are depersonalized patients who have little to no temporal disintegration, but those patients who have temporal disintegration almost always have some degree of depersonalization.

To give a flavor of the subjective experience of the interrelationship between temporal discontinuity and depersonalization, some quotes from our THC subjects are revealing: One subject, who prior to taking THC had discussed his extensive future plans about getting his PhD, said during THC intoxication that he was unable to think of the future because he "could not keep an idea long enough—I can't remember my future." When asked to give an example of a future event, he looked at a chocolate bar and said, "I'm going to take a bite of candy." This subject also felt he had "lost his usual self." Another markedly depersonalized subject on a very high dose of THC stated: "I have no self. My self is broken in time."

In summary, temporal disintegration appears to disrupt the timeline of temporal perspective, making the self feel unfamiliar over time. This lack of a feeling of self-sameness over time impairs the sense of identity and gives rise to the feeling of depersonalization.

IDENTITY DIFFUSION AND DISCONTINUITY

Identity diffusion is a phrase coined by Erikson (1956) to refer to a feeling of vagueness, confusion, and nonintegration with regard to the self. It is less severe than the feeling of unreality about the self as in depersonalization. Persons with identity diffusion are vexed with the question, "Who am I?"

Such a question commonly reaches it peak during adolescence when the individual is struggling to differentiate himself or herself from parental identifications and to separate from the family of origin to find his or her uniqueness among peers, and to make crucial decisions about intimacy and vocational pursuits. About 30% of adolescents struggle with identity diffusion, but the majority go through this phase of development with only minor difficulties in establishing their identities.

Identity diffusion may persist into adulthood, particularly in borderline personality disorders, but its pervasiveness in the exacerbations of most psychiatric illnesses makes it a nonspecific disorder that cuts across almost all psychiatric diagnoses. For a psychiatric definition of identity diffusion, Akhtar (1984) highlights the following clinical manifestations of the syndrome: (a) contradictory character traits (e.g., feeling like a chronic "misfit"); (b) temporal discontinuity of the self (e.g., being swayed by external events rather than having a sense of one's roots and future directions); (c) lack of authenticity (e.g., acting "as if" one is another person); (d) feelings of emptiness (e.g., feeling hollow "like a shell"); (e) gender dysphoria (e.g., feeling that one does not belong to his or her sex role); and (f) inordinate ethnic and moral relativism (e.g., repudiation of one's ethnic origins and extreme dependence on others' view for what is judged good or bad).

Identity diffusion has diverse biopsychosocial roots about which different theoretical schools often cross swords. Biologists point to emotional dysregulation and immaturity of the brain; behavioral-cognitive therapists highlight insufficient self-reinforcement and self-control such that the individual is overly dependent on the views of others for his or her self-concept; psychoanalysts emphasize lack of empathic tuning of the mother with the infant so that, during adolescence, the person does not feel that he or she has a secure base that will permit exploration and separation.

In psychoanalytic theory, individuals with identity diffusion are thought to suffer from "lack of object constancy." This means they cannot hold in mind a nurturant image of the mother (or other parental figure) when such a person is out of sight. From research on normal early development, it is interesting that the maturation of object constancy takes place in parallel with the child's increasing capacity to anticipate (Kagan, 1979). It is as though the child who can sustain separations from his or her mother has the ability to envision her future return.

This brings us to the focus of this section: the role of temporal perspective, particularly future time perspective, in the formation and maintenance of a sense of identity. Identity diffusion often goes hand in hand with a foreshortened and vague temporal perspective into the future.

The evidence for this assertion is wide-ranging. The elaboration of the past and future into spans of awareness stretching far beyond the present progresses over development. For normal individuals, an extensive temporal perspective matures during adolescence (Wallace & Rabin, 1960). Concomitant with this, adolescence also is the period during which the self-concept becomes more integrated. The extension of temporal perspective during adolescence cannot be accounted for by the advancement of formal cognitive operations during this period, but rather appears related to increasing awareness of future social contingencies and commitments (Greene, 1986).

Adolescents with a firm sense of identity, compared to those without it, often employ detailed rehearsals with regard to future events (Hamburg & Adams, 1967). In a study of coping during the Peace Corps, Ezekiel (1968) found that those volunteers who, prior to going overseas, wrote extensive "future autobiographies" that described complex contingency planning were eventually much more successful in their assignments. This was assessed by self, peer, and supervisor ratings. The future autobiography was highly predictive of success, much more so than a battery of commonly used psychological tests.

In addition, projective tests that indicate a more extensive and dense future time perspective in adolescents and young adults correlate with measures of psychological health. Using the Thematic Apperception Test, Epley and Ricks (1963) found that prospective time span was related to academic achievement (but not to Scholastic Aptitude Test scores), empathic involvement with others, and low anxiety. In contrast to this "foresight" syndrome, retrospective temporal span was related to sensitive imagining, openness to experience, and narcissism. Cottle and Klineberg (1974) found that well-adjusted boys, compared to those judged maladjusted, had much longer future time spans of awareness.

However, it should be noted that further extensions into prospective spans may indicate that the person has foreclosed other options and does not have a flexible and integrated identity. In this regard, Rappaport, Enrich, and Wilson (1985) used Marcia's (1975) measurement of identity status in male undergraduates to obtain four categories of identity formation, which they labeled *identity diffusion, moratorium, identity achievement*, and *foreclosure*. These groups were then related to how the subjects placed personal events on a timeline representing the past, present, and future of one's life. Those subjects with identity diffusion had the least future orientation, those with foreclosure the greatest, and those who had achieved a sense of committed yet flexible identity had high but not overly extensive future orientation. The latter contrasted to the foreclosures who essentially had "closed" minds with regard to their futures (Rokeach, 1960). These findings suggest that it is not merely the length of future time extension but rather it is a flexible orientation toward the moderate-term future that is related to a firm sense of identity.

In summary, a firm sense of identity is associated with a feeling of continuity from the past through the present toward a focus on a moderately extended but open future. By contrast, an important aspect of identity diffusion is discontinuity of temporal perspective with a lack of future orientation.

LACK OF AUTONOMY
AND FRONTAL LOBE LESIONS

Although it may stretch one's mind to leap from the previous psychological discussions to a neuropsychological approach, the role of the frontal lobes in identity and temporal perspective is relevant to my central thesis. The frontal lobes in humans are important way-stations for anticipatory functions of the brain, and thus are important for future time perspective (Melges, 1988a). Damage to the frontal lobes impairs these anticipatory processes and makes the person more dependent on present input. With frontal lobe lesions, there is a peculiar indifference toward the future. This is associated with a reduction of anxiety but at the high cost of loss of motivation and, in particular, loss of freedom from the demand characteristics of current circumstances.

In patients with frontal lobe lesions, Lhermitte (1986) pointed to this dependence on the present as giving rise to a "lack of autonomy." The patients appear to lack autonomy because they are dependent on immediate environmental input, rather than long-term goals, for their actions. For example, when a patient with a frontal lobe lesion was shown a bed with the sheet turned down, he immediately got undressed and got into bed. Another patient, when she was shown a tongue depressor, took it and then proceeded to examine the doctor's mouth. These examples portray how the patient's action is pulled by the stimulus at hand.

The feeling of autonomy comes from the sense of choice between alternative future directions. At least there is the illusion of the capacity to choose. It appears that this capacity is impaired in frontal lobe lesions because such patients are bound to present stimuli and are less able to consider and compare future alternatives. To the extent that autonomy is an important aspect of identity we can hypothesize that personal identity is compromised in patients with frontal lobe lesions because of their lack of alternative perspectives on their futures which would free them from the present.

SELF-REFLECTION OVER TIME
AND THE SENSE OF "I-NESS"

If a person were totally bound to the present, he or she would have great difficulty in observing himself or herself. He or she would have only present moments with no perspective on their linkages. His or her experience would be like beads strewn about without a thread to tie them together. Such a present-bound person would have little sense of self, or "I-ness," because he or she would lack the capacity to reflect on oneself over time (Melges, 1982). The capacity to self-reflect over time appears to be a fundamental aspect of self-consciousness (Brockelman, 1985).

It is interesting to speculate, in line with Comfort's (1977) proposals, that both the sense of I-ness and the sense of time may stem from different parts of the human brain observing each other after different timing delays. These different delays between parts of the brain may enable current experiences to be replayed in past memory contexts and future extrapolations while still being updated in the present. To be more specific, when there is a slight delay between the now and the then, it is possible for the function subserving the now to observe the function of then, and vice versa (Melges, 1988b). When the person observes the nows fading into thens, he or she perceives time and its directionality. The latter may be the core phenomena from which temporal perspective is elaborated. Moreover, it may be at the root of the sense of I-ness because it enables the person to observe oneself over time, to self-reflect from different vantage points of time.

Just how such observing systems are precisely mediated by the brain is beyond the scope of our present neuropsychological knowledge, but one could marshal evidence to show that there are delays in processing times between the left and right cerebral hemispheres, and between the brain stem, limbic system, cerebral cortices, and frontal lobes.

If this speculation proves to have merit, it suggests that I-ness and directionality in time are interwoven at the fundamental level of brain processes.

SUMMARY AND CONCLUSIONS

The central thesis of this chapter was that the sense of identity is related to the continuity of temporal perspective, particularly future time perspective. This thesis is supported by the findings that temporal disintegration appears to induce depersonalization, and that discontinuity of temporal perspective, especially future time perspective, is related to identity diffusion. In addition, patients with frontal lobe lesions, who have deficient future time perspective, lack the capacity for autonomous choices necessary for an identity that is independent of immediate environmental influences. Finally, the essence of self-consciousness may reside in the capacity to observe oneself through time.

REFERENCES

Akhtar, S. (1984). The syndrome of identity diffusion. *American Journal of Psychiatry, 141,* 1381-1385.

Block, R. A. (1985). Contextual coding in memory: Studies of remembered duration. In J. A. Michon & J. L. Jackson (Eds.), *Time, mind, and behavior* (pp. 169-178). Berlin: Springer-Verlag.

Brockelman, P. (1985). *Time and self.* New York: Crossroads.

Comfort, A. (1977). Homuncular identity-sense as a *déjà vu* phenomenon. *Journal of Medical Psychology, 50,* 313-315.

Cottle, T. J., & Klineberg, S. L. (1974). *The present of things future: Explorations of time in human experience.* New York: Macmillan.

Epley, D., & Ricks, D. R. (1963). Foresight and hindsight in the TAT. *Journal of Projective Techniques and Personality Assessment, 27,* 51-59.

Erikson, E. H. (1956). The problem of ego identity. In *Identity and the life cycle, selected papers* (Psychological Issues Monograph 1). New York: International Universities Press.

Ezekiel, R. S. (1968). The personal future and Peace Corps competence. *Journal of Personality and Social Psychology* (Monograph Supplement), *8,* 1-26.

Freeman, A. M., & Melges, F. T. (1977). Depersonalization and temporal disintegration in acute mental illness. *American Journal of Psychiatry, 134,* 679-681.

Freeman, A. M., & Melges, F. T. (1978). Temporal disorganization, depersonalization, and persecutory ideation in acute mental illness. *American Journal of Psychiatry, 135,* 123-124.

Greene, A. L. (1986). Future time perspective in adolescence: The present of things future revisited. *Journal of Youth and Adolescence, 15,* 99-113.

Hamburg, D. A., & Adams, J. E. (1967). A perspective on coping behavior. *Archives of General Psychiatry, 17,* 277-284.

Hicks, R. E., Mayo, J. P., Gualtieri, T., & Perez-Reyes, M. (1984). Cannabis, atropine, and temporal information processing. *Neuropsychobiology, 12,* 229-237.

Jacques, E. (1956). *The measurement of responsibility.* Cambridge, MA: Harvard University Press.

Kagan, J. (1979). The form of early development. *Archives of General Psychiatry, 36,* 1047-1054.

Kelly, G. A. (1955). *The psychology of personal constructs.* New York: W. W. Norton.

Lhermitte, F. (1986). Human autonomy and the frontal lobes. Part II. Patient behavior in complex and social situations: The "environmental dependency syndrome." *Annals of Neurology, 19,* 335-343.

Marcia, J. E. (1975). *Studies in ego identity.* Unpublished research monograph. Burnaby, BC: Simon Fraser University.

Melges, F. T. (1982). *Time and the inner future: A temporal approach to psychiatric disorders.* New York: Wiley.

Melges, F. T. (1988a). Time, timing, and the future. *Readings: A Journal of Review and Commentary in Mental Health, 3,* 13-17.

Melges, F. T. (1988b). Guyau on the illusions of time: Normal and pathological. In J. A. Michon, V. Pouthas, & & J. L. Jackson (Eds.), *Guyau and the idea of time* (pp. 213-231). Amsterdam: North-Holland.

Melges, F. T., Tinklenberg, J. R., Deardorff, C. M., Davies, N. H., Anderson, R. E., & Owens, C. A. (1974). Temporal disorganization and delusional-like ideation: Processes induced by hashish and alcohol. *Archives of General Psychiatry, 30,* 855-861.

Melges, F. T., Tinklenberg, J. R., Hollister, L. E., & Gillespie, H. K. (1970). Temporal disintegration and depersonalization during marihuana intoxication. *Archives of General Psychiatry, 23,* 204-210.

Michon, J. A., & Jackson, J. L. (Eds.). (1985). *Time, mind, and behavior.* Berlin: Springer-Verlag.

Rappaport, H., Enrich, K., & Wilson, A. (1985). Relation between ego identity and temporal perspective. *Journal of Personality and Social Psychology, 48,* 1609-1620.

Rokeach, M. (1960). *The open and closed mind.* New York: Basic Books.

Shalom, A. (1985). *The body/mind conceptual framework and the problem of personal identity.* Atlantic Highlands, NJ: Humanities Press International.

Tulving, E. (1984). How many memory systems are there? *American Psychologist, 40,* 385-398.

Wallace, M., & Rabin, A. (1960). Temporal experience. *Psychological Bulletin, 57,* 213-235.

Author Index

Subject Index